T0328336

The BASICS Lean Implementation Model

Lean Tools to Drive Daily Innovation
and Increased Profitability

The BASICS Lean Implementation Model

Lean Tools to Drive Daily Innovation and Increased Profitability

By

Charles Protzman, Dan Protzman, and William Keen

Routledge
Taylor & Francis Group

A PRODUCTIVITY PRESS BOOK

First edition published in 2019

by Routledge/Productivity Press
711 Third Avenue New York, NY 10017, USA
2 Park Square, Milton Park, Abingdon, Oxon OX14 4RN, UK

© 2019 by Charles Protzman, Dan Protzman, and William Keen
Routledge/Productivity Press is an imprint of Taylor & Francis Group, an Informa business

No claim to original U.S. Government works

Printed on acid-free paper

International Standard Book Number-13: 978-0-8153-8821-0 (Hardback)
International Standard Book Number-13: 978-0-8153-8794-7 (Paperback)
International Standard Book Number-13: 978-1-351-17272-1 (eBook)

Visit the Taylor & Francis Web site at
http://www.taylorandfrancis.com

Contents

We would like to dedicate this book to Eric Danielson, a great
Lean practitioner and even greater friend.

Foreword

Early in my career I was privileged enough to have the opportunity to participate in one of Charlie's famous five-day workshops. It was my first introduction to Lean manufacturing and to the BASICS methodology. I have since been a participant or assistant in three more workshops, have participated in or lead a handful of highly scoped projects or kaizen events within my company, and have helped to create a Lean-based production system that puts a lot of what is taught in this book into action.

"Do you know what you don't know?" and "Lean is a five-year journey that never ends" are two quotes that I hear from Charlie and Dan over and over again.

They never let me forget two main principles of Lean—Respect for people (or humanity) and Creating knowledge. The authors talk about both principles throughout the book by highlighting benefits of keeping everyone involved and respecting everyone's ideas. Put together with the rest of BASICS, these principles help create a culture of problem-solving and continuous learning.

BASICS was founded almost 20 years ago by Charlie and has become my go-to method. It can be used in a multitude of ways—from a small two-hour quick kaizen to a three-day rapid improvement to a larger five-day event, or even a multiyear improvement implementation.

In a recent event, my team and I were able to improve our production output by 20% and increase our efficiency by 30%. These improvements were achieved using BASICS. It is important though, that the sequential steps of BASICS be followed: Baseline, Analyze, Suggest Solutions, Implement, Check, and Sustain. The improvements mentioned above would not have been possible without the buy-in to the project by everybody at all levels of the plant. Following the authors' tools and experiences in this book helps make sure that you can get this buy-in.

To me, Baseline (*B*) is one of the most important steps in this process, and more importantly, it can be the hardest to get correct. This step is often overlooked, as it was by me early on in my career. I learned the hard way what the authors already knew and show in this book. If the project's problem, scope, and goals are not clearly defined ... then how do you know if your project was successful, or even worse, how do you know if it's complete? At the same time, if you do not know what the current-state metrics are, how can you measure if your improvements created positive results? The time must be invested up front to collect the data, scrub it—and then make sure there is an agreement from all parties involved. Without taking this important step, there is likely to be indecision at the end of the project on what percentage of improvement was attained, or when to move on to the next task. It is just as important to involve plant leadership during the baseline process, or, without a doubt, they will always resist the improvements and continue to pile more "in-scope" tasks on your team.

The second step of this method is to Analyze (*A*) your current-state process and to question everything that is being done today, or your "as-is" state. The authors present a comprehensive toolbox that helps to quantify this state, such as figuring out TTT (total throughput time), TLT (total labor time), and the difference between internal and external setup time.

Dan, Charlie, and Bill show how following a simple three-step process of analyzing the product, the operator, and changeovers will help make sure that there is a complete and comprehensive understanding.

Charlie and his team also introduce an old—and yet new revolutionary tool ... the video camera! Using a video camera alone has been one of the most important tools for us to get this step right. Sports teams have used them for years to learn and improve, however manufacturing tends to shy away. I'll be honest, I never even thought about videoing my operations in this way. This book will show you all the advantages, as well as the best way to get your company to buy-in to the thought of using a recording device.

From there, the book moves on to the "fun" stuff. This is one my personal favorite phases of a project: Suggesting Solutions (*S*) and then Implementing (*I*) those solutions. I find that many of the tools discussed lead to an interconnected system. The authors take this complicated concept and explain these tools in a way that helps the reader understand how they build upon each other, leading to an ever-growing Lean system. This phase helps you and your team to decide on the "right" layout, how to create one-piece-flow, sequencing the order of operations, workstation design, and much much more.

The authors then help define the best approach to implementing the improvements, such as setting up a pilot or test area and having the Lean Leader run the line first, while the line leader is being trained on running the line and all its processes. This also leads right in to creating standard work for the operators. The authors show their vast experience by providing best practices when it comes to standard work and leader standard work and helping to clarify what makes sense and what is most beneficial to those using it.

The book then moves into Check (*C*) and Sustain (*S*). In my experiences with BASICS, these last two sections rely heavily on your shop-floor management and their incorporation in this journey. We want to create a system of checks that makes sure the process continues to meet our expectations. It is also very important to realize that there needs to be a system in place that drives daily continuous improvement. While reading this book you will be introduced to a variety of ways to help make the transition into this phase as simple as possible.

Introducing Lean is hard enough; however, doing it without a roadmap is suicide. History shows us that many have tried, but few have succeeded. This book will help lay the groundwork for success by using BASICS as that roadmap. Whether you are a seasoned practitioner or being introduced to these concepts for the first time, this book is relevant. Charlie and his team go into companies with the idea of not only helping those companies succeed with Lean while using BASICS, but also training and teaching the companies' Lean team members how to continue this journey, even after they depart. They makes sure the company can rely on themselves to continuously improve. This approach to doing business is what keeps me going back to them time and time again. They are always willing to help and share their knowledge.

This book is an example of the vast knowledge this team has to contribute to the Lean and manufacturing community. Along with other books that the authors' have written such as *The Lean Practitioner's Fieldbook* and *One-Piece Flow vs. Batching*, this one will remain in my arsenal as a go-to point of reference when needed.

I want to thank Charlie, Dan, and the rest of their team for giving me the opportunity to contribute to this book through the foreword. I appreciate everything that they have done for me in the past and I look forward to continuing to work with them in the future.

Jeremy Horn
Operations Process Improvement Leader

Preface

I started working with Lean in 1985, but back then it wasn't called Lean; it had other names, like Total Quality (TQ) and Continuous Improvement.

At Bendix Communications Division, a group of us called the "hats" team began working with our GM, David Passeri, to find a way to improve our batch circuit-board facility. At that time, Jim Womack's book, *The Machine that Changed the World* and Joel Barker's *Business of Paradigms* video came out. These two methodologies were our springboard to starting Lean.

Eventually, under the direction of Vic Chance, Dan Daino, and Jim Robinson, we completed the conversion from batch to one-piece flow and turned the plant into a world-class Lean facility, where we eliminated the stockroom building, and were even benchmarked by Harley Davidson for self-directed work teams.

While at AlliedSignal, now Honeywell, I was exposed to a variety of different five-day kaizen event-implementation approaches by TBM and Shingijutsu, JIT institute, and others. We were also exposed to more analytical approaches through Demand Flow Technology based on a book called *Quantum Leap* by the World Wide Flow College of Denver, Mark Jamrog's SMC group's 14-step model, University of Tennessee's Lean Demand Management class by Ken Kirby, AlliedSignal's four-day Total Quality training by Coopers and Lybrand, AlliedSignal Lean Training from Mike Chan, along with Honda's Five Best Practices, GM Synchronous, and most recently the WCM approach being used by Fiat and Chrysler. I have received much training in change management and personality styles from a variety of sources over the years. I have also read well over 500 books on Lean, Six Sigma, and Total Quality.

In late 1997, I started Business Improvement Group, LLC (BIG), in Baltimore, MD. I used my past learnings to develop a simple model for Lean implementation, called BASICS, which is based on the sum total of my learnings above. We have continued to evolve, research extensively, and prove out this model for over 20 years.

Successfully implementing the BASICS model will improve quality, decrease safety risk, increase productivity, improve your working capital, increase your inventory turns, produce bottom-line savings, and improve cash flow.

BASICS is an implementation methodology for converting any batch process to one-piece (OPF) or small-lot flow and is also used for ongoing improvement to OPF lines and transactional processes. PDSA is still used for standard problem-solving.

I constructed the BASICS model (Figure 0.1) to provide a practical guide to approaching a Lean implementation. The foundation for this model is derived from much of my past experience but is primarily based on Frank Gilbreth's, Taiichi Ohno's, and Shigeo Shingo's books, among others (see Bibliography).

The target audience for this book is anyone, anywhere, who wants to make an improvement, big or small. Most of us, whether we realize it or not, have a deep-down need to find better ways to do things.

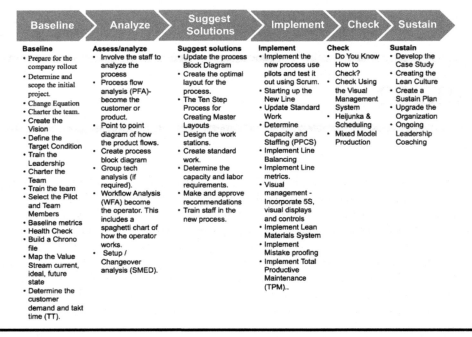

Figure 0.1   The BASICS six-step model for Lean implementation—short version. (Source: BIG Training Materials.) For more detailed information, see *The Lean Practitioner's Field Book* (Productivity Press, 2016).

Some of you have already implemented Lean and checked that box. But companies that really "get it" understand that Lean never ends and becomes a way of life.

Our Lean system implementations typically run six to ten weeks and we normally achieve productivity increases over 50% based on paid labor hours/unit and several hundred percent when looking at pieces per person per day.

Our line conversions from station balancing to baton-zone balancing can typically be accomplished in one to two weeks where we achieve 10%–30% or more increases in productivity.

Ranging from manufacturing to healthcare, we have saved clients millions of dollars in cost avoidance in new construction and savings at the gross-profit level as well as significantly increasing their cash flow and working capital.

This book has a proven, time-tested approach and methodology that will help you implement and sustain Lean thinking. Our approach has some subtle yet very powerful differences from traditional kaizen event-based implementation models. Our clients have profited greatly from this approach and some would not be in business today or would not have weathered the great recession of December 2007 to June 2009.

Because they embraced these techniques and realized true savings to their gross margins and bottom lines, our clients look at our BASICS approach as a strategic and highly effective weapon against their competition.

Charlie Protzman

Acknowledgments

We would like to thank all our clients for their contributions to the development of the BASICS model over the years.

We would also like to acknowledge the authors of *The Lean Practitioner Field Book*: Fred Whiton, Joyce Kerpchar, Pat Grounds, Chris Lewandowski, and Steve Stenberg; and *Leveraging Lean in Healthcare*—Dr. George Mayzell, Joyce Kerpchar—on which this book is based.

In addition, we would like to thank MaryBeth Protzman, James D. Root, P.E., C.P.I.M., Jeremy Horn, Deepa V. Kamat, Mike Oswald, Dr. Tom Brady, Maureen Harte, and Mike Meyers for their valuable feedback on and contributions to an earlier draft of the book.

We would like to thank Rhidian Roach and Cory Liffrig of Six Sigma Solutions for their contributions on their very popular leanEdit® software.

We would also like to thank Jeremy Horn, one of the best Lean practitioners we know, for writing the Foreword.

Lastly, Charles Protzman would like to acknowledge his sensei, Mark Jamrog, for introducing him to his Shingo/Ohno Lean implementation model and his learnings from Kawasaki. Eventually Mark went on to call this his 14-step model.

Acknowledgments

Chapter 1

The BASICS Model Overview

Baseline (B):

- Create the vision.
- Train the leadership and implementation team in Lean.
- Charter the team, scope the project.
- Select the pilot area and team members.
- Conduct five-day Lean training seminar.
- Baseline metrics, identify the "gaps" and set targets.
- Build a chronological file—take photos and videos of how it is today.
- Health check.
- Value-stream map: current, ideal, and future state.
- Determine the customer demand and takt time (TT).

Assess/Analyze (A):

- Involve all the staff to analyze the process.
- Process-flow analysis (PFA)—become the customer or product. This includes a point-to-point diagram of how the product flows.
- Create process block diagram.
- Group tech analysis (if required).
- Workflow analysis (WFA)—become the operator. This includes a spaghetti chart of how the operator works.
- Setup/changeover analysis (SMED).

Suggest Solutions (S):

- Update the process block diagram—one-piece flow vision for the process.
- Create the optimal layout for the process.
- The ten-step process for creating master layouts.
- Design the work stations.
- Create standard work.

- Determine the capacity and labor requirements.
- Make and approve recommendations.
- Train staff in the new process.

Implement (I):

- Implement the new process—use pilots.
- Start up the new line.
- Update standard work.
- Determine capacity and staffing (PPCS).
- Implement line balancing.
- Implement line metrics.
- Visual management—Incorporate 5S, visual displays, and controls.
- Implement Lean materials system.
- Implement mistake-proofing.
- Implement total productive maintenance (TPM).

Check (C):

- Do you know how to check?
- Check using the visual-management system.
- Heijuka and scheduling.
- Mixed model production.

Sustain (S):

- Document the business case study and results.
- Create the Lean culture.
- Create a sustain plan.
- Upgrade the organization.
- Ongoing leadership coaching.

Why Is the BASICS Model Different Compared to Point Kaizen Events?

Many of you reading this book have probably already implemented Lean or think you have already taken Lean as far as it can go. No matter how far down the Lean maturity path you may think you are, we believe, based on our past and current client experiences, you still have lots of opportunities and room to improve.

BASICS is a different implementation approach with a much higher sustain rate* versus tra- ditonal point kaizen events or WCM major kaizen. BASICS is a system-level approach designed to take more time up front to involve everyone in studying and analyzing the current process and set the target for the future state condition. It typically takes anywhere from one to ten weeks to

---

* Eighty to ninety percent of our past clients on average have sustained their Lean programs at some level over the past 20 years. Many of their examples are in *The Lean Practitioner's Field Book*, Protzman, Whiton, Kerpchar, Grounds, Lewandowski, Stenberg, 2017, CRC Press. In one client this methodology has been consistently out- performing WCM being used in some of their other plants.

study, implement, and run the line,* as well as getting 5S and lineside materials in place. We train the leadership, pick a pilot, and use small dedicated teams, with 100% operator and team leader involvement to manage the conversion from batch to flow.

This time frame is based on how much total labor time exists to produce one complete piece in a manufacturing line, one patient in a healthcare process, or one complete activity within a transactional process. For processes with very lowtouch-labor, i.e., less than three minutes per piece, we can analyze it and have the new line up and running in a week. Then we spend two to four weeks teaching team leaders how to run the line, create visual scheduling, standard work, and material flow systems. For lines or processes with longer total labor times it can run up to eight to ten weeks. This approach can also be used on converting station-balanced lines to bumping[†] lines.

In every case where we have applied this approach we have been able to obtain significantly better results in less than eight to ten weeks as compared to implementing using only five-day point kaizen events or major kaizen in WCM, which can take up three to five years or more.

The BASICS model yields much higher productivity in less time than traditional point kaizen events.[‡] BASICS has the added value of seeing the process from a systems perspective, which allows for very innovative solutions in healthcare that would virtually never be found using traditional point kaizen events.

We even use the BASICS model in hospitals, clinics, and laboratories, which takes on average 12–14 weeks to complete an implementation. This approach, because of the systematic view, applies to a variety of industries and services. One of the key concepts that separates BASICS from other approaches is its simplicity.

The BASICS Model and Transactional Processes

Within most companies, transactional costs are often hidden, not well understood but still included in overhead. There is little to no knowledge of current transactional capacity or current performance against that capacity and overhead costs are embedded in many locations on the traditional P&L statement.

For example, much of the waste in manufacturing and transactional processes is included in the time standards. The days of the official stopwatch man are now gone. What's left are five- or ten-year-old time standards that can no longer be met due to all the wastes growing in the process.

For example, in the general and administrative (G&A) section of the P&L statement, we often find costs for contracts, central accounting, legal, marketing, and the executive staff. The typical G&A costs can be large and are thought of as fixed.

The reality is the consumer considering a new car purchase would not want to pay for an option on the window sticker entitled G&A costs; however, those costs are real and are concealed in every car made by every manufacturer. Also, there can be overhead costs related to direct labor and they are shown as a separate line on the P&L.

Every business has transactional processes, while some businesses are virtually all transactional processes (i.e., banking and insurance). Every business, healthcare institution, financial services,

---

* The term study does not mean analysis paralysis. Back in 1996, during a Shingijutsu point kaizen event at Hitachi in Japan, Charlie Protzman learned from his sensei that the Japanese approach is always to study major changes and reach consensus (nemawashi) prior to implementation. This was not taught to Charlie at AlliedSignal during five-day point kaizen events at that time by Shingijutsu or TBM.
† Bumping lines are based on baton-zone line balancing techniques that we have been working on perfecting over 20 years. We normally see a 10%–30% increase in productivity converting from station balancing to bumping.
‡ *Leveraging Lean in Healthcare*, Protzman, Mayzell, Kerpchar, 2011. CRC Press: Boca Raton, FL.

and governmental agency can apply Lean, streamline their processes, and eliminate waste. By its very nature transactional processes are 95% non–value-added.

Financial, human resource, and sales and marketing processes are not activities a customer wants to pay for; but, they are required to keep a business viable and effective. These processes supply companies with the data necessary to make the strategic decisions required to stay in business and provide the customer with better products and services at a lower cost.

When implementing office or administrative-type processes, we yield the same results:

- 80% reductions in throughput times (weeks to days or days to hours)
- 80% reductions in work in process (WIP) (amount of paperwork, sometimes e-mails in the process)
- 30%–50% or more increases in productivity
- 80% reductions in (non-electronic) travel distances
- 10%–20% increases in quality

At many companies we see Lean savings charts, and when we ask, "Are those bottom-line savings?" we find most are paper-savings where, for example, they freed up 0.7 of a person. We see much of this paper-savings in WCM implementations. This doesn't get to the bottom line unless you can make that person productive somewhere else. The book and the movie by Goldratt called *The Goal** does a great job of emphasizing this point.

The BASICS model is 50% scientific management and 50% change management. It is a Lean approach, which targets an entire transactional process, i.e., accounts payable, or production line. In a hospital, for example, it will target an emergency room "system" or surgical "system."

The BASICS Model

The main objective of creating the model was to present an easy-to-use roadmap. This roadmap helps to guide the users on what should be occurring as you move through a Lean implementation.

BASICS is a simple method and stands for:

1. Baseline
2. Assess/Analyze (Study)
3. Suggest Solutions
4. Implement
5. Check
6. Sustain

Implementation Phases

In our approach there are four implementation phases, which are incorporated into the BASICS model. These phases are:

1. Implement the line: Includes Baseline, Analyze, Suggest Solutions, and Implement
2. Implement standard work and visual heijunka scheduling

---

* *The Goal*, Eli Goldratt, 1984. New York: Gower Publishing.

3. Implement the line side and supermarket logistics systems
4. Sustain the overall system implementation

At the end of Phase 1 we have the line up and running. This phase will realize 80% of the productivity results. In one large plant in Buffalo, New York, we rolled out phase 1 of this model on 14 lines over a 16-week period. Thirteen of these lines were already considered "world class for Lean" based on their Value-Based Lean Six Sigma Master Training. Overall we obtained 10%–50% increases in productivity and freed up 16 people,* which immediately impacted the bottom line.

There was one line that was originally batched where we obtained a 70% productivity improvement (units per hour) and on one of their world-class lines we obtained a 377% increase in pieces (pcs) per person per hour going from ten people on two shifts to 2.7 people on one shift. This plant outside of Buffalo is still sustaining at high levels and growing their business.

At another company in Buffalo, we were able to bring offshore business back to a union facility with one of the highest labor rates in the country.

We still use point kaizen events with the BASICS model for setup reduction, rapid kaizen, and sustaining, but we still follow the BASICS methodology during the point kaizen event.

Lean and Layoffs

Our goal has always been to never layoff any permanent employees as a result of continuous improvement, and to date we have lived up to that goal. We have, however, laid off contract/temporary workers.

This goal has been a key driver to sustainment and continued improvements. If you do layoff anyone due to improvements, the operators will stop helping you improve. If layoffs are looming due to a business condition or merger, etc., make sure they are not associated with your Lean efforts. Many times, we get the president to send a letter to employees that supports this prior to starting the Lean implementation.

The Lean Practitioner Principles

When applying Lean tools, in any capacity, it is important to keep Lean principles in mind. When I first started working with hospitals in 2001, outside the lab, there weren't any true benchmark sites or places to go and see. I was left to my own devices to figure out the best way I knew how to implement Lean in healthcare. I succeeded by following these ten principles as my guide, and they have not failed me yet. If you learn to apply these principles and tools from this book you can improve any process.

The Ten Fundamental Practitioner Principles

1. The customer must be willing to pay for it.

     Without the customer we don't exist. Everything must start with the customer. Do you really know your customer, and what problems are they trying to solve?

---

* We never lay off full-time people at companies when we implement Lean. We use attrition or in some cases early retirement. In this case we reduced 16 people because they were temporary workers, so the company saw immediate bottom-line results.

2. Start with the "system" and let the data be your guide.

   Systems thinking is a fundamental thought process for implementing Lean. Yet most of us are never trained in systems thinking. In systems thinking we learn everything is connected and to look for the systemic cycles of cause and effect versus, just looking at it as a linear relationship. So part of every implementation or kaizen is taking a step back to look at the overall system and identifying the systemic changes that may be necessary.

3. How can we make it run like an assembly line and eliminate batching?

   This was a key principle for me in healthcare. There is batching everywhere, in every industry and every process. We must eliminate it and strive to implement one-piece flow wherever possible.

4. Safety: Would I let a family member do the task?

   We like to tell our teammates that we would like to see them leave the same way they came in to work, i.e., with all their fingers, toes, eyesight, etc. We must mistake-proof this mentality wherever possible and work to eliminate the need for personal protective equipment (PPE)

5. Do you know what you don't know?

   You must learn to continually ask yourself this question. So often we think we know but find out we really don't know.

6. Quality: Never pass on a bad part or bad information. Do you know how to check?

   Ask yourself this question whenever following a part, information step, or patient through the process.

7. Focus on the process to get the result: Do the right thing regardless of the ROI. Don't let perfect get in the way of good.

   This is a fundamental paradigm shift for every company. But think about it. If every process was optimized, what would stand in our way of achieving great results?

8. Standardize everything (to the extent it makes sense).

   Imagine what life would be like without any standards. What if there was no standard for measurements, currency, etc. The only way to achieve quality is to have a standard. Our first question whenever we run into a problem anywhere in the company is "What is the standard?"

9. Implement visual management everywhere.

   Without visual management you cannot manage; you can only react to problems. This leads to firefighting, which becomes a systemic problem. We find many companies today are in need of returning to good shop-floor or department management systems.

10. Create the best possible experience for our team members.

    Experience is different than satisfaction. If we create a good team-member experience and continually develop the team members, it will be an enabler for a great customer experience. This concept engages people and demonstrates respect for people, which is an enabler for high-performing teams.

Why Are You Implementing Lean? What Problem Are You Trying to Solve?

PDSA

At the core of the BASICS model is the problem-solving method of plan–do–study–act (PDSA). PDSA comes from Walter A. Shewhart and was later revised by W. Edwards Deming and the

Japanese. Dr. Deming wrote his famous 14 points. Most companies still struggle with living these point today.

1. Create constancy of purpose toward improvement of product and service, with the aim to become competitive, stay in business, and to provide jobs.
2. Adopt the new philosophy. We are in a new economic age. Western management must awaken to the challenge, must learn their responsibilities, and must take on leadership for change.
3. Cease dependence on inspection to achieve quality. Eliminate the need for massive inspection by building quality into the product in the first place.
4. End the practice of awarding business on the basis of a price tag. Instead, minimize total cost. Move toward a single supplier for any one item, on a long-term relationship of loyalty and trust.
5. Improve constantly and forever the system of production and service, to improve quality and productivity and thus constantly decrease costs.
6. Institute training on the job.
7. Institute leadership. The aim of supervision should be to help people and machines and gadgets do a better job. Supervision of management is in need of overhaul, as well as supervision of production workers.
8. Drive out fear, so everyone may work effectively for the company.
9. Break down barriers between departments. People in research, design, sales, and production must work as a team, in order to foresee problems of production and usage that may be encountered with the product or service.
10. Eliminate slogans, exhortations, and targets for the workforce asking for zero defects and new levels of productivity. Such exhortations only create adversarial relationships, as the bulk of the causes of low quality and low productivity belong to the system and thus lie beyond the power of the workforce.
11.
    a. Eliminate work standards (quotas) on the factory floor. Substitute with leadership.
    b. Eliminate management by objectives (MBO). Eliminate management by numbers and numerical goals. Instead substitute with leadership.
12.
    a. Remove barriers that rob the hourly worker of his/her right to pride of workmanship. The responsibility of supervisors must be changed from sheer numbers to quality.
    b. Remove barriers that rob people in management and in engineering of their right to pride of workmanship. This means abolishment of the annual or merit rating and of MBO.
13. Institute a vigorous program of education and self-improvement.
14. Put everybody in the company to work to accomplish the transformation. The transformation is everybody's job.

Deming's 14 points embody problem-solving and the PDSA methodology (Figure 1.1). It is important to note that PDSA always starts with study. This is because you are assessing a problem after a plan, and action was already put in place. The outcome of the act of checking results in the discovery of a new gap from the A3. An A3 is a single sheet of paper, which we use to describe the story of how we solved a problem (Figure 1.2). An A3 can be used for not only problem-solving, but also deviation from the standard analysis, proposals, project status updates, i.e., new-product development, engineering design briefs, and more.

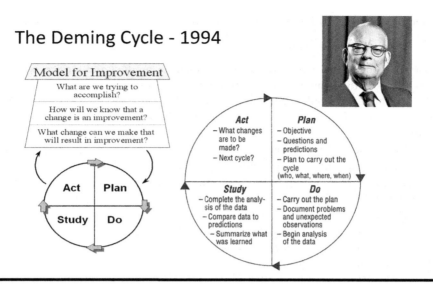

Figure 1.1 Foundation and history of the PDSA Cycle. (Source: Ronald Moen, Associates in Process, Improvement–Detroit (USA), rmoen@apiweb.org, https://deming.org.)

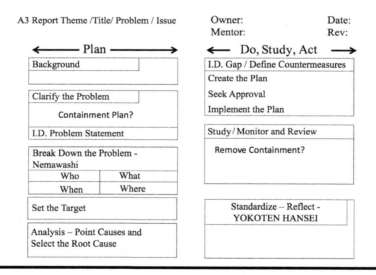

Figure 1.2 A3 problem-solving storytelling example. (Source: *Understanding A3*, Durward Sobek and Art Smalley, 2008. CRC Press: Boca Raton, FL; *Managing to Learn*, John Shook, 2008. LEI: Cambridge, MA; and Nigel Thurlow, Chief of Agile at Toyota Connected.)

The A3 report is a standardized report utilizing a storyboard format. The A3 helps one to organize one's thoughts and involve others in the problem-solving process. It normally takes two to three years to learn to do an A3 correctly for complex problems. For simple processes, we don't need the A3 form filled out but we do need A3/PDSA thinking. This prevents just "throwing solutions at problems."

The Problem Statement

Engaging in a continuous improvement initiative means everyone must learn and understand how to problem-solve. Problem-solving starts with understanding and being able to write down the problem or gap. The problem statement should identify what is wrong (as compared to a standard or expectation), where and when it is occurring, the baseline or magnitude at which it is occurring and what it is costing me.* Once that is done, then the objective statement can be written as follows:

> Improve some METRIC from some BASELINE level to some GOAL, by some TIME FRAME, to achieve some BENEFIT, and improve upon some CORPORATE GOAL or OBJECTIVE.

Set the Target Condition

As discussed, earlier the gap can come from anywhere. Once we define the gap we need to set a target. In some cases, management may set the new improvement target in their strategic plan or we find a need (mandated or innate) to do something better than it is today. We may solicit people's ideas, whether it be from an employee, customer, supplier, patient, etc. The idea is a target from which one can infer there must be a gap in the process.

The target should have a desired outcome and should also have a designated time frame. The target provides a framework against which to measure your progress. This target should be realistic and may take anywhere from two seconds to years to realize.

Root-Cause Thinking

Once we identify the gap we need to figure out why there is a gap. For this we use something called "root-cause analysis" or "A3" thinking.

When we are faced with a new problem, our first step should be to take a step back and look at the entire system that is at work. Ask yourself the following question: Is the person at fault or is it the system, which the person is a part of, at fault?

- Step 1 Analyze the problem, identify all the symptoms. We call these point causes.
- Step 2 Find the root cause or causes for each of the point causes. In some cases, one root cause may solve several point causes or there could be multiple root causes tied to one point cause.
- Rule 1 Fixing the symptom just manages the problem.
- Rule 2 Blame gets in the way of finding the real problem.
- Rule 3 Poka yoke to make sure the problem never comes back.
- Rule 4 If you can't prevent it, inspect it 100% by machine or sensor.

---

* Contributed by Jane Fitzpatrick, Executive Consultant, Success Staging International, LLC.

Do You Know What You Don't Know?*

We utilize the operators' talent and experience in every step of our improvement process methodology. However, many times we hear the saying: "The operators are the experts." This may be true for the majority of the time, but not always. Operators only know what they *know,* based on how they were trained and/or who trained them. Sometimes they don't know or understand everything the machine can do or what the final product looks like or how it works. We have created the following diagram. which divides knowledge into four quadrants (see Figure 1.3):

1. *You know you know*: The meaning behind this one is obvious.
2. *You know you don't know*: The meaning behind this one is obvious.
3. *You don't know you know*: Many times, we realize we knew something, which at first, we did not think we knew. For instance, many times we do Lean things without realizing it, or sometimes, just thinking about a problem, we can logically sort it out.
4. *You don't know you don't know*: This is the most dangerous quadrant. Many times, we think we know things, which we really don't. We call this knowing enough to be dangerous. The other interpretation is we don't know what we don't know. It behooves us to find an expert or continue to dig and research a problem, so we get to a point of knowing what there is to know.

Those with some Lean knowledge can sometimes be more destructive than those with none at all. One of the big obstacles with Lean is discovering, or helping others to discover, what they do not know they did not know.

At every company, when we start drilling down into processes and equipment knowledge, etc., we find people don't really know the process or why they do what they do. When we ask how the machine works they can't answer the questions. Then when we ask about machine manuals, they don't know where they are stored.

(1) Things You Know You Know	(2) Things You Know You Don't Know
(3) Things You Don't Know You Know	(4) Things You Don't Know You Don't Know

Figure 1.3   The four quadrants—Do you know what you don't know. (Source: BIG Training Materials.)

---

* The sayings, "Do you know what you don't know?" and "Do you know how to check?", are credited to Danilo Bruno Franco, Operation Director of MT China, ITT High Precision Manufactured Products (Wuxi) Co., Ltd.

For example, at a company in China, we asked them what the static-value readout on an electrostatic painting machine meant and why they recorded it every two hours. They were having a lot of quality issues with the machine. To make a really long story short, no one knew, not even the process engineers. It turns out they were constantly setting this value to some arbitrary number that someone thought in the past was the right number. It turns out the value should have never been changed once it was set. In addition, the length of the hoses from the paint to the machine played a role in the static value. Over time, maintenance was moving the equipment and would extend the hoses, which then changed the static value of the paint.

In another case, quality shut down a machine and rejected all the parts from a day's production because the torque angle reading wasn't good. When we asked what a torque angle was, the quality manager didn't know. When we asked how she knew it wasn't good, she said it was because the manufacturer of the control device told her it was not a good number. Upon further investigation we found that, at the time, the data in the report was erroneous.

Before you can start to problem-solve, the first question you have to always ask yourself is, do you know what you don't know?

Know How versus Know Why

How often have you had a problem where you just went and fixed several things all at once, and suddenly, it works? But which thing fixed it? Alternatively, when we have a problem with testing equipment on the shop floor, we tap it (or hit it with a hammer), and it works. Sometimes we know how to fix things, but we do not know why. Eventually the tapping does not work anymore. We must learn the *know why* in addition to the *know how* to truly fix the root causes of problems.

Chapter 2

The BASICS Model: Baseline (B)

The B in our BASICS model stands for Baseline, or determining "as-is" metrics. It is important to develop a true baseline prior to starting the project so we can ascertain how much we have improved later on (see Figure 2.1).

Getting Started with Lean

When working with new clients we start by understanding what problems they are facing. We then tour the plant, where we can immediately assess, as you will see later, whether the plant is batch or flow, and what opportunities there are to improve the productivity or efficiency in the plant. For office processes or hospitals, we start with a value-stream map to expose the gaps (problem areas). We then agree on a shared vision of what to expect from a Lean implementation.

If you are thinking about implementing Lean, the best place to start is to pick a pilot area as a project. Keep in mind, the most important thing for any pilot project is to be successful. The strategy behind the BASICS model is to build people's motivation by having small ongoing successes that make everyone feel like they are part of a winning team. We then work to introduce a problem-solving culture and eventually a Learning organization.*

The Change Equation

You have determined you need to change, or at least that you *want* to change, so what next? The first change tool we use is called the "change equation." We review this with all our clients, normally starting during the assessment phase. The equation is:

$$C \times V \times N \times S > R_{change}$$

---

* A Learning Organization is made up of five pieces: Personal Mastery, Mental Models, Shared Vision, Team Learning, and Systems Thinking. *The Fifth Discipline*, Peter Senge, 1990. Random House: New York.

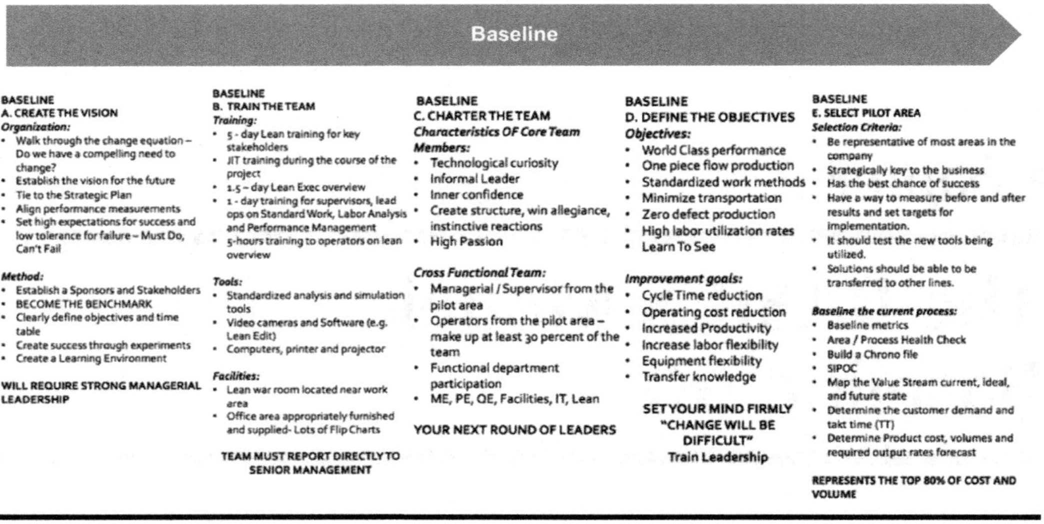

Figure 2.1 The BASICS six-step model for Lean implementation—baseline. (Source: BIG Training Materials.)

R_{change} = *Resistance to Change*

Notice there is a multiplication sign between each letter. This is because if any of the letters equal zero or are not addressed, we will not overcome the R_{change}, which stands for resistance to change; thus, effective change will not occur. In addition, each step needs to be followed in order.

C = *Compelling Need to Change*

We have learned Lean is generally not even pursued in most companies unless there is a perceived need to change. The question to ask is: Is there really a compelling need to change? If we could say this a thousand times louder, it would not even come close to how necessary this equation is for change. There are two ways to incentivize change:

1. One is to have an actual crisis or business case, where, without change, the organization will not survive.
2. The other way is to invent a crisis or to set very high goals (challenges or stretch targets) for the organization that cannot be achieved by doing it the way it has always been done.

We must find a way to drive Lean improvements and implement employee ideas every day. We have learned if you implement someone's idea then they will more than likely give you another. The CEO must create the compelling need to change for the organization. This means not only do we go through the change equation, but the CEO must determine a way to continuously repeat the change equation cycle to create a systemic way to drive continuous improvement every day.

V = Vision

The next letter in the change equation is *V* for vision. A shared vision is important in the change equation because without a vision, how can you chart a course? People must understand the vision and the why the change is required to support the vision. This includes the how, when, and what their contribution will be, as well as their role in the change. This will make the change easier to sell and adopt, thus reducing the resistance to change.

Communicate, communicate, and communicate. It is critical when you begin deploying Lean that team members communicate the vision and why the Lean transformation is needed.

N = Next Steps

N stands for next steps. Once we know we have a compelling need to change and know and understand the vision, we need to determine the next steps to reach the vision. These steps come from assessing where we are currently, relative to the vision, and then understanding and overcoming the gaps. This must be translated to what we call a Lean roadmap. The roadmap will outline how we are going to achieve the vision.

S = Sustain

The final letter, *S*, stands for sustain. This is the most difficult step of all. Sustaining is the true test of whether there was a compelling-enough reason to change and a sign as to if the other letters were implemented properly.

Train the Leadership Team

It is important to conduct a training session for the Leadership team. This varies in length but the executive overview is normally one to two days. We normally augment this training with a working session to start laying out the goals for the first pilot and to agree on a contract for change. The leadership team will require ongoing coaching and training, using benchmarking trips, gemba walks, Lean conferences, etc. Over time the leadership should all attend the five-day Lean training class.

Five-Day Lean Training Seminar and Kaizen

The next step is to train the core team and pilot team along with any related stakeholders, which will be crucial to implementing the project. We recommend the leadership participate in the training as well. This five-day Lean overview consists of lecture, videos, and includes real-life application by kaizening a small project. This five-day training just scratches the surface of Lean principles and tools but will motivate the team to find waste and achieve excellent implementation results.

The system's success absolutely depends on the entire organization's input and implementation of the tools and methodology, but it is up to the leadership team to drive the organization. This means at every level of implementation they need to be hands-on with the concepts and understanding of their team to make sure they align with the direction of the company. The highest success rates we have seen when it comes to Lean implementation is when the leadership team is involved as early on as the team charter.

Charter the Team, Scope the Project, and Select the Pilot Area

We always suggest starting small to create learning. We start by creating a team charter, picking a pilot and core team, and selecting the pilot area. One should think through the following elements when considering large projects:

1. Enter a clear statement of the problem or process to be improved.
2. The specific metrics to be targeted.
3. List the team members and the names for the champion, team leader, team members and their function, and the facilitator.
4. Describe how the project ties to the customer and strategic goals for the company.
5. Who is the principal owner of the process?
6. Who are the primary stakeholders that will be affected by the project deliverables?
7. What are the baseline and targeted metrics?
8. What is the process scope: input boundary—the starting point of the process to be improved: output boundary—ending point of the process to be improved?
9. Budget: List any budget available if applicable or list tools or equipment that may need to be purchased or modified.
10. Potential benefit: List any non-monetary or intangible benefits expected from improvements to the process.
11. Exit criteria: List specifically at what point the team will be considered "done" the event, where any and all changes or open actions transfer to the team leader.
12. Empowerment level for the team: At what empowerment level the team is chartered. i.e., are they empowered to recommend changes, implement changes, etc.?
13. Is there any pre-work required?
14. Support functions required: this could be maintenance, IT, etc.
15. HS&E: Is there a checklist for environmental and safety that needs to be filled out?
16. Risk mitigation: Are there any potential risks from the kaizen we need to assess and mitigate?
17. Steering group/Review council: List what group the team is going to report out to and at what frequency.

The purpose of the core team is to stay together during the implementations and become the future Lean practitioners. The goal of the consultant is to transfer the knowledge to the Lean practitioners. The pilot team is made up of members from the line, including the supervisor, whose job is to sustain the line when the core team exits.

The purpose of the pilot is to experiment and provide a starting point for the Lean implementation. This gives the team a chance to see how the Lean tools work and what results can be obtained. We then gather lessons learned from the pilot prior to implementing in the next area. The criteria we use for the pilot are as follows:

- Be representative of most areas in the company and strategically key to the business.
- An environment where the implementation has the best chance of success and sustaining.

- The supervisor and staff are willing to make the necessary changes and lead the area with the new changes in place.
- People in the pilot area have a positive attitude toward change.
- Have a way to measure before and after results and set targets for implementation.
- It should test the new tools being utilized.
- Solutions should be able to be transferred to other lines.

Many times companies want to "jump" right into the biggest problem area, or where there is major crisis. This criterion doesn't mean you can't pick the biggest problem area; but remember, the ultimate goal of the Lean implementation in the pilot area is simple: It must be successful! Sometimes it is better to go with an area where both the attitudes are good and there is a compelling need to change.

The implementation team should have members from the pilot area and can include persons from the next area to be worked on in addition to those subject-matter experts you are working to develop, that is, the Lean core team or kaizen promotion office (KPO). The team should be no larger than six to eight persons.

We then select the team and team leader. Team leader characteristics should include:

- Can lead a team and manage to a project deadline
- Is familiar with the business and open to change
- Has the respect of both the senior leadership, the organization as a whole
- Is technologically curious, imaginative, and insightful and has good common sense
- Is a critical thinker and not afraid to ask why (dumb question), admit error, create structure where no structure exist, and identify good talent
- Is not afraid of confrontation, and has good communication skills, presentation skills, and good interpersonal skills
- Has detailed process knowledge and has grown up in the system promoted from within
- Is dedicated and committed and does whatever it takes to get the job done with respect to effort and time commitments

Team member characteristics should include:

- Have good communication skills and interpersonal skills
- Provide 110% effort
- Conduct constructive critical evaluation of their own work
- Have a good positive attitude and are open to change
- They are curious and continuous learners
- They are team players

Baseline Metrics, Identify the "Gaps," and Set Targets

It is important to first understand the gaps between where we are today and the voice of the customer (VOC). We then create the scope, goals, and problem statement prior to starting the analysis phase. If not, it will create a high amount of confusion and frustration for the team.

Also included in the project plan must be a concept of how we will measure the success of the new process. This will be utilized in the *check* phase of the BASICS model.

We start with defining the problem and establishing the baseline, which includes the metric definition, source of the data, owner, frequency it is updated, and the calculation(s) used.

We then need to understand and create a list of what problems we have today. This exercise does two things. It lets people "vent" about the problems and we get a good list of opportunities to improve. When we finish the initial phase of the implementation we then go back to this list to see how many of the problems we solved and, more importantly, those we didn't solve.

Then we brainstorm the ideal state of what the process could look like in five years. This is the beginning of building what we call a shared vision or true north. This shared vision provides the targets for our Lean implementation. Our vision always includes the following:

- Create one-piece flow (OPF)
- Eliminate waste everywhere in the process
- Build in quality to every step
- Create leader and operator standard work
- Create visual-management systems

Next, we identify the gaps between where we are today and the vision. This is what we need to root-cause and solve. We always find most companies, even Lean ones, are batching. This is true in the information-flow world as well. This is called "push" production. Batching, or push systems, are the root cause of the seven wastes we will discuss later.

The Change and What's in It for Me

Change can be a difficult adjustment for many individuals. Whenever challenged with a new initiative, it is important to develop and agree upon answers as an organization to the questions it will receive from its workforce. This means that the Leadership must drive the team to make sure the same answers are being given at every level to ensure uniformity in the organization. These are just a few of the possible questions employees will ask. If not answered correctly they will be left in the dark, creating an unnerving void:

- What is the change we are making?
- Why are we making the change?
- How will it affect the employees? Now and in the future?
- How will it affect the company? Now and in the future?
- What is in it for the employee if we make the change?
- What is in it for the company if we make the change?

Share as much of the implementation plan as possible to provide when, where, and how the change will be implemented. People feel much more secure knowing there is a plan in place and that they have a future role in the company. Not to assume selfishness, but it's natural for the biggest concern of people to be "what is in it for us and how will it affect us."

Contract for Change

Once all the answers have been agreed on for how to roll this out to the workforce, it is important to have a group understanding on the initiative being taken. One way to do this is with a contract for change. This document has been extremely useful from a culture standpoint to ensure everyone is on the same page and having them literally sign and date the contract-for-change document. The contract should contain the vision, goals, and objectives, an escalation plan, methodology, and commitment. It can be used at any level for any project. It is critical to have an escalation process in place to help the improvement teams or supervisors remove barriers to improvement. The escalation process should proceed all the way to the CEO.

Resistance to Change*

In Jerald Young's book *Not Now Not Ever* he breaks resistance to change into two categories:

1. Logic-based resistance, which presents a problem to be solved. For example, voicing a valid objection to the idea being presented. This does not mean the person is being negative; but, we must overcome this objection in order to get their buy-in and, in many cases it will make the implementation of the idea better. This type of resistance can actually be reviewed as good.
2. Emotional-based resistance, which presents an emotional reaction to be dissolved. For example, a friend of mine, when they were a teenager, had a bit too much rum to drink and since then they refuse to drink rum again.

Young points out that the person is not the enemy, the resistance is the enemy. Young suggests we must dissolve the emotional-based resistance (EBR) before attempting any logic-based resistance. It's people with this emotional-based resistance that we would have termed "concrete heads" in the past. We also described this EBR in the past as the following:

> You can lead a horse to water
> The horse likes the water
> The horse refuses to drink the water

If you can dissolve the emotional-based resistance and then win the logic-based objections, the person generally will not only go along with the change but tends to become a zealot.

Dr. Young also points out that opposition is different than resistance.

Over the years we have learned that people share two different perspectives on change:

1. I'll believe it when I see it.
2. I'll see it when I believe it.

Think about the difference between these two statements. In many cases, for people that share the type 1 view, we need to benchmark other companies, read books, use YouTube®, etc. to "show" them what is possible. Once they see it, you can't stop them from going after it.

For people that share the type 2 view, they use a very misunderstood gift called intuition to see or even know the possibilities before they see it.

---

* *Not Now Not Ever*, Jerald Young, PhD, 2003. Center for Stable Change: New York.

The Impact of Barriers: Removal Degree of Difficulty (✗)

Whenever implementing change we run into barriers. We classify these barriers as cultural, process, and technical. We describe these below:

Cultural barriers (100✗) result in entrenched habits, behaviors, and attitudes. They have a degree of difficulty = *100×*. Cultural barriers can only be removed by the senior leadership team.

Process barriers (10✗) are best removed by using cross-functional teams and championed by senior leadership. These are good candidates for Lean system-wide kaizen projects or in some cases point kaizen events.

Technical barriers (1✗) are those specific to machines or the industry. Technical barriers can normally be removed by individuals or cross-functional teams.

To remove these barriers one must identify the barrier and question if there is a compelling need to change the barrier. If there is, then categorize the type of barrier and choose the appropriate method or approach to deal with the barrier.

What Is Batching?

We define batching as, "where one operation is done to multiple parts prior to moving the parts to the next operation." So, this means that one doesn't see the first completed piece until the entire batch, of whatever it is you are making, is completed. However, sometimes we still have to batch (see Figure 2.2).

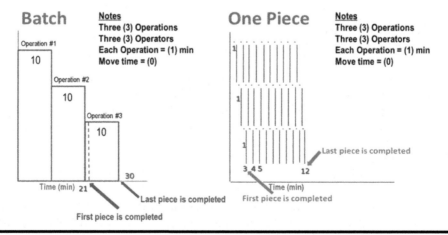

Figure 2.2   Batch versus one-piece flow example. When processing ten pieces we get our first piece in batch at 21 minutes versus three minutes in flow and our last piece at 30 minutes in batch versus 12 minutes in flow. With one-piece flow we average a part per minute off the line or office process. (Source: The effect of lot delay reductions—Shigeo Shingo, *The Shingo Production Management System*, Productivity Press © 1990, page 17, 116 used with permission, Taylor & Francis.)

Batching Is Bad

No matter what we do in life, how we do it matters. Batching drives tremendous inefficiency. This is a difficult concept for many of us to accept, since we all seem to be born with the mindset that batching is the most efficient way to do anything. The book *One-Piece Flow vs. Batching** explores this paradox in detail. Suffice it to say that batching drives waste and waste creates problems for all of us.

How many of you would rather take a highway versus a road with a stop sign or red light at every crossing? Stop signs impede our ability to flow. Red lights are called period batch systems, because they let a batch of cars through, determined by a certain length of time on green, before the light turns back to red.

Think about the systems in which you work or live. We find most are full of stop signs and red lights. We consider every stop sign a "gap" or a problem to be solved.

One-Piece Flow

One of the key concepts in Lean is one-piece flow (OPF), or small-lot processing. OPF refers to the processing or servicing of each component part, product, or piece of paper, one at a time through each step until it is completed. In the hospital we call it one-patient flow. One-piece flow or small-lot systems are always faster and result in a decreased opportunity for errors in comparison to processing in batches. Processing in batches essentially makes people robots, i.e., doing the same small step repeatedly over and over again. But please remember, for processes to flow we must eliminate the reasons or need for the batching.

The questions we always ask whenever we identify this gap is: "How can we get this process as close to an assembly line as possible?" In the hospital, we had to add: "… without calling it an assembly line."

It's not always possible, and sometimes we are forced to batch;[†] but, our end goal should always be to create systems with overall or master layouts that flow from beginning to end.

Why Do We Batch?

We have been studying batching behavior for over 30 years. We have developed the following eight reasons why people feel they "must" batch.

1. *Your mind*: Our minds are programmed from birth to believe batching is more efficient than one-piece flow. If we have any opportunity to batch, we will, and some of us will literally fight (and have fought) to protect our ability to batch. This is why only 20% of companies have any real success with Lean.
2. *Setups/changeovers*: The larger the lot, the more we need to batch. This is the basis of EOQ.[‡] We cannot reduce the lot size or get to one-piece flow on a piece of equipment until we reduce the setup time. However, we do not need to eliminate long setup times to

---

* *One-Piece Flow vs. Batching*, Protzman, McNamara, Protzman, 2016. CRC Press: Boca Raton, FL.
[†] See *One-Piece Flow vs. Batching*, Protzman, McNamara, Protzman, page 77.
[‡] EOQ is the economic order quantity.

achieve one-piece flow. We can do one-piece flow by setting up kanbans before and after the batching equipment.

3. *Variation*: We can handle all sorts of variation in one-piece flow implementations. However, the introduction of many new models is a frequent reason shops of all sizes lose one-piece flow.

4. *Travel distance*: We must decrease the travel distance or people will batch. This means machines must literally be next to one another. In some cases this means cutting in new access panels behind the equipment or moving parts of the equipment (i.e., pumps) on top of the equipment.

5. *Equipment*: We can do one-piece flow by using standard WIP before and after the equipment, i.e., a batch washer or oven. The goal should be to evolve to one-piece flow equipment using right-sized machines. This is called chaku–chaku.*

6. *Process*: Here our goal is to use smaller batches where it makes sense, with a goal of transitioning to continuous flow.

7. *Idle time*: If people are idle and can continue to build WIP, they will. People hate to be idle. So if they can build a subassembly, or have parts that they can partially assemble, they can't help themselves, and will build as much as they can or have space available for. Note: We can eliminate the idle time when we implement bumping in a one-piece flow process.

8. *Space*: Where there is too much space, eliminate it or people will fill it up with WIP, and where there is too little, we add space. If not, people will batch. This is a big problem for companies that implement Lean, cut down the workstations to do one-piece flow, and then start batching again. Because, now there is no room for the WIP. In this case, it can actually produce worse results than the original batching process.

Let Data Be Your Guide

The secret to implementing Lean is to start with the system and let the data be your guide. The data will tell you which way to go and what you need to do. It is a great objective tool. By videoing the process, we can collect data on the as-is process. The video can solve many arguments because it removes the opinions of people and replaces them with facts.

Non-Negotiable Guidelines with Lean System Implementations

- We must always strive to run one-piece flow. No batching.
- Create a pull system with level-loaded scheduling.
- Avoid conveyors between workstations. Only use conveyors to convey … not to store.
- Use baton-zone line-balancing (bumping).
- Standing/walking lines—utilize anti-fatigue mats† or operator insoles.
- Day-by-hour charts in place.
- All materials within operator ergonomic striking distance.

---

* Chaku–chaku stands for place place or load–load lines. They will take operations done on large machines and break them up to several small machines.

† This is the best anti-fatigue mat we have ever encountered. There is much science behind it: www.smartcell-susa.com. For insoles—I, Charlie Protzman, personally have been wearing these insoles for six years: ALINE Systems, www.aline.com

- Standard WIP in place, visual controls exist, and audited.
- The end goal is no forklifts, cranes, or hoists.
- The end goal is done right the first time—zero escapes to the customer—mistake-proofing first, 100% visual machine inspection second, human inspection is last resort.
- Operators do not leave the cell or line.
- Product does not leave the cell until it is completed.
- No process reversals. Product never goes backward.
- Standard work in place, followed and audited.
- The end goal is zero work orders released short. Systems and standard work must be in place to prevent shortages.
- Active cross-training—everyone can do everything.
- No trash containers in the cell. Use reusable packaging. No paper or cardboard in the cell. Goal is zero landfill waste.
- The end goal is a moving line used as a pacemaker for the process.
- The end goal is no unplanned downtime.
- Quick/real-time problem-solving demonstrated for line downtime
- Use MRP to drive high-level scheduling requirements—not spreadsheets. Do not use MRP as the shop floor control system.
- Use kanban, i.e., empty bins, empty spaces, card systems, to trigger replenishment—not MRP.
- Daily checks and TPM carried out routinely—quality control process checks (QCPC) have been internalized and are routinely used to improve quality.
- Value-stream maps exist—ongoing, daily improvements are clearly identified and prioritized.
- The end goal is no pits dug into the floor or platforms. Build right-sized equipment in-house.
- Multiple persons should not be required to lift the product.
- Everything less than 1.5 m (5 ft) in height.
- Work to eliminate the need for inspection. Inspection means you fundamentally don't trust the process.
- Subassembly lines used as required. Goal is eventually to have them in-line or directly feeding main line. These can also be laid out in parallel to the main line. There should be no offline batching of subassemblies.
- Andon/QCPC system used. Operators empowered to stop the line for any quality/safety issues.

Management and operators/staff must sustain these principles throughout the entire product life cycle.

Baseline Metrics

Why Is Baselining Metrics Important?

This is a critical step. If we don't baseline the metrics before the project begins, we will not be able to determine how much we have improved.

Unfortunately, many times, there are no standard procedures or metrics available. Sometimes this is because the metrics are kept at a high level or people frequently move in and out of various lines. In this case we may take a week or two to baseline the metrics or we estimate metrics to the best of our ability, which everyone agrees to at the time.

In addition, once you get done a Lean implementation there will be those that don't believe the new system is better than the old one. This can be a huge problem for those starting the Lean journey because without qualitative and quantitative results, people will not buy-in to Lean and will fight the effort moving forward.

Baseline Metrics

Typical metrics we collect are:

- Units per hour
- First-pass yield
- Rolled throughput yield
- Pieces per person per day or per hour (UPPH)
- WIP count and dollars
- Travel distance for the part and operators
- Space
- Current EHS work station rating—ergonomic risk factors
- Overtime as a percent of units produced

We may also collect any other process or industrial engineering data, drawings, procedures, as well as their overall operational metrics, i.e., on-time delivery, quality etc. See Figure 2.3.

Assembly Line - Feb 2010

Baseline Metrics – Station Balanced	
Operators (for two shifts)	10
Cell Lead (for two shifts)	1.5
Units per day 11/30 – 2/13/10	518
Paid Minutes Per Unit includes OT	11.72
Thru-put Time (Working days)	2.3
Cycle Time (min - Est.Batch)	1.73
Overtime #hrs 1/1/10 – 2/14/10	203
Space (sq. ft)	616
Travel Distance (ft)	84
WIP #	1562
Pieces per person per day	45

Baseline Product Flow

Actual After Lean Metrics June 2010 Data		
Operators (eliminated 2nd shift)	2.7	73%
Cell Lead	.9	40%
Units per day	261	49.6%
Paid Minutes Per Unit	6.6	43.5%
Thru-put Time (Working days)	.1	96%
Cycle Time (min)	1.72	9.9%
Overtime #hrs	0	100%
Space (sq. ft)	558	9%
Travel Distance (ft)	42	50%
WIP #	74	95.3%
Pieces per person per day	72.5	74%

After Lean Flow

74% Increase In Productivity & Eliminated Need For 2nd Shift

Figure 2.3   Before versus after metrics template example. (Source: BIG Archives.)

Health Check

We use a self-assessment tool to assess the current state of the line or area's behaviors, management system, and culture. The assessment tool should measure more than the use of Lean tools; it must measure behaviors at each level of leadership and how engaged employees are in the changes to processes they perform (see Figure 2.4).

We like to say the Lean tools, while they have to be learned, are easy compared to the change-management piece. There must be a balance between tools and people. It is just as important to focus on the philosophy as it is the tools. Without the philosophy, the tools, by themselves, will not sustain.

What Is a Second Worth?

Every company should have Finance calculate what a second of improvement is worth? Once you have the answer, this is an easy concept for all employees to understand and can answer the question: "Why should I worry about saving a second?" In any process, seconds, over the course of a year, add up to hours, and sometimes days, weeks, or months of savings. Improve your seconds,

Health Check	SCORING RULES		Score		
	Best Practice		4 to 6		
	Needs some improvement		2 to 4		
	Not addressed well or at all		0 to 2		

	Area	Operations Manager	How to measure?	Weighting	Score	Group Average
1	Environment	Is a DBTH system in use in the area	Observation	6	2	
2	Environment	Does visual management system make performance available for all to see	Observation	6	1	
3	Environment	Does a Cross Training Matrix and Training Plan exist?	Observation	6	5	2.75
4	Environment	Are cross training levels where they should be as per the cross training plan?	Observation/Feedback from Sups	6	3	
5	Ops Mgmt	Does the manager or GL attend morning line meetings more often than not	Observation/Feedback from Sups	6	6	
6	Ops Mgmt	Is the supervisor clear on make up of PFM available time (set up times, breaks, etc...)	Discussion & Agreement	6	2	
7	Ops Mgmt	Is there a clear picture of area metrics to form a baseline for project (actual downtime, actual % performance to standard work, Yield,) Note : this is Not expected performance, but actual performance	Discussion & Agreement	6	2	3.00
8	Ops Mgmt	Are supervisor Roles & Responsibilities clearly defined - is there enough time in the day to perform all tasks? i.e. is there standard work	Discussion & DILF	6	2	
9	Ops Mgmt	If managers understand how their available time is made up, is there alignment between Operations manager, supervisors and 14 step team	Discussion & Agreement	6	2	
10	Supv & TL	Do supervisors understand std work and its importance (including WIP limits, targets, labour balance, batoning, etc...)	Survey	6	2	
11	Supv & TL	Can the supervisor reconcile their DBTH board (on an hourly basis)	Observation	6	2	
12	Supv & TL	Can supervisor display sound RCA skills on reconciled units	Observation	6	3	
13	Supv & TL	Are supervisors able to review operators performance against standard work (and use Timer Pro if needed)	Discussion & Agreement	6	3	
14	Supv & TL	Do supervisors understand what their bottleneck stations are	Discussion & Agreement	6	4	
15	Supv & TL	Is there good meeting structure at morning meeting (is visible agenda followed, etc...)	Observation	6	5	3.00
16	Supv & TL	What % of supervisor time is on line (vs. target of 70%)	Discussion & DILF	6	3	
17	Supv & TL	Is there a structured supervisor handover meeting/checklist between shifts	Discussion & Agreement	6	2	
18	Supv & TL	Do supervisors have a basic understanding of Lean theory	Survey	6	5	
19	Supv & TL	Is there good behaviour on line - do operators return in time from breaks, do they leave early at end of shift	Observation	6	2	
20	Supv & TL	Are PFMs accessible on line (and clearly visible)	Observation	6	3	
21	Supv & TL	Do supervisors adhere to agreed headcount guidelines (max heads for holidays, etc...)	Discussion & Agreement	6	2	
22	Operator	Do operators understand what pace they need to produce parts at per hour	Survey	6	2	
23	Operator	Is the area set up to allow the operator count parts efficiently	Observation	6	2	
24	Operator	Is there adherence to standard work by the operators	Observation	6	2	
25	Operator	Do operators Baton when their WIP level is full?	Observation	6	3	2.17
26	Operator	Do operators understand the CI process and what they can do to solve problems in their own area?	Discussion & Agreement	6	3	
27	Operator	Do operators understand std work and its importance (including WIP limits, targets, labour balance, batoning, etc...)	Survey	6	1	
28	Gen'l Behaviour	Are lines working outside agreed timelines to hit targets (e.g. breaks)	Observation	6	2	
29	Gen'l Behaviour	Is there good Lean engagement - LPIS, A3s, std work audits on track etc..	Review metrics	6	3	
30	Gen'l Behaviour	Are CI Huddles in progress in the area - and are the results displayed	Observation	6	3	2.67
31	Gen'l Behaviour	Is there good morale on line (may be affected by overtime)	Survey	6	4	
32	Gen'l Behaviour	Are huddles happening weekly?	Survey	6	2	
33	Gen'l Behaviour	Is there a strong communication process in the area?	Survey	6	2	
34	Support staff	Are priorities for support staff aligned with operations (e.g. prioritisation of tasks, on line support availability, etc..)	Survey	6	2	2.00
35	Support staff	Do support staff have an understanding of the Lean production system	Survey	6	2	
		Total		210	0	

Figure 2.4 Health check template example. We use scoring for companies that are beginning since this is what they are used to. As the company matures in Lean we eliminate the scoring, otherwise it always becomes more about "the score" than learning the tools and changing the behaviors. (Source: BIG Archives.)

inches, cms, and save your pennies; save a little bit every day and watch the savings add up. This is daily kaizen which is at the heart of establishing a Lean culture.

Build a Chrono File

Take photos and videos of how it is today. You cannot take enough pictures of how things are today. People will quickly forget, once you go down the continuous improvement journey, how things used to be. We later use these pictures in what we call a chrono file, which documents the BASICS process you followed as well as all your team's improvements. It is important to build this document as you go or else you will forget a lot of it.

Map the Current-State Process

One can use a simple flowchart, process diagram, swim-lane map, or create a value-stream map (VSM). Normally for manufacturing implementations we just use a simple process map. However, we have found value-stream mapping to be extremely useful for visualizing information flow and trans-actional processes for administrative, hospital, government, and banking/insurance applications.

Seven Wastes*

The following seven wastes are attributed to Taiichi Ohno.[†] These wastes are primarily driven by batch systems or imperfect flows:

1. Waste of Overproduction
   This waste is the number one waste in the batch system. It manifests itself two ways: Making or buying more than you need or making or receiving it before you need it.
2. Waste of Time on Hand (Idle)
   Whenever someone is waiting with nothing to do.
3. Waste in Transportation
   Transporting people, things, or paper or electronic transactions.
4. Waste of (Too Much) Processing
   We define this as doing more to a part or paperwork (electronic or paper) than nec-essary to meet the customer-defined specifications, and customer-perceived quality needs. Inspection is a waste of too much processing.
5. Waste of Stock on Hand (Inventory)
   This can be raw materials, work in process (WIP), or finished goods. i.e., too many canned goods in the pantry.
6. Waste of (Worker) Movement
   We define this waste as follows: whenever someone has to reach outside their normal path of motion while sitting or standing, including having to get their own parts or supplies.
7. Waste of Making Defective Products
   This waste includes rework as well as defects.

---

* The first seven wastes originated with Toyota's Taiichi Ohno.
[†] There are many acronyms to help people remember these wastes, i.e., DOWNTIME, TIM P WOOD, etc.

Three Additional Wastes:

8. Waste of Talent (An Organization's Most Valuable Asset)

    We see this waste when organizations do not tap their employees' brainpower, ideas, and experiences or they have no respect for their people. The engagement of an organization's talent is critical in making Lean initiatives successful. The talent in your organization will drive innovation and change by identifying and eliminating all waste.

9. Waste of Resources

    Whenever we don't fully utilize or recycle our resources or we dump hazardous or every day waste into a landfill.

10. Context-Switching Waste

    This waste is encountered when someone is trying to multitask, which then results in batching the tasks. i.e., Emergency Room doctor batching three to four patients at a time results in 40%–60% waste.*

The Root Cause of Most of These Wastes Is Batching!

Ohno said the worst waste is the waste we don't see. We typically can't see hidden wastes because they are hiding behind or are masked by other wastes. You really have to hunt for them! These are the hardest wastes to find and yet the most dangerous. Reviewing videos is the best way to discover hidden waste.

Transactional Process Improvement

When implementing transactional processes, we utilize all the same tools in the BASICS and PDSA models. Like other Lean initiatives, in general, people are not the problem; the *system* is normally the problem. The office personnel are like other staff throughout the firm; they are always busy. However, what are they busy doing?

We video the office (transactional) process just like the shop floor and utilize the same analysis tools for information flow as we do for physical products. We always use analysis tools based on the problems to be solved and their complexity.

The Transactional Ten Wastes

1. Waste from overproduction of goods or services—waste of excess reports, both paper and electronic, batch copying, too many brochures printed, information duplicated across forms or not needed. Gathering, sorting, and saving more information than is really needed.
2. Waste from waiting or idle time—is either the information itself or the person waiting for it, time to secure (rubber-stamped) approvals for contracts, equipment ordering, repairs in the office, unplanned interruptions, unbalanced workflow, lack of capacity for volume, etc.
3. Waste from transportation—(unnecessary) document flow/movement between offices for processing, routing, and poor office layout, placement of adjacencies, travel time, unnecessary copying/approval of information to people who do not use it.

---

* *Certified Scrum Master Training Book*. Scrum Inc.: Cambridge, MA.

4. Waste from overprocessing (inefficiency), multiple, redundant, and undefined approvals; or multiple reviews and inspections. Elaborate filing systems for documents.
5. Waste of motion and effort—rework of requests, calls for following up on approvals if multiple people are involved, searching for information, centralized printers, etc. Waste driven in computer systems.
6. Waste of inventory—unnecessary stock on hand, too many supplies, duplicative files, multiple file storage, just in case storage, etc.
7. Waste from defect—lack of training documents, completion of company errors in capturing data, errors in transferring data, supplies and equipment ordered incorrectly or in the wrong quantities, missed deadlines, rework, clarifications, etc.
8. Waste of talent—frustration of employees, no one listens to their input, right person in wrong position, talented people spending time on rework, lack of empowerment to correct processes, lack of training on process improvement, unclear roles, task interruptions, multitasking, underutilization of talent, etc.
9. Corporate staff waste—creating report-out presentations and ongoing requests for data. Sometimes we receive the same requests from various positions of corporate staff. These people create no value yet justify their positions by creating work for people already busy.
10. Waste driven by centralizing processes.

Waste Exercise 30-30-30 or Ohno Circle

Taichi Ohno worked his way up the ranks at Toyota from machinist to vice president. He was known for drawing a chalk circle around managers and making them stand in that circle until they had seen and documented all the problems in an area that he wanted them to see; sometimes for an entire shift or longer (see Figure 2.5).

Figure 2.5 The Ohno circle—managers would spend many hours, sometimes over a shift or more, until they saw the waste Ohno wanted them to see.

Today this exercise is known as the Ohno circle or the 30-30-30 exercise, i.e., 30 minutes' watch: find 30 problems, and spend 30 minutes solving one of the problems so it doesn't come back. This is a great first step to train someone's eyes to see waste and to provide structure for the group leader/supervisor or manager to carry out daily improvement.

Ritsuo Shingo* says the busy executive with limited time must "go to the Gemba and Watch" (not see) what is really happening. We must eliminate batching and always work toward one-piece flow.

Lean Maturity Path Visualization

As we make improvements throughout the process, we should go back and update the VSM. As the value stream evolves from year to year, it can be used as a method to keep track of your progress throughout your Lean journey.

Definition of a Process

A process is defined as anything with an input that is transformed into something else which becomes the output (see Figure 2.6). An input can start with raw material from the ground or from the brain. It is then converted as part of the process to the output desired (or sometimes not desired, i.e., defect). It can be physical or mental; it can be a manufacturing step for a product or a series of manufacturing steps. It can be cocoa turned into hot chocolate, or hot chocolate where milk and/or marshmallows are added to it to make it more creamy and delicious. A process can be information that is transformed into a different output by a particular input.

SIPOC

We use the SIPOC tool at the beginning of the workshop or when we are working on the team charter (see Figures 2.7 and 2.8). The tool can be very useful if there is any confusion surrounding the process, its inputs, outputs, or customers. The SIPOC can help a team get a high-level understanding and gain consensus of the basics that make up the process before doing a value-stream map (VSM). The tool is used to obtain clarity around:

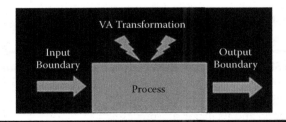

Figure 2.6   Definition of a process. (Source: BIG Archives.)

---

* Ritsuo Shingo Speech at LLI Santorini Seminar August 2017, hosted by George Trachilis.

	Supplier	Input	Process	Output	Customer
What are we trying to accomplish? Competed charts and ready patients.					
Process Step	**Supplier**	**Input**	**Process**	**Output**	**Customer**
1	Surgeons Offices	Patient referred to Pre-Testing	Registration - Full and Partial with Copay Request (hall patients only)	Patient registered and ready to complete Pre-Testing	Patient, Surgeons, PreOP
2	Pre-Testing Nurses (retrieves patient)	Interview patient in person, vital signs, PICIC assessment, Med Rec, HOM entry	Nursing Assessment	Patient determined to be ready for surgery, identify any Ancillary testing needed	Patient, Surgeons, PreOP
3	Pre-Testing & Ancillary Staff	Complete blood draw, EKG or X-rays	Ancillary Testing (as indicated)	Lab, EKG, X-ray results	Patient, Surgeons, PreOP
4	Pre-Testing Nurses (obtains patient name from phone list)	Interview patient over the phone, vital signs, PICIC assesment, Med Rec, HOM entry	Nursing Assessment (phone patients only)	Patient determined to be ready for surgery, identify any Ancillary testing needed	Patient, Surgeons, PreOP
5	Pre-Testing Staff	Next Day Surgery Charts, Consult Notes, H&P, Orders	Pre-Testing Chart Completed	Chart has all required contents and patient is ready to go to PreOp	Patient, Surgeons, PreOP

Figure 2.7 SIPOC—example from healthcare. (Source: BIG Archives.)

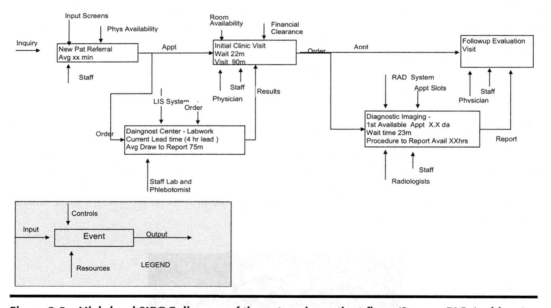

Figure 2.8 High-level SIPOC diagram of the enterprise patient flow. (Source: BIG Archives.)

- Defining the inputs and outputs of the process
- The high-level process and its major sub-processes
- Defining the true customer and their requirements

We generally start filling in the SIPOC with the process box. We have the team list the processes and try to keep it simple. Typically it is around five steps. Next we have the team list the outcomes expected from the process along with the customers. The customers can be internal and external. The team then identifies the inputs and suppliers. Because it is only a high-level view, there's still a need to do detailed process mapping whether it is a VSM and/or product process-flow analysis (PFA).

Value-Stream Mapping (VSM)

VSM has become an important tool in Lean implementations, particularly in understanding the current state of a process and identifying the opportunities where a process can be improved. VSM techniques are explained in two books, *Learning to See** and *Seeing the Whole*.

Since the introduction of these books, many subsequent books utilize VSMs as part of their instruction. This book is no exception. VSM is included initially as part of the baseline toolset (the *B* in the BASICS model), but it can also be used as an assessment tool (*A* in our BASICS model).

The VSM Tool

The VSM is much more powerful than a flow chart and has been successfully applied across many types of business, such as manufacturing, any office setting, services, healthcare, and government. The VSM is the best tool for mapping transactional administrative processes including order entry, scheduling, human resources, purchasing, sales, marketing, engineering, finance, and new business development.

The VSM is a dynamic tool that allows one to see the overall system and clearly understand the components of a process, subsystems, and interrelated dependencies at work as it follows the value stream across departmental silos (see Figure 2.9).

Over time the VSM can be used to track the progress of the Lean journey (see Figure 2.10). The VSM also helps one visualize the information and material flows across departments There should be an executive position in the organization that is assigned to continually look at how the value streams (processes) function and work together and assess improvement opportunities to stream-line the overall organization.

There are many benefits of VSM, including:

- Visualizes the flow and focuses on the big picture/system(s)
- Helps see areas to improve across silos
- Identifies the current state of the process
- Helps highlight and determine the source of the waste in the process
- Provides a common language for discussing problems and improvements
- Makes necessary decisions about flow very apparent
- Enables innovation brainstorm ideal and future states that leave out wasted steps while introducing smooth flow and leveled pull
- Provides a visual roadmap of prioritized opportunities to the strategic plan (i.e., projects and tasks) necessary for improvement as a management tool to track progress
- Enables opportunities to see where information systems should be able to talk to each other
- Creates employee objectives for their evaluations

The current-state VSM shows the "as-is" processes, which make up the overall system, and provides a focus on opportunities for improvement. Annually, updating your value-stream maps is a great way to keep track of your progress over time.

---

* *Learning to See*, Mark Rother and John Shook, 2003. LEI: Cambridge, MA; and *Seeing the Whole*, Jim Womack and Dan Jones, 2002. LEI: Cambridge, MA.

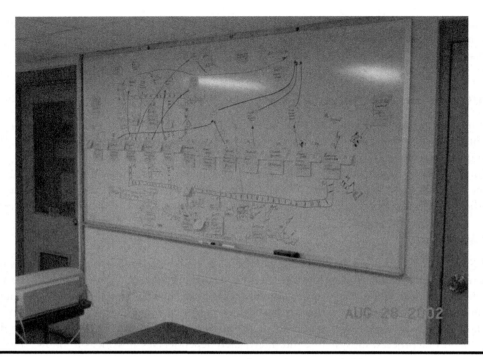

Figure 2.9 VSM on whiteboard with stickies. (Source: BIG Archives.)

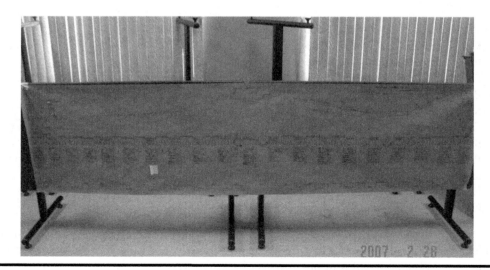

Figure 2.10 VSM in main conference room, which is updated every time improvements are made. (Source: BIG Archives.)

Parts of a VSM

VSMs started at Toyota and were informal tools, many times written on a napkin, used to describe the supply chain. They have four major parts: see example in Figure 2.11

1. In the middle of the map are the process boxes, which is how the part, product, or information flows.
2. At the top of the map are information system boxes, which outline what information, whether electronic or paper, is required to make each process work and the connection to the process box.
3. The third part is the timeline information at the bottom of the map. The timeline is a sawtooth, which includes the storage times on top and process CTs on the bottom. The results box shows the overall storage time (non–value-added time) versus the process time.
4. The fourth part is the materials flow from supplier to customer.

There are many references to VSM icons. Figure 2.12 depicts some standard icons, as well as lines to show manual information flows, i.e., someone hand-carrying information verbally or written, and communication such as fax, e-mail, snail mail, and telephone. Use colored lines for information flow: use red for automated, green for manual, and blue for snail mail, e-mail, fax, text, etc.

How to Create the VSM

Our approach is to make the VSM as realistic as possible. The process box also includes a data box (see Figure 2.13). We try to obtain statistically accurate data to populate the boxes where we can; however, the entire process map is a snapshot in time. While some simple maps can and have been done in a day, we find that when combined with teaching a VSM team and collecting real

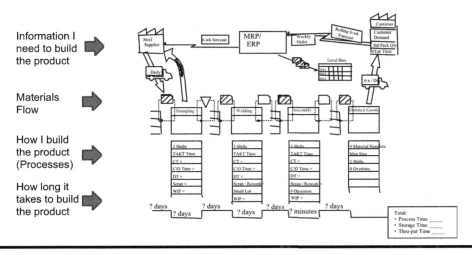

Figure 2.11   Parts of a value-stream map (VSM). (Source: BIG Archives.)

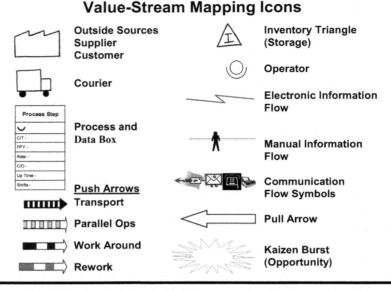

Figure 2.12   VSM icons. (Source: Learning to See and BIG Archives.)

data, doing the ideal and future states and developing a list of projects tied to the strategic plan normally takes a week.

Current State Map

As discussed previously, the first step is to create the VSM based on the current state (see Figure 2.14); this requires walking the process, pretending to be the "thing" (or information)

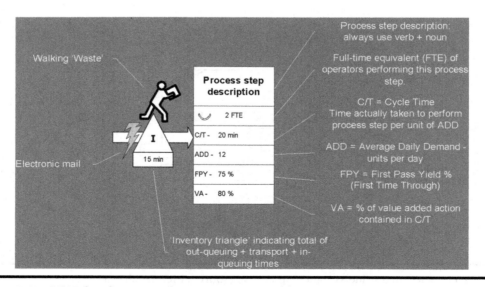

Figure 2.13   VSM data box example. (Source: BIG Archives.)

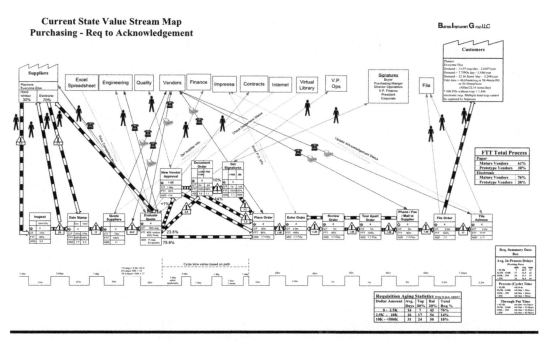

Figure 2.14   Current-state VSM example. (Source: BIG Archives.)

going through the process with a team of subject-matter experts consisting of frontline staff and those familiar with the process.

The VSM must describe what occurs in the process, not what is written in policies or how supervisors or managers may believe the process is occurring. It is critical to capture reality to truly identify waste and non-value activity, as described, as well as the supporting data.

We use stickies to map the process with one step per sticky (see Figure 2.15). A process step is easy to see; think about the stop lights. First you are driving, then you stop, then you go. When a product or service stops, the activity before the stop was a step, the stopping is a step, i.e., storage, and the activity after the stop is another process step.

At the bottom of each sticky we have a data box normally consisting of process cycle time (for one-piece), changeover time, lot size, number of people, number of shifts, etc. Mapping the flow is easy, collecting the data takes time because most of the data doesn't exist at this level. This means the team has to collect the data thoroughly.

We then add the information required to make each box work, which can include everything from major computer systems to manual logs kept in employees' pockets.

Next we add the material flow and finish it up by adding a timeline to the bottom. The timeline is a sawtooth, with the storage time, represented by triangles in the map, on the top, and process times on the bottom. We then add whatever notes make sense to describe what happens in the process.

The ERSC Process

The ERSC process is a review of every step in the current state map to determine the following:

- Which activities can be ERSC (eliminated, rearranged, simplified, or combined)?
- What is the critical path? Which events can be done in parallel?

Figure 2.15 VSM on paper with stickies—pink stickies is information flow and yellow is process flow. (Source: BIG Archives.)

- How many people touch the product or information, and are there handoffs?
- Are there activities duplicated by the same or another person or department?

Ideal-State Map

The second step is to create the ideal-state map (see Figure 2.16). It should be constructed as part of a brainstorming session in which the team determines what the process would be like if they were starting with a clean slate and all barriers are removed. Mapping the ideal process sets the target condition and looks at the process with what it could look like five or ten years from now if:

- All "sacred cows" were removed
- You had all the money in the world
- You had all the new technology available
- It was your company and you wanted to make money

Teams should not spend more than 30–60 minutes on this step. The purpose is to get teams to brainstorm, get the team "out of the box," and shift paradigms to envision the possibilities and to set an ideal-state target condition.

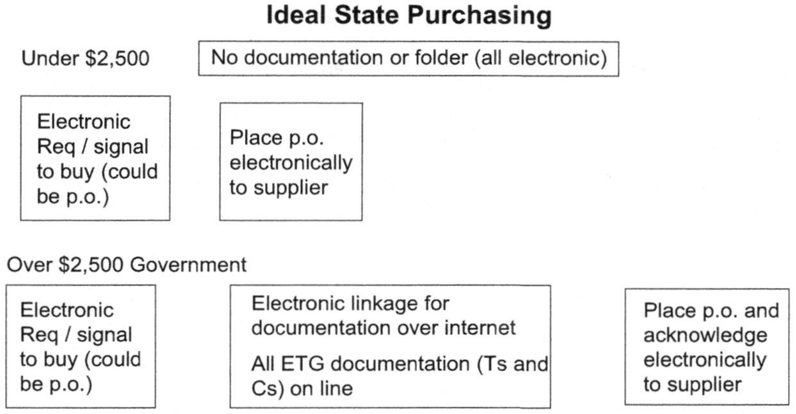

Ideal State Purchasing

Under $2,500 | No documentation or folder (all electronic)

Electronic
Req / signal
to buy (could
be p.o.)

Place p.o.
electronically
to supplier

Over $2,500 Government

Electronic
Req / signal
to buy (could
be p.o.)

Electronic linkage for
documentation over internet

All ETG documentation (Ts and
Cs) on line

Place p.o. and
acknowledge
electronically
to supplier

Figure 2.16   Ideal-state VSM example. (Source: BIG Archives.)

Future-State Map

The final step is to construct a future-state map (see Figure 2.17). The future-state map is created by the same team and normally determines what could realistically be accomplished from the ideal-state map over the next year but can forecast out even two years.

The team creates kaizen bursts* (sometimes known as improvement bursts) or potential projects and identifies quick wins (immediately changes to improve the process, usually unnecessary waste activities), which can be implemented, to get the process from its current state to future state.

As the team reviews and designs the future-state process, the opportunities are placed in a project list. Each opportunity is ranked based on impact to the strategic planning goals (Figure 2.18) (which may include service, people, finance, clinical, operations, ease of deployment, and cost).

In addition, priority-ranking is used to understand the risk and impact to other departments for each solution that is proposed. The list of potential opportunities provides a road map of CI activities the team can work on and track progress over the next year.

Value-Stream Layout Maps (Sometimes Referred to as Skitumi Maps)

During our VSM teachings, we always use the phrase: the process boxes are a process, not a place. However, the information in VSMs can help guide layout revisions to help optimize flow. Skitumi maps leverage the VSM data by overlaying the process boxes (data) on top of the existing master layout (see Figure 2.19).

This is an excellent way for leaders to help visualize how their overall layouts create bottlenecks and waste. This is also a good way to look at your overall master layouts or block diagrams of the company and develop high-level systemic approaches to improvement.

---

* Kaizen bursts can be placed on the current state or future state maps.

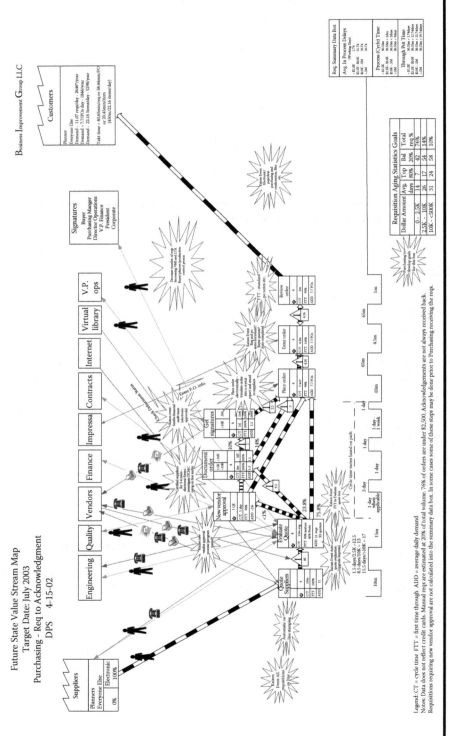

Figure 2.17 Future-state VSM—purchasing requisition to acknowledgment. (Source: BIG Archives.)

Lean Project Selection

Proposed Projects	Ranking 1-low impact 3-medium impact 5-high impact			Financial Perspective	Internal Business Process Perspective	Improve External Customer/ Stakeholder Perspective	Organization Enabler Perspective	Future Perspective	Totals	Costs	Potential Savings/ROI	
	Project or Task	Owner	Resources Required									Benefits
1 Kaizen Event - Auto quote evaluation, (upgrade Impresa, requires $30K Oracle udpate, Impressa is included in maintenance contract) and Electronic / paperless purchasing & confirmation, files etc.	Project	Purchasing	IT	5	3	3	1	5	17	$30K		Improved data collection
2 Buyer / planner / production control person	Project	Purchasing	Operations, L&P	5	3	1	5	1	15			
3 Kaizen event - FTT in evaluate quote process	Project	Purchasing	Cross Functional	1	3	1	3	1	9			
4 Kaizen Event - All requisitions on line	Project	Purchasing	IT	1	3	1	1	1	7			
5 Kaizen new vendor approval process, investigate program teams, standard form or	Project	Purchasing	Quality	1	3	1	1	1	7			
6 Kaizen event Smiths financial audit team - signature authority	Project	Purchasing	Smiths Financial	1	1	1	1	1	5			
7 Place order electronically - translate order into a crystal report and email to suppliers	Task	Purchasing	IT						0			
8 Req and po same document? Buyer queues? Auto completed	Task	Purchasing	IT						0			
9 FTT - standard po notes etc.	Task	Purchasing	IT						0			
10 Decrease number of reqs - Increasing VMI and LTA	Task	Purchasing	Purchasing						0			
11 Certified suppliers 3-4 years to cut down paperwork, on line DCAA audits	Task	Purchasing							0			
12 Purchasing to develop goals for this cycle time / aging req box	Task	Purchasing							0			

Figure 2.18 Decision matrix of tasks and projects prioritized to their strategic plan goals. (Source: BIG Archives.)

Conducting Value-Stream Mapping on Transactional Processes

We have found value-stream maps in the office environment to be unsurpassed as a continuous improvement tool. It is very difficult to *see* an office process because all you can see are cubicles, computers, and paperwork. The waste might be more streamlined now (i.e., e-mailed, texted, and twittered vs. paper documents in inboxes or in file cabinets) but it is still there. The process may pass through many people, floors of a building, across buildings, counties, states, or even across countries. VSMs are a great way to map, review, and discuss linkages between your customers' and suppliers' processes and yours.

The BASICS Tools Hierarchy

There is a definite hierarchy to how to implement the BASICS tools. The reason is, if one can eliminate a step at the value-stream level then no further analysis (i.e., product, operator, or setup) is needed for that step and it hastens the improvement process. This reasoning cascades to the product-flow analysis (PFA). If we can eliminate a step at the PFA level, we don't have to do the next step of the analysis, which is the workflow analysis of the operator, or, in some cases, the setup step is eliminated as well.

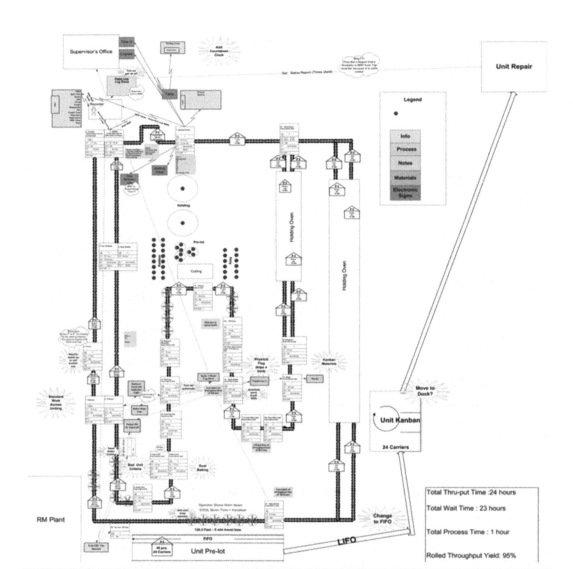

Figure 2.19 Skitumi map—VSM overlaid on the cad layout. (Source: BIG Archives.)

What Is Customer Value-Added in the Office?

As the team works through the current state, they should ask themselves the following question: Is what I am working on right now adding value for the customer? It must meet the following criteria:

■ Does the customer care? Are they willing to pay for it?
■ Does it physically change the data package?
■ Is it done right the first time?

During the ideal-state brainstorming we ask the team, if it was their business or company, how they would set up the process, even though it is paper- or electronic-based, to be as close to an assembly line as possible and make money! During the ideal-state brainstorming we force people to think "out of the box."

The first thing to pop out will be all types of IT systems–based ideas. Capture these IT suggestions and record them as options. While these are normally very good long-term suggestions, they tend to get expensive quickly, involve training hurdles, and can take a long time in the IT queue to implement. This does not mean they should be discouraged.

Next, ask the team for creativity versus capital ideas. What can we do to fix the process, first with no money and then look at automating the solutions?

Value-Stream Maps Key Points

- You must walk the process! This is also true for the office. The VSM cannot be done in isolation in a conference room, on a computer, or in a cafeteria. (Some recommended that you start at the last step in the process and go backward. This engages a deeper thought process).
- You must become the product as you outline the process. Make sure everyone is clear on what you are following (i.e., the product) otherwise everyone will become confused and discouraged.
- We always start by doing hand-drawn maps and obtain agreement from everyone involved in the process, and then we may put it into the computer.
- It is best to map the current or baseline state by reviewing the entire process versus a piece of the process.
- Don't confuse value-added and process times. They are different. At the VSM level, process CTs include both value-added and non–value-added.
- Don't be afraid to change or update the map during the year. It is good practice to have every stakeholder review the map, make changes, and track their progress throughout the year.
- Ensure the map is as close to reality as possible. If you can acquire accurate historical data, it is better than timing the process and calling it a "snapshot in time"; however, sometimes there is no other choice.
- Hold the process owner accountable to run the VSM event and to meet the actions agreed upon during the mapping event.

Determine the Customer Demand and Takt Time (TT)

Production Smoothing

Calculating the takt time starts with understanding the customer demand. Since the customer demand may only be available as a monthly total we use a tool called production smoothing. It is important to understand customer demand at the lowest possible level, especially if there are wide swings in demand cycles, such as in a seasonal business or hourly arrivals in an Emergency Room.

As we begin to relate demand to activities performed, we must be able to analyze demand in terms of how and when it is needed, that is, if a customer wants 1000 pieces per month and we have 20 working days, then the daily demand is 1000 pieces divided by 20 working days which equals 50 pieces per day. This is called production smoothing or leveling.

Peak Demand

Some companies may experience spikes in volume at various times throughout a shift, day, month, or year. Our goal is to totally level-load the demand, but in some cases, this may not be possible.

Therefore, we need to account for the highest volume the system will need to handle to create a successful Lean implementation. We call this demand variation—peak demand. We then use peak demand for the takt time where we can't level load the system.

Available Time*

The next thing we need to calculate is available time. This is equal to the actual working time of the team members. It is determined by taking the total clock time per shift and subtracting the time for breaks, meetings, cleanup, lunch (if included in the eight hours), etc., where the entire work area shuts down.

In some continuous manufacturing processes (i.e., casting or government or healthcare environments), the areas don't shut down, so available time equals the total shift time as staff and managers cover breaks.

In the following example, we assume an eight-hour or 480-minute shift. We subtract the following:

- 20 minutes—two 10-minute breaks
- 10 minutes—5-minute morning and afternoon exercise break
- 5 minutes cleanup time
- 10 minutes daily + QDIP or huddle meeting

This equals 45 minutes of the daily lost time from the workday so we would subtract it from the 480 minutes:

Takt Time Calculation

Many people, while they are familiar with the term takt time (TT), cannot recite the formula. TT allows us to review a process or a group of activities and determine, based on customer demand and available time, how fast a process needs to run related to time. This is just as true for a transactional process as it is for a shop-floor process. TT is equal to the available time or actual working time to produce a product or service divided by the customer demand required during the available time:

$$TT = \text{Available time} \div \text{customer demand}.$$

Here is an example: (Figure 2.20).

---

* Available time = 480 minutes – 45 minutes lost time = 435 minutes.
  Note: Planned downtime should be excluded from the available time calculations. If the cell is planned to be shut down, it does not count as available time; however, setup times and unplanned downtime are all included in available time.

Time Available		Customer Demand
One Shift	480 min.	If the customer demand is 8,700 units per month we turn it
Breaks	−20 min	into daily demand by dividing by the number of working days
Exercise	−10 min	in the month (in this case 20) which equals 435 units / day. If
Clean-up	−5 min.	there is one shift then we need 435 units / shift.
Daily meeting	−10 min	Takt Time
Total	435 min.	= 435 min available time / 435 units /day = 1 min/unit

Figure 2.20   Takt time example. (Source: BIG Archives.)

How to Interpret Takt Time

This calculation shows we must produce one unit every minute to meet the customer demand. However, what does this really mean? Let's assume it takes five minutes of total labor time to build the product. If the TT is one minute, many of you may at first think we cannot meet the TT because it takes longer than one minute to build the product. However, this is not the case. If it takes five minutes to build the product, you would need to staff the line with five people, each with one minute of work.

Let's think about what TT is really calculating, as it is not really measuring anything. When we calculated one minute per unit, it must be looked at for what it is, which is customer demand: no more ... no less. TT describes the time needed for the system, whether on the floor or in the office, to complete one unit of product or one paperwork task. TT takes nothing else into account.

Important Metrics to Understand

Process-Focused Metrics

The BASICS methodology primarily focuses on building-in quality and eliminating waste. To do this we suggest using process-focused metrics versus results-oriented metrics.

Process-focused metrics include value-added percentage, number of operators, total labor time (direct and indirect), first-pass yield, safety, product travel distance, operator travel distance, work-in-process (WIP) inventory, throughput time, cycle time, setup time, and productivity, i.e., pieces per person per hour and hours per unit.

It should be noted we don't discriminate between direct and indirect labor. Any labor required to produce a part, including indirect labor, should be accounted for when calculating productivity.

Desired versus Actual Cycle Time

Most companies don't know their real customer demand so we use required cycle time instead. Cycle time is calculated in different ways, but each should have the same result. There are two types of cycle time—desired and actual.

Desired cycle time is computed by dividing available time by required *factory* demand (versus customer demand), while the actual cycle time can be determined as follows:

- The time each team member/operator on the line *must* be able to meet.
- The amount of time each person *actually sp*ends completing their part of the operation if the work is evenly distributed.
- It can be computed by dividing the total labor time by the number of operators (assuming the work can be balanced evenly, i.e., there is no idle time).
- The amount of time between units coming off the end of the line or out of the process. This is the real, actual cycle time.
- It can be dictated by the time of the slowest machine or person in the line environment.

Determining the current state CT early in the Lean initiative provides a baseline of the activity or process. It is a very important data point since it can be used as an in-process metric versus a results metric.

Throughput Time: A Key Metric

Throughput time is the measure of time from the beginning to end of a process. We say it is the time it takes the product, paper, or thing, to move from its raw-material stage to shipping or finished goods. The throughput time is the sum of all the time the product, patient, or information spends in the process. This means it includes all the wait and/or queue times in the process. The book, *Lean Thinking** (Womack and Jones), describes how a can of soda, from mining the ore to reaching the customer, has a throughput time of 319 days.

Throughput time, sometimes referred to as lead time, or overall cycle time, can be used to describe the length of time the thing is in the process. This length of time is from whatever input (beginning) to output boundary (end) you choose.

Every leader should understand that each extra second of throughput time adds costs, which can be defined in a variety of ways. This metric is seldom tracked as a formal KPI and mostly hidden inside of traditional cost accounting methods. Performance goals should be tied to reducing throughput time throughout the year.

Remember, throughput time is your material flow velocity. It represents how fast you can respond to your customer's or patient's needs. Throughput time directly ties to inventory turns and dollars and affects your company's cash flow and working capital.

In the hospital world this metric can mean literally the difference between life and death. The longer the person or product is in the value stream the more resources it ties up and the more opportunity there is for defects to occur. In the hospital world these are known as nosocomial infections.

Man-to-Machine Ratio

What is your man-to-machine ratio? Do you measure it? Is it a KPI? Most companies around the world think they are world-class if they have one operator for two or even three machines. However, these pale in comparison to the Toyota statistics below:

---

* *Lean Thinking*, Womack and Jones, 1996, 2003. Simon and Schuster: New York.

- In 1896, Toyoda Loom Works averaged over 50 machines per operator.
- In 1940s, Toyota Motors averaged five machines per operator.
- In 1993, Toyota Motors averaged 16 machines per operator.

We will discuss a tool called jidoka later, which is the tool that makes these types of man-to-machine ratios possible.

Sales per Employees

Sales or revenue by itself can be a misleading metric for companies, as the prices charged or product mix can change from year to year or during a year; however, sales per employee is a good overarching metric for companies implementing Lean. This is a results-focused lagging metric. This is determined simply by dividing the sales dollars for a given period by the number of employees working.

Contribution margin or gross profit per employee is also a good overarching metric for Lean. This is a high-level look at the contribution per employee, and we should set a percentage goal to increase this each year.

Productivity versus Efficiency versus Effectiveness

Our Lean principles strive for the best utilization of man, machine, methods, and materials. We call these the four M's. When analyzing a system, it is important to understand the definitions below:

1. *Productivity*: Productivity is the number of products produced in a certain amount of time with a certain amount of labor. The products could be physical products or transactional, such as processing an invoice, or internet blogs. Productive means getting things done, outcomes reached, or goals achieved, and is measured as output per unit of input (i.e., labor, equipment, and capital) or pieces per person per shift/day.
2. *Efficiency*: Efficiency is based on the energy one spends to complete the product or service, as well as timing. For example, we all know of the learning curve. The more one performs a new task the better one becomes each time the task is practiced. As one becomes more efficient one reduces stress and gain accuracy. A person has achieved efficiency when they are getting more done with the same or better accuracy in a shorter period, with less energy and better results.
3. *Effectiveness*: Effectiveness is the ability to achieve stated goals or objectives, judged in terms of both output and impact.

One example is an air conditioner. It can be efficient but not effective if the windows are open. A line can be considered productive, but if it is batching it may not be as efficient or effective.

Improvement Paths May Lead to Innovation

If you think about it, all improvement can be considered a form of innovation, so daily kaizen could be also considered daily innovation. Regardless of the improvement path, for businesses to progress, they must keep improving.

Sir John Harvey* Jones said, "If you are not progressing, you're regressing; because the rest of the world is moving against you." The more successful we are, the more complacent we tend to get. No matter how successful we are, we must have a system to guard against complacency.

Steven Spear,[†] MIT Senior Engineering Lecturer, states, "They (Toyota) constantly worry about who is going to catch up and if they can't figure out about whom to worry, they worry that they can't worry. This is why Toyota as an organization, routinely, is always worried about something and looks at having no problem as a big problem! This constant worrying is referred to as ongoing healthy paranoia and is designed to guard against complacency. This is why there were no parties thrown when Toyota became number one in overall vehicle sales in the world."

The need for improvements, "gaps," can be generated through the development of new targets or the discovery of existing problems. Once this gap is identified we need a process to overcome the gap.

This improvement process could be simple, as described by Paul Akers[‡] in his book, *2 Second Lean*, or it could be a much more complicated process, such as reducing the warranty cost by 50% over the next three years.

The thought process is the same for both. Even a two-second Lean project has a baseline, target condition, and a gap. So, no matter the size, we still must think through this process, or, as necessary, document it on paper for larger projects.

---

* Sir John Harvey-Jones MBE was an English businessman. He was the chairman of Imperial Chemical Industries from 1982 to 1987. He was best known by the public for his BBC television show, *Troubleshooter*, in which he advised struggling businesses.
† Steven Spear is a Senior Lecturer at the MIT Sloan School of Management and at the Engineering Systems Division at MIT.
‡ Paul Akers is an American author, the president of Fastcap, and an internationally recognized expert on Lean manufacturing principles.

Chapter 3

BASICS Model: Assess/Analyze (A)

The A in our BASICS model stands for Assess and Analyze, and the goal of this chapter is to introduce the tools and methodology in order to understand the current condition or what we call "as-is" state. The purpose is to document and question every step in every process and see if it can be eliminated, rearranged, simplified, or combined to make the operator's job easier (see Figure 3.1.)

The rest of this book will now introduce a structured approach for problem-solving regardless of how the problem originated. You do not have to use every tool, but you do need to get to the root cause if you are going to solve the problem.

The Importance of Video

For any of you that have played or know anything about football, you know the importance of watching game tape! The pros use it to better understand their opponents and to improve their game from both a team perspective and an individual perspective. The same should go for manufacturing and office processes. The video camera was even used by Frank Gilbreth back in the early 1900s for his company's bricklayers, and by the surgeons doing tonsillectomies on his children (as portrayed in the original movie *Cheaper by the Dozen*.) In our opinion, the video camera was the greatest industrial engineering tool ever invented, but hardly ever used.

Why Video?

There is no way one can observe everything that goes on in a football play from the football sidelines or from the stands (see Figure 3.2). If so, we wouldn't need *instant replay*. How many times do we all see and observe the same play on the field only to find out that during the instant replay, we were indeed so wrong. Of course, admitting to it is another story.

The same is true for manufacturing. If you are visiting the gemba and filling in a typical point kaizen key-observation sheet with a pencil, you cannot possibly capture everything the operator does down to a second or in some cases fraction of a second.

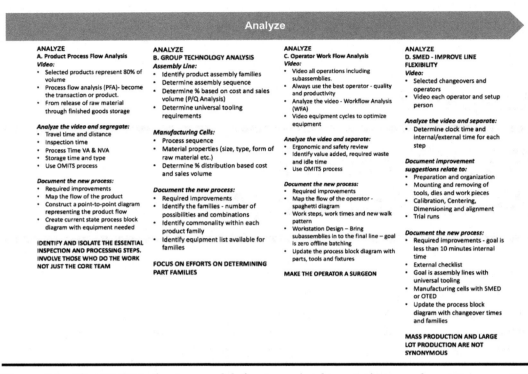

Figure 3.1 The BASICS six-step model for Lean implementation—analyze. (Source: BIG Training Materials.)

This doesn't mean you cannot make improvements by observing the process. However, one cannot possibly see all the waste in a more complex process by just observing or truly understand the process without videoing and reviewing it with the operators you filmed.

Videoing is a great way to get the operators and supervisor involved in the change and subsequent buy-in to the resulting standard work. We utilize video for both office and shop-floor processes.

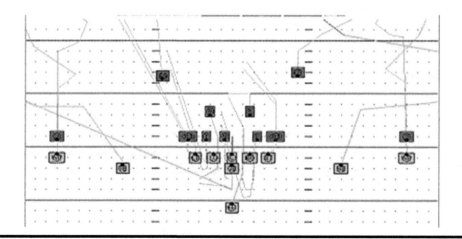

Figure 3.2 Football play example. (Source: BIG Archives.)

In unionized facilities, it pays to let the union know ahead of time and get someone from their leadership on the team with you. It is best to put a communication plan together and get HR and the union involved from the start. Again, get all the stakeholders involved before starting any video or improvement initiative. We have never had a problem implementing in union or nonunion facilities.

Video Guidelines for the Product

- Never turn off the camera.
- Some information must be collected by hand. One must use common sense when videoing. If the operator puts the batch in a washer then you need to go to the next operation as opposed to filming the washer.
- Follow the product not the operator. Make sure you can always see what the product is doing.

Analysis Tools Hierarchy

As discussed earlier, when we analyze a process we look at three things, and in this order:

1. Product
2. Operator
3. Setup

PFA—Process-Flow Analysis or TIPS (see Figure 3.3)

1. Video.
2. Analyze the product steps.
3. Follow the (ERSC) process (sometimes referred to as the Omits process because we Omit steps or update the "to be" or future-state estimated times).
4. Reorder the steps.
5. Determine the total throughput time.

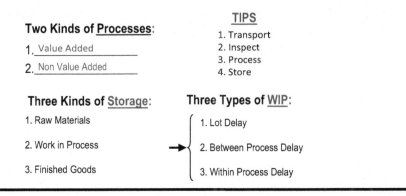

Figure 3.3   Process-flow analysis (PFA) breakdown. (Source: BIG Archives.)

To conduct a PFA analysis correctly, one must become the *thing* going through the process, whether it is a product, a patient in health care, a person in a government agency, or information (paper or electronic).

This may sound easy, but in practice it is very difficult to do. This analysis is much more detailed than the value-stream map process analysis. In the past, most of us have been focused on what the operator does and not the product itself. When we follow the product, we don't care what the operator is doing. Note: this doesn't mean we don't care about the operator as a person, but, they are not a factor in this analysis. We only follow the part.

The PFA looks at each individual step a product takes. This includes when a part or information (paper) is moved, inspected, processed, or stored. We include the time it takes for each step and the distance traveled by the product (not the operator).

If you want to improve the material or information flow in any process you must perform what we call a TIPS analysis. TIPS refers to the four basic steps that occur with a product:

Transport (T)

Transport occurs whenever the product is physically moved from one place to another. Transportation is non–value-added and we should work to eliminate each transport step or reduce it as much as possible. Transport is recorded in in our analysis as time and distance. This is one reason why we try to eliminate forklifts, cranes, conveyors, and even simple movement from one part of the plant or office to another.

Inspection (I)

Inspection occurs whenever the product or information (paperwork or electronic) is reviewed for any reason. Many times, operators (which can also be a senior executive reading over a report they are ready to submit) don't even realize they are inspecting.

We believe Shingo separated out inspection (which also could be considered a non–value-added process) because whenever you need to inspect part of the information, it means you don't trust the process and it is not capable of making the transformation right the first time.

Inspection Means You Fundamentally Don't Trust Your Process!

A fundamental question should always be asked: How do we make sure we don't pass a bad part from one step to the next? The goal in Lean is not Six Sigma; but, zero defects or 100% first-pass yield, which is built-in quality.

Process (P)

Processes are broken down into two categories: value-added and non–value-added. The industry definition for value-added was part of an AMA* (American Management Association) video

---

* http://www.crmlearning.com/time-the-next-dimension-of-quality.

called *Time, The Next Dimension of Quality*. For any process step to be value-added it must meet all three criteria:

1. The customer must care about the step and be willing to pay for it.
2. The step must physically change the thing going through the process, whether it is a part or information. It must change form, fit, shape, size, or function. In the healthcare world, we say it must change the patient physically or emotionally for the better.
3. The step must be done right the first time.

Some steps may meet one or two of the three criteria but not all three. We call these steps necessary but non value-added.

The Customer Must Be Willing to Pay for It

When we make improvements, we are always focusing on what we can do to increase value-added to our customer. This starts with our external customer but also includes our internal customers.

Voice of the Customer (VOC)—Does the Customer Care?

Too often, when we go into companies, the staff tell us their customer expectations; but when we probe a bit, we find the expectations communicated were not really those of the customer. They were what the staff thought the customer wanted. It is important to understand what makes a good customer experience through the customer's lens, *not* the lens of the staff. One must clearly define the customer's expectations to ensure the organization does the right things to meet those expectations. Anything else is waste!

Physical Change

A process has an input and an output, with some transformation occurring in between where the material or information is somehow physically changed. This means some transformation, physical or mental, is occurring to the part or information flow.

Done Right the First Time

Rework and defects do not count as value-added. The process must be done right the first time. This ties back to our goal of zero defects.

Storage (S)

We break storage into three parts: raw material storage (RS or RM), work in process (WIP), and finished goods stock/work (FS):

- RS is considered any part that has not had any direct labor added to it.
- WIP is defined as any raw material received with direct labor added to it.
- FS is defined as the completed product/work, ready for sale to the customer.

WIP Categories

We differentiate WIP into three categories.

1. Between process delay
2. Lot delay
3. Within-process delay

When using leanEdit®* these subcategories need to be added using the customization feature, as they are not currently part of the default list.

Between-Process Storage (B)

Between-process storage is defined by products sitting and waiting individually or as an entire lot for the next process, that is, they are stored in between two sequential processes.

Lot Delays (L)

Lot delays are where we are waiting for the rest of the batch or what we call *our buddies* to be processed. We refer to them affectionately as *buddies* (when we are pretending to "be the part" during the PFA) because we find it is easier for people to remember that we are the product in this way. Lot delays are "batch" delays because, whether we are the first or last piece in the lot, we are waiting for the entire lot to be completed before moving from one step to the next.

Within-Process Storage (W)

The first two delays are standard industrial engineering categories. Charlie Protzman created "within-process delay" back in 2003 when he was working with hospitals. He discovered that some products did not fit the criteria for between-process or lot delays.

Within-process storage (delay) occurs after a process is started on a part or a lot, where the part, person, or lot is delayed because the process is interrupted for some reason. It could be a machining operation interrupted for lunch break or a machine that breaks down or a tool bit that breaks, and the piece has to wait during the repair. It could also be someone stuck in an elevator or a requisition being placed. It could be having to stop the process to check the status of that or another part in a different MRP screen or window. It could be a patient where the doctor exam started but was interrupted by a phone call.

Why Separate out These Delays?

To truly obtain the fastest velocity possible for material or information flow requires understanding the nature of the operation and where the waste exists. It is imperative to break down each step the product goes through on its journey from RM to the shipping dock. Again, this is your cash flow or patients who are stuck waiting in the process.

---

* leanEdit.com—the author uses this software and has contributed ideas to its development. leanEdit is the property of leanEdit LLC, © 2017.

Roles

When we are reviewing the PFA we assign roles to the participants. These can include:

- Drawing a point-to-point diagram
- Listing major equipment in the process and utilities required
- Listing any improvement ideas
- Keeping track of the distance traveled by the product

PFA Example

To illustrate a simple PFA, let's walk through getting a cup of coffee. Keep in mind the first step is always to decide on what you are following. If you don't, you will have problems during the analysis.

Let's say in this case we are following the coffee cup and that the operator is making two cups of coffee.

1. Pick up both cups—Transport—½ foot 1 sec.
2. Put the cups down—Between-process—1 sec.
3. Pick up the coffee pot, what step is this? Many of you just thought transport. But in reality, it is still between process storage—2 sec.
4. Pour the coffee in the first cup—Value-added—2 sec.
5. Pour the coffee in the second cup—Lot delay—2 sec. Note: this is a batch delay and the first cup is waiting while the second cup is poured.
6. Put the coffee pot back-between process—2 sec.
7. Take the cups to the people that wanted them and deliver to first person—Transport—5 ft, 5 sec.
8. Transport to second person—Lot delay—5 sec.
9. Taste the coffee. This could be value-added or inspection for temperature.

While this is a simple example; it proves the TIPS analysis tool can be applied to anything. We could have expanded the example using cream and sugar.

ERSC—Omits Process and Improvement Questions

Think about how this process could be improved. What ideas do you have? We always walk our team through four questions, as we did during the VSM, which we call the Omits process. Look at and question each step and ask if it can be somehow be:

- *Eliminated*: If we can eliminate the step, we do not have to do an operator analysis on that step, and we immediately speed up the process without adding any additional work. This is what we were referring to earlier in this chapter when we said we could improve productivity without even looking at the operator!
- *Rearranged*: If we can't eliminate it, we look to see if the step is in the proper order, makes sense, and allows the product to flow smoothly.

- *Simplified*: If we can't eliminate it, or rearrange it, our next option is to try to simplify. By removing the complexity in the operation, we expose the waste and simplify the process.
- *Combined*: The next option is to combine it with another step, assuming we can reduce the time or improve the flow by finding a better method.

Walking the Process

To walk the process, you first need to involve the operations director of manufacturing and department managers to let them know you are going to be in the area and you will be interrupting their operators.

We then need to decide what part of the product we are going to become. We generally try to find a component part that travels through the entire process, starting with unloading from the truck in receiving. If you choose to start somewhere else in the process, then we have to scope the flow from start (input boundary) to finish (output boundary). For the first one you conduct, we suggest starting at the receiving dock and ending at the shipping dock. This will give you the total throughput time within the facility. For office processes we start from order received to collecting the money.

PFA Worksheet

We use a worksheet to capture the PFA steps (see Figure 3.4). We capture each step and note where it fits into our TIPS definition. We break down each process step as to whether it is value-added, non–value-added, and, if it is a storage step, we identify which type of storage the step fits. We accumulate the times the product spends in each step and the distance traveled.

Every step is questioned as we capture it as to why we do what we do and whether we really need to do it. We then look for opportunities to eliminate (omit), rearrange, simplify, or combine each step. We are left with a before and an after analysis that gives us an *as-is* versus a *to-be* number of process steps and times within each part of TIPS. The process analysis should yield a 20%–40% productivity improvement to the overall process versus a batch environment.

Video Analysis Software leanEdit®

There are a variety of software packages available today but leanEdit® is the first that works specifically with our analysis methodology and approach. leanEdit® is a software program we use, which is designed to streamline the analysis of video thereby allowing the user to quickly edit and categorize process steps as described above.

The user simply uploads their video (single video or multiple videos for merging) into the software, selects the appropriate tool—Process-Flow Analysis, Labor (workflow) Analysis, or Setup Reduction—and then carries out the analysis. The software comes in desktop, web, and server versions and includes features such as "favorite" clip capture, search functionality, clip download, standard work generation and spreadsheet export capability. leanEdit® takes advantage of the cloud to facilitate collaboration between users and is 50%–60% faster than manual methods (see Figures 3.5 through 3.7).

No. of Steps	OMIT	Flow Code	Flow Symbol	Description	Alt. Start Time (sec) (optional)	Cumulative Time (sec)	Baseline Time (sec)	Baseline Time (min)	Post Lean Estimate Time	Distance (in feet)	Distance Post (with omits)	Machine	Department
								This totals of these columns become our baseline and post Lean throughput time					
1		rm	◻	Received as an e-mail				0	0		0		Customer service
2		b	◻	Waiting to be opened			21600	360	21600		0		
3		b	◻	Open e-mail			1	0	1		0		
4		nv	○	I am opened as an attachment			2	0.0	2		0		
5		nv	○	I am printed on the printer			10	0.2	10		0		
6		1	■	Waiting on the printer while other POs are printed			270	5	270		0		
7		b	◻	Waiting while Kathy walks to the printer			10	0	10		0		
8		t	◉	I am picked up			1	0.0	1	2	2		
9		nv	○	Sort through the papers to make sure others are not with us			3	0.1	3		0		
10		t	◉	We are walked back to the desk			10	0.2	10	30	30		
11		nv	○	I am stapled			2	0.0	2		0		
12		1	■	Wait while others are stapled			13	0	13		0		
13		b	◻	Wait while oracle opens			5	0	5		0		
14		b	◻	Checking if i am available in inventory and status checked			120	2	120		0		
15		b	◻	Waiting while looking up the "opportunity #" is looked up and files saved to the smart team file			1800	30	1800		0		
16		b	◻	Waiting while an EAR is created and attachments downloaded onto EAR			2100	35	2100		0		
17		b	◻	Waiting while EAR is e-mailed to engineering			30	1	30		0		
18		b	◻	Waiting while EAR sits in engineering e-mail box			28800	480	28800		0		Engineering
19		b	◻	Waiting while EAR's application data is reviewed			300	5	300		0		
20		b	◻	Waiting while application sizing program is being performed			600	10	600		0		
21		b	◻	Waiting while p/n is being assigned from book			300	5	300		0		
22		b	◻	Waiting for the simulation program to be performed and orifice designed			900	15	900		0		
23		b	◻	Waiting for counter-drill calculations			300	5	300		0		
24		b	◻	Waiting for drawings and solid works models to be created			900	15	900		0		
25		b	◻	Waiting for design folder to be created in smart team			300	5	300		0		
26		b	◻	Waiting while drawing folder is linked to the EAR			600	10	600		0		
27		b	◻	Waiting while the drawing folder is linked to the EAR			480	8	480		0		
28		b	◻	Waiting while the part number is added to the			180	3	180		0		
29		b	◻	Waiting while the EAR is updated with "hours worked" and e-mail sent to Kathy with p/n			60	1	60		0		

Figure 3.4   PFA analysis sheet example. (Source: BIG Archives.)

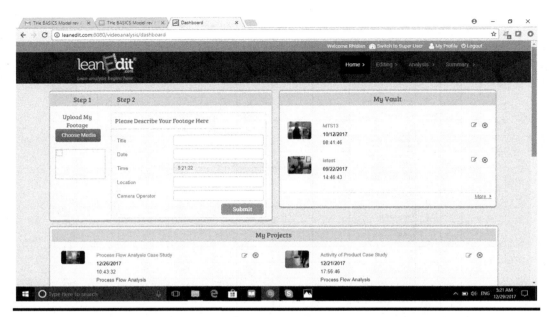

Figure 3.5   The leanEdit.com web version main dashboard. (Source: © 2017 leanEdit LLC.)

Figure 3.6   The leanEdit® desktop tool selection screen. (Source: © 2017 leanEdit LLC.)

Point-to-Point Diagram

Point-to-point diagrams (see Figure 3.8) are utilized to show the path of the product through the layout of the area. This differs from the spaghetti diagram we use for operators. The steps are numbered to identify the step-by-step product-flow path.

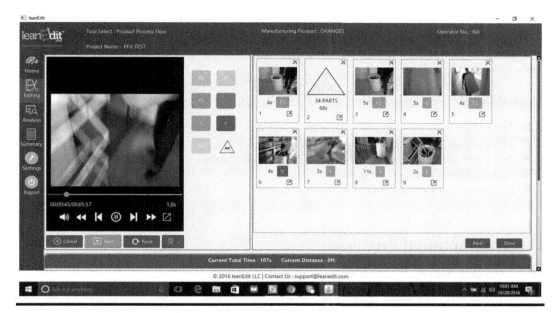

Figure 3.7   Editing clips using the leanEdit® desktop process-flow analysis tool. (Source: © 2017 leanEdit LLC.)

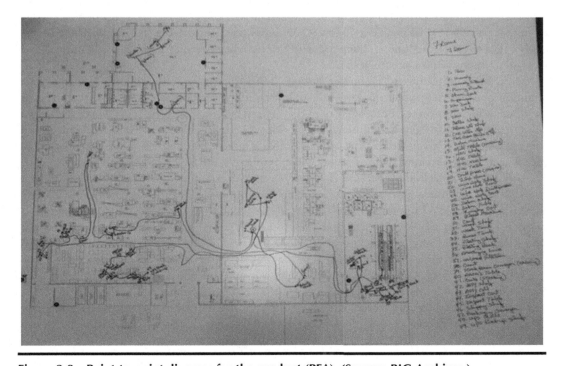

Figure 3.8   Point-to-point diagram for the product (PFA). (Source: BIG Archives.)

Our future layout will come from the PFA, so this point-to-point diagram is useful to guarantee the product always moves forward in the layout.

If any stations are out of order, they will immediately show up as you draw the point-to-point flow of the product.

Questions After Completing the Point-to-Point Diagram

- Does the product see one smooth continuous flow?
- Does the product go backward at any time?
- Are there areas where the product crisscrosses as it travels through the layout?
- Is the product flowing one piece at a time?
- Is there excess inventory or idle time on the line?

The Transactional Processes

The Current State

Transactional processes often tend to be more inefficient than manufacturing and we observe much more overprocessing waste in offices than in manufacturing.

The data packages move through the transactional process the same as in a manufacturing line; however, it is difficult to see this *transactional line*. The movement of the transactional line is via paper, files, e-mail, texts, scanners, computer reports, workflow tools, in and out of database management, and other types of storage systems. The product almost always changes from one type of form to another as it travels through the process, often generating large amounts of paper or electronic forms.

Many changes to transactional process are via mandate, corporate, or legal requirements. New computer systems require people to follow screen inputs that enforce the changes but don't necessarily mistake-proof the inputs. There are many times where we find procedural definition, and roles and responsibilities, are unclear.

Most newly implemented computer systems lack sufficient training dollars, so many times countless hours are lost while employees try to learn and use the new systems.

There is no entry on the P&L or entry in the chart of accounts for orders lost due to inefficient computer systems. In Tom Peters' *Speed is Life* video,* he talks about the 0.055 rule which says: "most products and many services are actually receiving value for 0.05 to 5% of the time they are in the value delivery system of their company which implies 99.5% to 99.95% is non-value."

The authors of the book *Competing Against Time* give an example of an insurance company that takes 22 days to process a new application. Peters goes on to say: "In the course of those 22 days there is a good solid 17 minutes of work done ... This is the world's greatest good news bad news story. The good news is, what an awesome opportunity, if you're 99.95% screwed up and you just start looking at the thing you might get better; the bad news is if someone else starts looking at it before you do; you can get your hide nailed to the wall. The issue is Get Fast or Go Broke!"

The challenge with transactional processes are the constant barriers to change, starting with "this is the way it has always been done," to all the "sacred cows" embedded in the system.

The best way to conquer these barriers is to create the pull from the top management for change, and assemble cross-functional teams to run through the BASICS model with a Lean

---

* http://www.enterprisemedia.com/talent/tom-peters/?gclid=Cj0KCQjwjN7YBRCOARIsAFCb934IMJ38tbGt
  ph7BMjK7y7sm8LdBxVOoQ_8aBfCRSyTYvqaCSzcDevIaAiuBEALw_wcB.

practitioner. Every transactional process, even in an office, should have a safety, quality, delivery, inventory, and productivity (+QDIP) board, just like in the factory.

The greatest opportunity for the highest levels of net profit-margin improvement and customer satisfaction is to design all processes Lean from the beginning, whether it is manufacturing based or transaction based. If companies had great engineering and informational processes up front, the waste in the factory would already be greatly reduced.

Transactional-Process Wall Map

A great tool for transactional processes is called a process wall map. To create a process wall map (see Figure 3.9) we first layout either flip-chart paper or a roll of butcher-block paper on the wall. We then decide what we are going to follow or become, since we are now the product. We begin in a conference room with each of the participants who actually perform the jobs on the team and ask them to write down on yellow stickies step by step what they do in the process.

The wall map:

- Shows what is happening to the product
- Shows all the details of every step the product goes through, including transport, storage, and inspection, no matter how small (TIPS)
- Shows the number of activities and the time required for each activity
- Shows who touches the product and does each step
- Shows overall length of the process (throughput time) by having each yellow sticky represent a standard amount of time

How to Construct a Process Wall Map

Have the team start by putting yellow stickies on the left-hand side with who or what position does the job. This is similar to a tool called swim lanes but more detailed.

Then we have each person write each individual step in the order that they perform them on a different sticky with a magic marker. As soon as they write the first step, for example, *match up the paperwork*, we have them break the step down (a big bucket) into finer detail (granularity of

Figure 3.9 Process wall map of order entry to collect with every piece of paper required to process an order from quote to ship to collecting the cash. (Source: BIG Archives.)

big bucket) of what is really involved in the step. For instance, broken down "match up the paper-work" is:

- Move the receiving and invoice folders to the desk (transport).
- Get the incoming mail and move to the desk (transport).
- Open all the mail (process NV).
- Wait while the rest of the mail is opened (lot delay).
- Sort out the invoices received by the vendor (process NV).
- Wait while the rest of the mail is sorted (lot delay).
- Search through the receiver folder until you find the receiver to match the invoice (process NV).
- Staple the invoice and receiver together (process NV).
- Wait while the rest of the invoices are matched (lot delay).
- Wait while invoices that can't be matched are put back into the invoice folders (lot delay).

Note: It is important to follow up the PFA by then walking each step of the product on the floor or through the office with operator/staff participation. No matter how good the person is at doing the job, there will be steps missed when just listing them out in a conference room. Sometimes we will walk through these maps, including VSMs, backward from the end to the beginning to make sure we have captured all the steps.

Yellow Sticky Legend

Each of these steps is now recorded on a yellow sticky (see Figure 3.10). We then label each sticky with the type of TIPS step noted previously. We also add the following:

- Who does the step?
- How long the step takes (cycle time)?
- The distance the product travels.

Analysis of a Wall Map: ERSC

When the map is completed the team reviews (Figure 3.11) the following:

- Which activities can be eliminated, rearranged, simplified, or combined (ERSC)?
- Which events can be done in parallel?

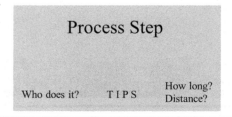

Figure 3.10   Process wall-map yellow sticky. (Source: BIG Archives.)

Omits
"X" sets
estimated
time to zero

No. of Steps	OMIT (X)	Description of Product Step	Baseline Time (sec)	Post Lean Estimate Time	Distance (in feet)	Distance Post (with omits)	Machine	Person who touches it (job class)
1	x	Parts sit as bar stock	14400	0		0		
2		Mori	125	125		0	Mori	Eric
3	x	Sits in parts tray in Mori	16	0		0		
4		Move to hand to inspect	3	3	1	1		
5		Inspect part	19	19		0		
6		Lathe	80	80	5	5	Lathe	
7	x	Sits on lathe - lost FIFO	1260	0	2	0		
8		To Gear Cutter	3	3		0	Gear Cutter	
9		Gear Cut	300	300		0		
10		Sits on Gear Cutter	29	29		0		Joe

Figure 3.11   Process-flow analysis with Omits. (Source: BIG Archives.)

■ What is the critical path?
■ How many people touch it?
■ Where are the handoffs between participants (mistakes, waits)?
■ Where are the duplicated activities by the same or another person or department?

Map the Ideal Process

Next map the process with no barriers.

■ What could it look like?
■ How would you set this process up if it were your business or if you were a small business?
■ What happens when you must get something through this process right away?
■ List the major problems preventing you from realizing your ideal process.
■ Identify the real purpose for the process you are improving.
■ Do we even need the process?
■ What would it take and how long to put this new process in place?

Identify and Rank Improvements to the Process

After reviewing and designing the *to-be* process, do the following:

- List all the ideas and opportunities discussed in the ideal state to improve process speed/velocity.
- Filter each idea to determine first if it is a task or project. If it is a task, it should be able to be assigned to one person with a due date. This ensures accountability and point of contact. Record these as action items from the project. What will be left are the projects that generally require a cross-functional team to work on them. Next, consider the amount of resources available and the strategic planning goals, and identify each project with the time horizon. That is, can it be completed within a year?
- Is it 2 to 3 years out? Is it 5 years out?
- Then list all the projects that can be completed in a year with the expected results and anticipated project cost.
- Now categorize each of these projects using a decision-matrix chart, and prioritize them according to your strategic plan goals (see Figure 3.12). Which one should we work on first? The answer is low-cost, high-benefit.
- Make sure to consider the risk and impact to the other departments for each project.
- Then create an implementation plan and action item list (see Figure 3.13) for improvements and expected results phased in by month.

Conducting Process-Flow Analysis on Transactional Processes

Just like in manufacturing, every second counts and every second we waste threatens our company's competitiveness. When we follow the product (TIPS) in administrative processes, 95% of steps are non–value-added, with the majority being storage and inspection. This may sound harsh, but in virtually every process, we have mapped less than 5% of the steps, and 1% of the time is value-added to the end customer.

	Proposed Projects or Tasks Description	Ranking 1-low impact 3-med impact 5-high impact / Project or Task	Financial Impact	Ease of implementation	Customer Satisfaction	Cycle time impact	Growth	Totals	Status
1	5S OR equipment storage area	T						0	75% complete
2	5S OR hallway	T						0	Open
3	Unclamp each instrument before sending to CS	T						0	100% complete
4	Eliminate instrument container washing process	T						0	100% complete
5	Improve pre-op patient information FPY	P	5	3	5	5	5	23	Open
6	Demand and supply matching for frequent used instrument sets	P	3	5	1	3	3	15	Open
7	OR scheduling process	P	3	1	3	3	3	13	Open
8	Improve 7:30 case start on-time	P	3	1	3	3	3	13	Open
9	Cross training for Pre-op, PACU and PreTesting staff	P	3	1	3	3	3	13	Open
10	Assess block time effectiveness	P	3	1	3	3	3	13	Open
11	Case cart assembly process standardization	P	1	5	1	3	3	13	90% complete
12	Level loading cases by : service line, instrument type, patient type	P	3	1	3	3	3	13	Open
13	Reassess PreTesting demand and staffing need	P	1	5	1	1	3	11	Open
14	Visual control for processes (KPIs)	P	1	5	1	1	3	11	Open
15	OR room stock standardization	P	1	5	1	3	1	11	100% complete
16	CS demand and staffing need study	P	3	3	1	1	3	11	100% complete
17	Reduce unnecessary flashing	P	3	3	3	1	1	11	In Process (new equip purchase)
18	Align supply area to resource map (preference card)	P	1	5	1	1	1	9	80% complete (bin locations ID'd but needs to be uploaded by Surgery IS)

Figure 3.12   Decision matrix prioritized to the strategic plan goals. (Source: BIG Files.)

Machine Shop Kaizen Action Registry

ITEM	ACTION	Task or Project	Impact on Problem (A) Impact from 1 to 10 (1-Low, 5- Medium, 10- High)	Mistake Proofing potential (B) Impact from 1 to 10 (1-Low, 5- Medium, 10- High)	Ease of Implementation (C) Impact from 1 to 10 (1-Hard, 5- Medium, 10- Easy)	Priority Number (A x B x C)	Rank (Ascending order of Priority Number)	RESPONSIBLE	DUE	STATUS
	PRODUCT CELL:	Machine Shop								
	TEAM LEADER:	JOE								
1	Dedicate person to pre-stage setups	Task	10	10	10	1000		Joe	8/15/2012	In Process, Person Identified, TBA on 08/09
2	Develop format for Gauge List that will be used for each order. Add to or similar to tools sheets. This will be the "recipe" for the job.	Task	10	10	1	100		Mike		
3	Develop kanban bins for all good candidates that run through the shop	Task	5	1	10	50		Jim		
4	Determine inspection sampling plan to be used by shop. Decide whether last piece inspection is still needed and if so, can it be done after the machine is already running the next job to move it to external time.	Project				0		JOe	Ongoing	First batch of parts handed to QC to develop IPs (on 08/03)

Figure 3.13 Action registry for a machine shop. What's missing? (Source: BIG Archives.)

Most administrative jobs are support jobs for the factory and service industry and, while necessary, do not fit the classic definition of value-added (i.e., physical change, done right the first time, and customer is willing to pay for it). We have yet to run into a process where we could not take at least 50% or more out of the overall internal lead time (or throughput time) of the process just by eliminating the storage steps in the process. (This would not include a process with a significant amount of external time like an outside supplier lead-time.) Administrative process should *flow, flow, flow*, just like the factory.

The leanEdit® software has a specific set of codes that are unique to the office environment to support transactional processes. You can also create your own customizable categories. Figure 3.14 is an example of the video editing screen, which creates movie clips as small as one second that can be selected as favorites for later use or shared with others (Figure 3.15).

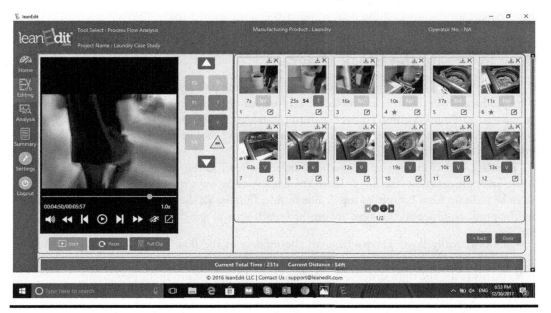

Figure 3.14 Video editing screen which creates movie clips as small as one second. (Source: © 2017 leanEdit LLC.)

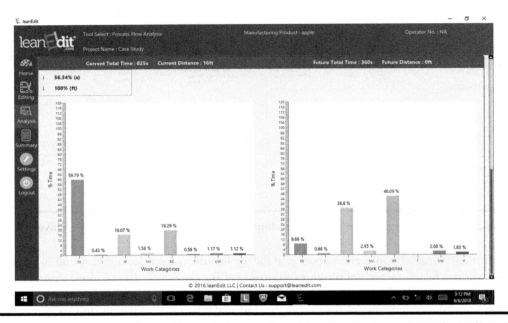

Figure 3.15 Before and after summary bar chart for each code. (Source: © 2017 leanEdit LLC.)

Create the Process Block Diagram

Once the initial analysis is completed, we construct a block diagram. The block diagram takes the output from the (to be) PFA and (to be) workflow analysis (WFA) and combines them into one flow. We develop the block diagram with the operator and supervisors present. The block diagram sets the stage for the workstation design and layout (see Figure 3.16).

How to Create the Block Diagram

We start on a whiteboard or piece of paper and lay out the process in the order of how the part is to be produced, whether it is assembled, machined, or both. At this point, we don't worry about the current tooling, fixturing, layout constraints, and the size of each part or model, or if you have enough space, equipment, operators, etc. We want to make sure we line up each step in the proper order based on the process.

This is a very difficult step for some because we tend to let our current state influence our future-state process-flow decisions. There are usually many ways to build a product. For instance, it can be built up from bottom to top or side to side. Discuss all the different alternatives for building the product. Once all the steps are on the board, start to ask the following questions:

- Does it really flow? Do we have all the models in the flow? Can we change the flow to streamline it even more?
- Is this really the right order for each step from the part or product's viewpoint?

Note: where there are subassemblies (or pre-assembly operations):

- Are the subassemblies in the right order?

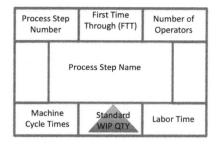

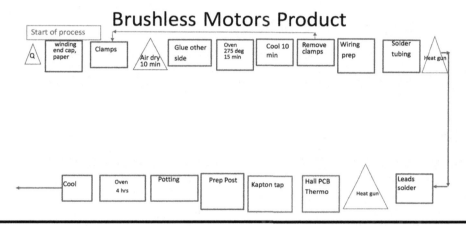

Figure 3.16   Start of block diagram. Listing out the current state product flow. The triangles represent storage spaces for WIP (Source: BIG Archives and Andrew McDermott.)

- Can they be incorporated into the line?
- Do we have to carry a subassembly with us? Can we deliver it without carrying it (i.e., gravity conveyor)?
- Is there a way to build the subassembly into the product directly?
- Is there a way we could rearrange and/or combine steps that make more sense or make it easier to assemble?
- Would changing the order of steps help in mistake-proofing?
- Would simplifying steps help in mistake-proofing?

For a mixed-model line, we need to review each model and add any unique steps (in a different color) where they fit in the block diagram for each model as necessary. Many times, it is surprising that very few, if any, steps must be added.

The Quality Paradox

Every step in the PFA we can remove or simplify eliminates the step and thus the opportunity for a defect to occur. This can and almost always will improve quality. This leads to the paradox, often scoffed at, which is that it is possible to do a job quicker and still have better quality.

We cannot express how important it is to separate the product flow from the operator steps when analyzing or assessing a process in any area. It is this principle that allows process improvement in any situation, and in any environment at work or at home. In addition, the product and operator provide different pieces of the Lean puzzle.

While simple in understanding, Shingo's discovery* that processes are a network of operations—i.e., product vs. operator—is truly remarkable. When we teach people this, they find it extremely difficult to conceive that it has such implications for improvement.

The priority must start, first, with looking at the product flow; second, the operator(s), whether they are on the shop floor or in an executive office; and then, third, applying the setup reduction tools or in conjunction with the operator step if there is unloading and loading involved.

Conducting PFAs on Machines

One can also conduct a PFA or WFA on a machine where we follow the product through the machine. We start by picking the first piece and note each step. Where there is external loading and batching on or around machines, one will find many in-between process and lot delays.

What We Get from Analyzing the Product Separately

To our knowledge, no one has broken down these processes into the actual pieces of Lean Thinking each one provides. We studied this for literally years before we concluded that each analysis tool (product vs. operator's axis plus changeover) provides different answers for the Lean improvement puzzle.

Analyzing the product will provide the following pieces of the Lean implementation:

- Total throughput time
- Flow, flow, flow
- Layout and workstations location and the proper sequence for equipment and supplies
- The location for standard WIP (waiting rooms in hospitals)
- Machine times (running time of the process within a piece of equipment)
- Routings sequence of steps the product or patients follow
- Percent transport, inspect storage, non–value-added and value-added for the product
- Capacity analysis when combined with operator and setup analysis
- Travel distance for the product

Total Throughput Time

A primary goal of the process-flow analysis (see Figure 3.17) is to determine the total throughput time of the process. This is a process-focused metric. The total throughput time is the sum of all the time the product, patient, or information spend in the process. Using Little's Law† we can take throughput time and divide it by the cycle time to determine how much inventory should be in the system.

---

* Shingo reported this during a speech to the JMA Engineering Conference, 1945.

† Little's Law provides a simple but powerful method to understand the relationship of steady-state production systems. The law has deep-rooted mathematical underpinnings; however, we can use the law as a tool for Lean. The textbook by Hopp and Spearman refers to Little's Law as "… an interesting and fundamental, relationship between WIP, CT and throughput" and states the law as: TH = WIP ÷ CT.

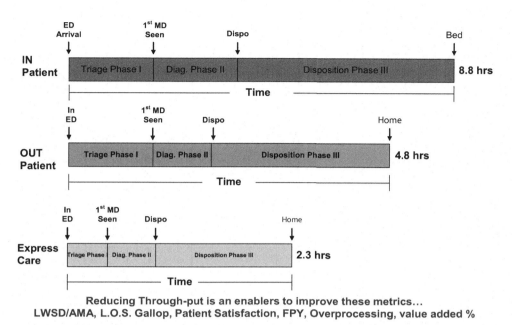

Reducing Through-put is an enablers to improve these metrics...
LWSD/AMA, L.O.S. Gallop, Patient Satisfaction, FPY, Overprocessing, value added %

Figure 3.17 ED throughput time detailed analysis. (Source: BIG Files.)

World Class and the Product (PFA)

Our world-class goal for the product throughput time is three times the value-added time.

Group-Tech Matrix

The group technology matrix, sometimes referred to as the process-family matrix, is the process of identifying the processes and characteristics for each part and then dividing products into families or similar/like groups or services based on those process steps or product characteristics or profiles.

The first step is to determine which path the parts follow. We do this by putting an X where the parts hit a certain process (see Table 3.1). When some of the parts follow the same process steps or use the same equipment or are subjected to the same operations in a similar order, they can be considered a family. We then take the equipment and line it up and form a cell for that family. Some parts may skip certain machines but they can still work in the cell. Most shops can set up at least one cell, and normally more. Parts that don't fit any cells or simply will not flow one-piece or small lot are relegated to what we call the misfit or model-shop cell or some parts may have to cross cells, which means we still have to batch them between cells.

The group-tech matrix is created by listing down all the part numbers on the left side and all the processes, machines, operations, volumes, etc. on the top columns. This tool even works for assigning operating rooms for surgery in the hospital. In some cases, where there are thousands of parts, one can use the Pareto rule to help narrow it down to the 20% that make up 80% of the volume.

A company was working on their master layout and had the group-tech matrix pictured (Table 3.2). We ran the data through a pivot table and then sorted it multiple ways to see if we could find a family of parts. Some families did pop out as well as some questions. What questions would you ask? The first one we asked was:

Table 3.1 Group Tech Example with Xs

Part/Machine	Machine 1	Machine 2	Machine 3	Machine 4	Machine 5	Machine 6	Machine 7	Machine 8	Machine 9	Machine 10	Machine 11	Machine 12
Part 1				X	X	X		X		X		
Part 2				X	X	X		X		X		
Part 3				X	X	X		X		X		
Part 4				X	X	X		X		X		
Part 5				X	X	X		X		X		
Part 6				X	X	X		X		X		
Part 7				X	X	X		X		X		
Part 8				X	X	X	X		X	X		
Part 9				X	X	X	X		X	X		
Part 10				X	X	X	X		X	X		
Part 11				X	X	X	X		X	X		
Part 12				X	X	X	X		X	X		
Part 13				X	X	X	X		X	X		
Part 14				X	X	X	X		X	X		
Part 15				X	X	X	X		X	X		
Part 16				X	X	X	X		X	X		
Part 17				X	X	X	X		X	X		
Part 18				X	X	X	X		X	X		
Part 19				X	X	X	X		X	X		
Part 20			X		X	X	X	X		X		
Part 21				X	X	X	X	X		X		

Source: BIG Archives.

Table 3.2   We Ran the Data through a Pivot Table and Then Sorted It Multiple Ways to See if We Could Find a Family of Parts

Part Number	Centerless Grind 1	Centerless Grind 2	Furnace	Cut Off	Polish	Round	Hard Tumbling
Part 15		X	X	X		X	X
Part 16		X	X	X		X	X
Part 17		X	X	X		X	X
Part 22		X	X	X		X	X
Part 54		X	X	X		X	X
Part 59		X	X	X		X	X
Part 65		X	X	X		X	X
Part 70		X	X	X	X	X	
Part 71		X	X	X	X	X	
Part 14			X			X	X
Part 7	X		X	X		X	
Part 10	X		X	X		X	
Part 11	X		X	X		X	
Part 27	X		X	X		X	
Part 8	X		X	X		X	
Part 9	X		X	X		X	
Part 60	X		X	X			
Part 61	X		X	X			
Part 62	X		X	X			
Part 63	X		X	X			
Part 64	X		X	X			
Part 38	X			X			
Part 39	X			X			
Part 40	X			X			
Part 41	X			X			
Part 42	X			X			
Part 43	X			X			

(Continued)

Table 3.2 (Continued)   We Ran the Data through a Pivot Table and Then Sorted It Multiple Ways to See if We Could Find a Family of Parts

Part Number	Centerless Grind 1	Centerless Grind 2	Furnace	Cut Off	Polish	Round	Hard Tumbling
Part 44	X			X			
Part 45	X			X			
Part 32	X	X	X	X			
Part 33	X	X	X	X			
Part 34	X	X	X	X			
Part 35	X	X	X	X			

Source: BIG Files.

Note: Some families did pop out, as well as some questions. What questions would you ask?

- What is the difference between polish and hard tumbling?
  - We were told the parts could go to either. This immediately freed up the polish machine.
- We asked what was the difference between the grinders?
  - We were told one machine is a larger diameter. Cutoff was essentially a manual operation.
- Why does part 14 not hit in either grinder?
  - We were told that the supplier grinds them to size.

So we came up with the following potential families:

- Grinder 2, furnace, cutoff, round, tumble
- Grinder 1, furnace, cutoff, round
- Grinders 1 and 2, furnace, cutoff

We can take the group-tech data and use it to determine the families of parts. If we have enough equipment we can set up dedicated cells for each family and sometimes eliminate the setup times and normally reduce them significantly. The next step is to create a cell composed of machines or process steps that will support the family or parts. The next step is to process them through the cell using OPF or small lots, noting every part may not hit every process step or machine (see Table 3.3).

Creating the Group-Tech Matrix

Group technology falls in the middle between batching and OPF and generally leads to segmented batch processing.* An example is having cells set up that work on a family of parts using the same tooling with a limited number of parts and tools; thus, we can run the cell with no setup time impact.

Take note that over time, this matrix must be updated, especially in small-volume, high-mix machine shops, as machines and customer requirements change over time.

---

* Segmented batch processing is running 100 of part A OPF followed by 100 of Part B OPF. This is different than pure mixed model which would be part A followed by part B.

Table 3.3 Same Group-Tech Matrix as Table 3.1 with Average Daily Demand Multiplied by the Machine Run Time with the Total Hours per Day Required to Run the Parts without Considering the Impact of Setups

Work Center	99722	99723	99721	99720	96201	99017	24600	91630	91620	533A1	533B1	533C1
Part/ Machine	Machine 1	Machine 2	Machine 3	Machine 4	Machine 5	Machine 6	Machine 7	Machine 8	Machine 9	Machine 10	Machine 11	Machine 12
Part 1				0.012	0.004	0.033		0.039		0.024		
Part 2				0.188	0.107	0.499		0.613		0.492		
Part 3				0.000	0.000	0.000		0.000		0.000		
Part 4				0.244	0.102	0.681		0.823		0.527		
Part 5				0.064	0.018	0.186		0.219		0.104		
Part 6				0.012	0.004	0.033		0.039		0.024		
Part 7				0.000	0.000	0.000		0.000		0.000		
Part 8				0.020	0.008	0.056	0.047		0.103	0.044		
Part 9				0.549	0.231	1.531	1.289		2.837	1.199		
Part 10				0.006	0.003	0.017	0.015		0.032	0.014		
Part 11				0.008	0.002	0.023	0.017		0.042	0.014		
Part 12				0.283	0.082	0.822	0.602		1.494	0.484		
Part 13				0.007	0.002	0.019	0.014		0.035	0.011		
Part 14				0.014	0.005	0.040	0.032		0.073	0.029		
Part 15				0.632	0.237	1.789	1.433		3.299	1.302		
Part 16				0.015	0.006	0.042	0.033		0.077	0.030		
Part 17				0.001	0.000	0.002	0.002		0.004	0.002		
Part 18				0.000	0.000	0.000	0.000		0.000	0.000		
Part 19				0.000	0.000	0.000	0.000		0.000	0.000		
Part 20			0.001		0.000	0.002	0.001	0.002		0.001		
Part 21				0.007	0.003	0.021	0.017	0.025		0.012		
Part 22			1.650		0.689	4.603		5.561		3.571		
Part 23				0.091	0.035	0.256		0.309		0.186		
Part 24			0.001		0.000	0.002	0.002	0.002		0.001		
Part 25				0.235	0.079	0.671		0.793		0.469		
	13.22	6.87	5.95	6.32	5.30	34.07	8.79	42.24	11.02	34.86	24.19	0.32

(Continued)

Table 3.3 (Continued)   Same Group-Tech Matrix as Table 3.1 with Average Daily Demand Multiplied by the Machine Run Time with the Total Hours per Day Required to Run the Parts without Considering the Impact of Setups

Work Center	533A1	533B1	533C1	53519	53514	53925	53924	91640	54231	24802	26412	26501
Part/Machine	Machine 13	Machine 14	Machine 15	Machine 16	Machine 17	Machine 18	Machine 19	Machine 20	Machine 21	Machine 22	Machine 23	Machine 24
Part 1	0.024			0.031		0.031			0.004			
Part 2	0.492						0.159	1.022	0.112			0.424
Part 3	0.000						0.000	0.000	0.000			0.000
Part 4	0.630			0.761		0.761		1.396	0.107			
Part 5	0.104						0.030		0.019			
Part 6	0.24						0.007	0.067	0.004			
Part 7	0.000						0.000	0.000	0.000			0.000
Part 8	0.055					0.063			0.009			
Part 9	1.511					1.728			0.243			
Part 10	0.017					0.020			0.003			
Part 11	0.019					0.017			0.002			
Part 12	0.689					0.616			0.086			
Part 13	0.016					0.14			0.002			
Part 14	0.039					0.39			0.006			
Part 15	1.765					1.769			0.254			
Part 16	0.041					0.041			0.006			
Part 17	0.003					0.002			0.000			
Part 18	0.000					0.000			0.000			
Part 19	0.000					0.000			0.000			
Part 20	0.001			.002		0.002			0.000	0.002		
Part 21	0.012			.020		0.020			0.002			
Part 22	4.258			5.152		5.152		9.436	0.689			
Part 23	0.237			.263		0.263		0.524	0.037			
Part 24	0.001					0.002			0.000			
Part 25	0.469			.591		0.591			0.086			0.521
	51.02	24.06	0.32	68.53	0.89	68.02	3.48	51.19	12.27	1.37	7.47	15.38

Source: BIG Archives.

Cross Cells Issues

The first sign of a cross cell part is when a part in a family has to leave the cell to run on another machine in another cell. This is known as cross-cell processing and results in batching the parts up to transfer them to the outside cell. The more cross-cell parts required, the sooner one needs to revisit the families and update them. There will always be parts that don't fit any family, and normally, a model-shop cell is set up to handle such misfit parts, noting some parts will always go across cells no matter what families are created.

Results

Figure 3.18 shows one of the cells resulting from a group tech matrix. The company had requisition in process to buy more centerless grinders. After studying the project for less than 3 hours we were able to form cells and free up two machines and reduce the setup time to zero. They canceled the requisition to buy the additional machines, saving $2 million in cost avoidance. They used the machines they freed up to do TPM. We also doubled the output by reducing the time to load and unload the machines. Even on very quick operations and machines, Lean tools facilitate the continuous improvement process. This company (see Figure 3.19) uses high-volume serializing machines. Even though their operators were only spending 8.75 seconds in labor time on each card using the Lean tools, we were able to reduce the time to three seconds.

In this transaction example, the accounts payable department in this company receive invoices from all over the world. Unfortunately, as the business has grown the method of processing each type of invoice has evolved slightly. The group-tech matrix provided by Rhidian Roach* (see Figure 3.20), shows the different processes that the invoice will follow depending on its origin,

Figure 3.18 Grinding machining cell realized a cost avoidance savings of $2M, increased capacity, and freed up machines. (Source: BIG Archives.)

---

* Rhidan Roach is the designer of the leanEdit® software.

Figure 3.19   Results at a card solutions processing company. (Source: BIG Archives.)

Group Tech–Process Family Matrix

COUNTRY OF ORIGIN	LOG IN	TAKE COPIES	PROCESS	REVIEW	APPROVE	PAY	FILE	%
LATIN AMERICA	X	X	X		X	X	X	30
EUROPE	X		X	X	X	X		15
USA	X		X		X	X	X	40
ASIA			X		X	X		15

The Process Family Matrix is a tool that's used in the transactional space to help determine where to focus when faced with multiple processes or process types. It's a simple form of Group Technology and is usually applied in advance of a mapping exercise or product flow analysis activity. The process steps are documented on the matrix together with any relevant quantitative data therefore enabling the user to factor in to their decision how representative a process may be.

In the above table, the Accounts Payable department in Company X receives invoices from all over the world. Unfortunately as the business has grown the method of processing each type of invoice has evolved slightly differently. The Process Family Matrix shows the different processes that the invoice will follow depending on its origin along with the percentage of total invoices made up by that country. The USA has the highest percentage of invoices with 40%, but Latin America is the most representative. Mapping the USA will cover 55% of the total invoices since process steps in the USA are also present in Asia. Mapping Latin America, on the other hand, will encompass both the USA and Asia, making up 85% of the total number of invoices. In this example this is clearly the place to start.

Of course quite often there are other factors to consider when selecting a process and common sense must always be applied in conjunction with the application of this tool.

Figure 3.20   Accounts payable group tech matrix. (Source: BIG Archives.)

along with the percentage of total invoices made up by that country. The United States has the highest percentage of invoices with 40%, but Latin America is the most representative. The group-tech matrix will work regardless of the number of parts or lot sizes involved. The goal of the group-tech matrix is to determine what, if any, families exist and to what extent of the parts they will cover. We have created group techs with 30 parts and some with thousands of parts.

Converting the Group-Tech Matrix to a Kanban and Capacity Planning Model

The group tech may start with Xs where a part runs across a machine or operation. We can then turn the Xs into machine run-cycle times for each part (Table 3.3). If you multiply these times by the average daily demand, it will immediately provide an idea of the loading hours (capacity) on each machine. As the project progresses, the same matrix can be used to develop the kanban lot sizing for each part (Table 3.4).

Table 3.5 is the same group-tech matrix where we are now able to use it to create the capacity analysis, i.e., average daily demand multiplied by the machine run time with the total hours per day required to run the parts without setups.

The Group-Tech Matrix and Layouts

Once we do a group-tech matrix and determine a cell can be created, we do a process-flow analysis (PFA) on the part(s) in the cell to make sure we have the steps in the correct order (Table 3.6).

Many times routers will have steps in a different order for similar parts. We have found that this is normally due to different engineers designing the routers. Most times the steps can be changed on routers to put them in the same order. A PFA and point-to-point diagram (cell layout with point-to-point part-travel paths drawn on it) are the best tools to double-check that you have the right equipment/machines in the cell and they are in the right order. Once we get done we can analyze the results (see Table 3.7).

Workflow Analysis (WFA)—Following the Operator

Our second analysis step is to conduct a WFA on the remaining steps of the product- process flow (see Table 3.8). While somewhat tedious, it is critical to go through each step and document it. Going through this analysis on video with the team and questioning each step helps to build that compelling need to change. Many times, we find all kinds of opportunities to improve production and transactional processes. Most of the steps we find were probably necessary at one time but with the changes in technology may no longer necessary.

WFA Steps

1. Video.
2. Analyze the operator steps.
3. Follow the (ERSC) process (sometimes referred to as the Omits process because we Omit steps or update the "to be" or future-state estimated times).

Table 3.4 Same Group-Tech Matrix as Table 3.1 with Kanban Analysis

| | | | | Work Center | | | | |
Part/Machine	Greenstock #	Base Number	Total Parts per Run	Kanban Qty (Parts per Tub)	# Tubs	Tubs in Process (on Hand)	Number of Weeks between Setups	Working Days Worth of Parts per Tub
Part 1	1172057	1118548	1,010.92	3,661.80	0.28		7.2	36.2
Part 2		1118835	15,330.65	2,365.05	6.48		2.0	1.5
Part 3		1118835		2,365.05				
Part 4		1118861	20,944.94	3,509.98	5.97		2.0	1.7
Part 5		1119051	5,731.91	4,771.05	1.20		2.0	8.3
Part 6		1119064	1,004.46	3,719.73	0.27		7.4	37.0
Part 7		1119065		4,339.06				
Part 8		1122090	1,709.37	3,322.36	0.51		3.9	19.4
Part 9		1122090	47,091.85	3,321.72	14.18		2.0	0.7
Part 10		1122090	535.75	3,321.09	0.16		12.4	62.0
Part 11		1122110	706.48	4,675.56	0.15		13.2	66.2
Part 12		1122110	25,262.22	4,674.59	5.40		2.0	1.9
Part 13		1122110	590.21	4,673.60	0.13		15.8	79.2
Part 14		1122120	1,222.59	3,849.07	0.32		6.3	31.5
Part 15		1122120	55,001.30	3,848.30	14.29		2.0	0.7
Part 16		1122120	1,283.79	3,847.52	0.33		6.0	30.0

Source: BIG Archives.

Table 3.5 Same as Table 3.1 with Capacity Analysis Derived from Group-Tech Matrix

Available Time	16.50	16.50	16.50	16.50	16.50
Takt time (TT) per machine minute	5.45	2.86	11.21	4.30	3.24
Avg. run cycle time per machine (minute)	3.00	1.75	3.00	3.00	3.00
Demand on the machine (hour/day)	9.08	10.08	4.41	11.51	15.29
Setups 3/week (avg. hours per day)	1.20	1.20	1.20	1.20	1.20
Total demand per day run time + setups	10.28	11.28	5.61	12.71	16.49
Lost time due to inspections (internal time)					
Grand total demand on machines	10.28	11.28	5.61	12.71	16.49
Capacity available	6.22	5.22	10.89	3.79	0.01
% at capacity based on hours	62.3	68.4	34.0	77.0	100.0
No. of parts per day	181.52	345.68	88.29	230.21	305.89
# of parts available capacity per day	306.00	524.57	306.00	306.00	306.00
% at capacity based on # parts	59	66	29	75	100
Available time less setups and inspect downtime	180.32	344.48	87.09	229.01	304.69
Additional parts that could be produced per day per machine	3424.95	11,465.15	1653.43	4349.92	5787.89

Source: BIG Archives.

4. Reorder the steps.
5. Determine the total labor time (TLT).
6. Create standard work for the operator and the supervisor.

It is better to film your best person at the job, and sometimes we will film the fastest, the slowest, and someone in between. With rare exceptions, it is important not to talk to the operators or have them talk to you when filming them.

Table 3.6 Process-Flow Analysis After

No. of Steps	Omit (X)	Description of Product Step	Baseline Time (s)	Post Lean Estimate Time	Distance (in ft)	Distance Post (with Omits)	Machine	Person Who Touches It (Job Class)
1	x	Parts sit as bar stock	14400	0		0		
2		Mori	125	125		0	Mori	Eric
3	x	Sits in parts tray in mori	16	0		0		
4		Move to hand to inspect	3	3	1	1		
5		Inspect part	19	19		0		
6		Lathe	80	80	5	5	Lathe	
7	x	Sits on lathe – lost first in, first out (FIFO)	1260	0	2	0		
8		To gear cutter	3	3		0	Gear cutter	
9		Gear cut	300	300		0		
10		Sits on gear cutter	29	29		0		Joe
11		Inspect gear cut	11	11		0		
12	x	Sits in egg carton	300	0	1	0		
13		Sand	51	51	8	8		John
14		Lathe deburr	45	45	1	1	Lathe	
15		Mill	22	22	5	5	Mill	
16	x	Sits in egg carton	11520	0	2	0		

Source: BIG Archives.

Table 3.7 Process-Flow Analysis Results Before and After

Summary	Baseline	Post Lean Projected	Reduction	Reduction (%)
Total steps	16.0	11.0	5.00	31%
Orig sec:	28,184	688	27,496	98%
Minutes	469.7	11.5	458.27	98%
Hours	7.8	0.2	7.64	98%
Days	1.1	0.0	1.05	98%
Weeks	0.2	0.0	0.2	98%
Distance	20.0	20.0	—	0%
# of people	3.0	1.0	2.00	67%
# of machines	5.0	5.0	—	0%
VA (%)	1.8699	76.60	−74.73	
NVA (%)	0.34	13.95	−13.61	
Storage (%)	97.66	4.22	93.45	
Inspect (%)	0.11	4.36	−4.25	
Transport (%)	0.02	0.87	−0.85	

Source: BIG Archives.

Step 1: Video the Operator(s)

The first step is to video the operator. Our goal is to capture the total labor time to produce *one* piece of the product or the transactional process. If they are batching, you will need to keep the camera running until the batch is completed. The other option is to force them to build one piece from start to finish and video it.

> If they are batching, then we only analyze the first piece of each batch and then review and compare the total time for each piece after that (like a 10-cycle analysis). If we see a big difference in time we will go back and examine that cycle in more detail.

Step 2: Analyze the Video

Hold an analysis session in a conference room or on the shop floor if there is room, and project the video up on the wall. Invite the operators, supervisor, engineer, and someone unfamiliar with the process to the session. We then assign roles to each person. These can be:

- Draw the spaghetti diagram.
- Keep a list of tools used.
- Keep a list of part used.
- Keep a list of ideas for improvement.
- Check the distance each person travels.
- Check the current documentation against the video and look for discrepancies.

Table 3.8   Workflow Analysis (WFA)

OP Step	Omit (X)	Description	Key Points Quality and Safety	Analysis Codes Enter Either VA, RW, PW, MH, UW, R T I	Current Time (sec)	Estimated Time
1		Open door Mori	Mori	RW	1	1
2	x	Press button		RW	2	0
3		Pick up pliers		RW	3	3
4		Pull out bar		RW	2	2
5		Close door Mori		RW	2	2
6		Press start/cycle machine		RW	1	1
7		Open part catch		RW	1	1
8		Take out part		RW	4	1
9	x	Grab mic		RW	2	0
10	x	Inspect		RW	2	0
11	x	Put down mic		RW	1	0
12	x	Pick up mic		RW	1	0
13	x	Inspect		RW	13	0
14	x	Put down mic		RW	1	0
15		Move to lathe	Lathe	RW	2	2
16		Remove from chuck		RW	1	1
17		Reach for hose		RW	1	1
18		Blow off		RW	3	1
19		Put down hose		RW	1	1
20		Reach for deburr		RW	1	1

Source: BIG Archives and Ancon Gear.

We may initially use a flipchart to capture the steps and times so people get used to the process. Then we use leanEdit® to carry out the analysis using the "Labor Analysis" tool. This software has the advantage of integrating the video and analysis sections into one seamless interface. During video analysis, it is a good idea to identify sections of video to be referenced later as best practices or examples of waste. Traditionally, finding clips can be a tedious process, involving time-consuming video editing. leanEdit® automates this process with the "favorite" clip-capture feature allowing the user to identify these clips in real time as they analyze the video! These "favorite" clips can also be merged for convenience. Find out more at leanEdit.com (see Figure 3.21).

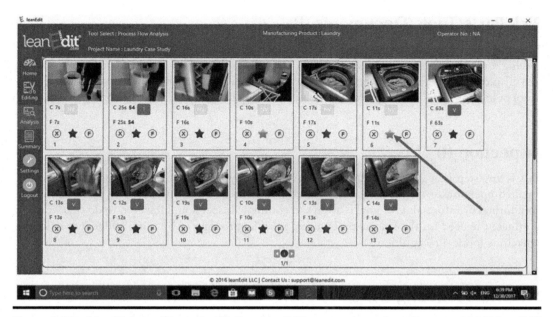

Figure 3.21   Identifying a "Favorite Clip" on leanEdit.com web version. (Source: ©2017 leanEdit LLC.)

The first thing we always look for when reviewing videos is anything unsafe or that results in poor ergonomic positions. It is *extremely* important the operator be present during the analysis. When the operator is not involved, they do not benefit from the on-the-spot learning discussed during the video and many times we really don't know what or why the operator is doing what they are doing. Dr. Shingo called this "*knowing what*" versus "*knowing why*." We will discuss this more later.

The WFA analyzes the operator steps while the product is flowing through the system down to the second. We break the operator steps into two categories:

■ Value-added
■ Non–value-added

We have the same definition for value-added we had for the product piece which is as follows:

Value-Added (V):

1. Customer cares, that is, is willing to pay for
2. Physically changes the product (form, fit, shape, size, or function)
3. Done right the first time

We break operator steps into the elements listed in the following and sometimes other elements, depending on the process. Eventually one can get to the Therblig elements of motion study.

Pick Parts/Tools/Documents (P)

This is any step that involves reaching for, grasping, and picking up a part, tool, or document and moving it to the unit. It must immediately be placed into the unit to be considered a value-added step. This category is also used when reaching for a tool being used right away or loading a part into a tool or loading a tool onto a part. This includes loading the part onto a fixture or into a machine.

Inspection (I)

This is any step that includes inspection whether it is by a final inspector, in-process inspector, certified operator, or neighbor operator (successive checks), etc. It includes any operator inspection, formal or informal. Our goal is always to eliminate inspection. However, to do this we must eliminate the need for the inspection by using mistake-proofing or by using 100% inspection by a machine (optical recognition).

Material Handling (H)

Whenever an operator gets a part but does not put it immediately into the unit or grabs a tool but then sets it down before using it, it is considered material handling. It should be equal to 0 seconds in the after condition. Tests for this code are: Is this step something we can hand off to a water spider (material handler) to do for the line, or could the operator have put the part directly on the assembly or used the tool immediately after he/she picked it up?

Non–Value-Added Work (NV)

These steps do not meet all of the three value-added criteria in the current condition (i.e., searching or over-processing waste)! Sometimes we don't have a clue, nor does the operator, why they did what they did. We see this especially in transactional-type settings; for example, circling information on an invoice for data entry or putting a payable date on an invoice which is already assigned by the computer system.

As an example, in the assembly area, you will see the operator sit down and just start making wholesale changes to their workstation area, moving this, moving that, etc., for really no reason other than getting settled and ready to start working.

The test for non–value-added steps is they should be equal to 0 seconds in the after condition (i.e., we should be able to *omit* the step in the after condition). If it cannot be omitted it must be considered required work. For instance, if the operator has to change bits on a screw gun or change a fixture over because they only have the one screw gun or one arbor press, it is required work because in the current condition it is required.

Idle Time (IT)

This step denotes where the operator is doing nothing but sitting or standing idle and waiting. This is not used for an operator searching for parts, etc. That would fall under material handling (if we can't get rid of it right away) or non–value-added work (if we can get rid of it right away). Operators should never be idle.

Load Machine (L)

Loading the part in the equipment or machine.

Unload Machine (UL)

Unloading the part from the equipment or machine.

Activating Machine (A)

Activating a machine.

Aligning (AL)

Aligning the part to be processed by the equipment or machine.

Changing Set Up (CS)

Changing the setup of a workstation from one product to another.

Walking (W)

Time when the operator is walking.

Other (O)

Work that does not fit into any other category. This can be used for specific work steps depending on the analysis.

For the Office

For the office, we may require categories like computer time, paperwork, telephone talking, etc. They can be classified using the "O" category described above. When using the leanEdit® "Administrative" mode the L, UL, A, AL, and CS categories are replaced by a general equipment category (E) since detailed equipment activity is rare in these situations. You can also create your own categories if desired.

WFA Example

Let's revisit our coffee cup example.

1. Pick up both cups—Required work (RW) —1 sec.
2. Put the cups down—Required work (RW)—1 sec.
3. Pick up the coffee pot—Required work (RW)—2 sec.
4. Pour the coffee in the first cup—Value-added—2 sec.
5. Pour the coffee in the second cup—Required work (RW)—2 sec.
6. Put the coffee pot back—Required work (RW)—2 sec.
7. Transport to second person—Required work (RW)—5 sec.
8. Taste the coffee (V or Inspection)—1 sec.

Once you assess the existing process, you must figure out and agree on what the new process will be and then compare the cycle times and other metrics you have chosen to forecast the improvement.

When we have finished analyzing the process, we must determine the new process and create and document the standard work.

The standard work must include the sequence of operations, including key points and reasons for key points, cycle times, and standard WIP (based on takt time) for each process. It is important to follow up with a *check* to make sure the improvements are taught to the rest of the users. It is not unusual to have to create or modify the roles and responsibilities matrix when working on transactional processes. Many times the process owner of a decision or activity in the matrix are not clear, so the ownership needs to be decided based on who has the most at stake by the process being improved.

Analyze to the Second

Do not shortcut the process. If you take steps larger than a second you can end up combining steps that mix up different codes, which affects true content of the work and eventually impacts the standard work, which is derived from this analysis.

As we engage employees in redesigning their workstations and eliminating excess motions to provide safe and ergonomically designed jobs for our shop-floor and administrative team members, we realize increased productivity, morale, and job satisfaction, which usually leads to higher profits.

Video Guidelines for the Operator

- Communicate to everyone about the videoing ahead of time (see Figure 3.22). Let them know they will be invited back to review the videos. No one is ever "written up" for what is on a video. It is not about the person but the process. If there are any violations it is management's not the operator's fault.
- If possible, do not make the filming voluntary. Add a clause into your HR forms that people are accepting videoing as one of the expectations and conditions for hiring.

Figure 3.22　The power of video. (Source: BIG Archives.)

■ Remember to make clear what you are following with the video, i.e., product or operator. Many times, people forget or get confused and stay filming the machine instead of following the operator wherever they go.

■ Never stop the camera. Operators will make a mistake and tell you to turn off the camera because they must go get something. Don't do it. The only time we stop the camera is when they are headed to the restroom. We need to explain to the operator ahead of time that if we need to remove a step, we can do it when we review the tape, and if they must get something that is not at their station, it is exactly the point of the video. We need to see the stupid things on the video that we (management) make them do every day. The other problem is the analog times do not convert to digital format. So the only way to know the true time is to keep the camera running all the time.

■ Film as far away as possible but close enough to be able to see exactly what the operator's hands are doing. This is a big advantage of videoing over traditional time study. Instead of standing over top of someone with a stopwatch, you can normally be a good distance away and still see everything the operator's hands are doing. Sometimes the operators even forget you are there.

■ Keep in mind when videoing you can have fun, but not too much fun. When you video, there are those who love to be filmed and others who truly hate it. Be aware of this fact and compassionate to those who don't like to be filmed. Empathize with them but still insist on filming them. Some operators will actually try to lose you as they travel through the plant trying to find what they need. Others will joke around and tease the operators as being film stars, wanting rights and royalties to the video, etc. Some of this can't be prevented but too much joking around will possibly result in someone getting upset.

■ Let people know that eventually everyone will be filmed. The first time being filmed is the hardest. Once people see everyone getting filmed, it will eventually become second nature and people won't even think about it. In some cases, they come to us now and even request to be filmed to rebalance the line (if it was station balanced) or show a problem in the process or to highlight someone who is not working.

■ Resist the temptation to zoom in and out constantly, and if doing so, do it slowly. There is nothing worse than reviewing someone's first video. Many times, you feel like you are on a boat and feel seasick.

- Make sure to follow the operator's hands or you will find yourself moving your head trying to see what the operator's hands are doing, which are just out of view. When you ask the operator what they did, most times, they don't remember.
- Try not to have the operators talk to you while you are filming. This slows the operator down and sometimes they forget the steps because they are talking. It can remove the normalcy from the video and not show what truly happens each day.
- Don't give operators advance warning. This normally results in them getting ready to be filmed and they go and retrieve all their parts, etc., which defeats the whole purpose of filming. This is especially true in setups.
- When panning an area, do it very, very slowly like walking down the aisle at a wedding. When we initially start the Lean process on a cell, the first thing we do is document the area with digital photos and video pans of the area. This is so we have a *before* video and pictures to compare once the area has been improved. People tend to forget very quickly what the area used to look like.

Always Involve the Operators

Always involve the operators from the beginning when viewing the video. Don't analyze the video and then bring them in. This is a trap everyone falls into. Two things lead to this trap.

1. The first is the thought process that the engineers are too busy to be bothered with watching the videos and we should find the problems and then hand them over to them. This almost never works. If you don't involve the engineers during the process, they can't possibly hear directly from the operators or feel their pain. We always insist the engineers go to the floor and build what they have designed. The operators love this!
2. The other pitfall is when we are told that management can't afford to free up the operators to review the videos. There is too much pressure on production. Our response is, "What do you do when they call in sick?" If you don't take the time to fix the process, you will never get out of the firefighting. Whenever we have given into this argument, it inevitably impacts the overall quality and outcome of the project during and after, and it becomes much more difficult to sustain because the operators weren't involved.

If you don't have the operator with you explaining during the video analysis, you can't possibly understand what they are doing. You miss steps, tribal knowledge, learning about the tools they developed, and all the other problems in the process like the interruptions from quality or planning or engineering. You don't learn why they do what they do or the way they do it. The output lost by having the operators involved is always quickly made up, and then some when the process is Leaned out. We always say:

"You can either do it to them or with them!"

Calculate Total Labor Time for One Piece

One of our major deliverables of WFA is the total labor time (TLT), i.e., the sum of V and NV labor or work performed during the process by the operator(s) to produce one completed piece.

Some refer to this as touch time. Machine time is not included in the labor time. This is part of the principle of separating man from machine work.

Calculating the TLT will give you a picture of how much labor and, ultimately, how many operators or staff are required to complete one piece of whatever is being processed.

Step 3: Conduct the Omits Process

(Eliminating, Rearranging, Simplifying, and Combining [ERSC])

The Omits process is crucial to the analysis process and it should be done with the operator(s) present. If we can omit the step we reduce the time to zero. If we can't completely omit it we change the time for the step to a new estimated time.

The employees participate in the process so they can help contribute their ideas and understand how we arrived at the new times for the overall work. It not only incorporates their improvement ideas, but the estimated times now come from them.

For example, if we can't omit the step but we think we can improve it, we ask the operator, "How long do you think it will take with this new process?" When we end up with a 30%–50% reduction in the TLT, they understand why and how it was calculated and agree to and accept it. In this way, they are included in determining their standard work, which will be the resulting process after the steps are reviewed. The next step is to review and question each step and ask if it can be somehow:

- Eliminated
- Rearranged
- Simplified
- Combined

The WFA can be viewed as time-consuming, but can be done fairly quickly. In fact, we have run through all of the analysis steps and implemented and run a new layout in as short as six hours.

If done properly, it is where all the value of performing the analysis resides. We want to continuously ask these questions whenever possible for each step. Much can be learned from motion study and questioning every step in the process. The WFA leads ultimately to our work instructions and standard work process for doing the job.

In the leanEdit® Analysis page, the user has the ability to eliminate/omit the step or improve it by entering a new future time (see Figure 3.23).

Action items, to enable the improvements, are captured along with optional fields for initials and completion dates. The application's summary page has the functionality to create preliminary standard work by offering "Edit," "Move," and "Add" row capability (see Figure 3.24). The software will also generate the workflow analysis spreadsheet, summary table, and pie charts, which can be exported to Excel® if desired (see Figure 3.25).

Spaghetti Diagram

A spaghetti diagram (see Figure 3.26) is like a point-to-point diagram. The point-to-point diagram follows the product from point to point through the process, where the spaghetti diagram follows the operator or staff person doing the work through each step of the process. It is constructed by following the operator for one complete cycle of their work. This can be done by following the operator on the floor, or in the office, or by mapping it off the video.

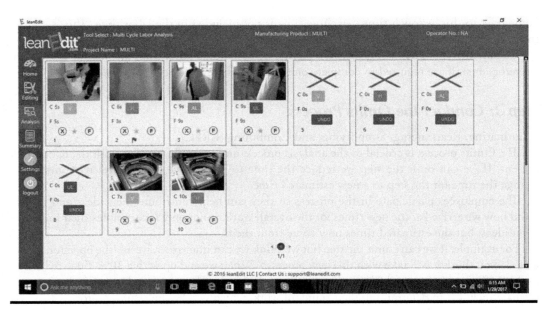

Figure 3.23   Analyzing process steps on the analysis screen ©2017 leanEdit LLC. (Source: ©2017 leanEdit LLC.)

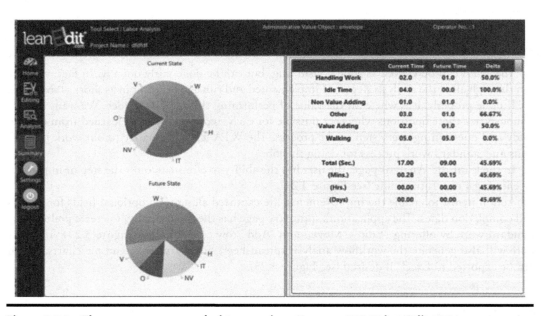

Figure 3.24   The summary screen desktop version. (Source: ©2017 leanEdit LLC.)

Operators in manufacturing essentially work in four environments:

1. Assembly
2. Machining (or automation)
3. Transactional

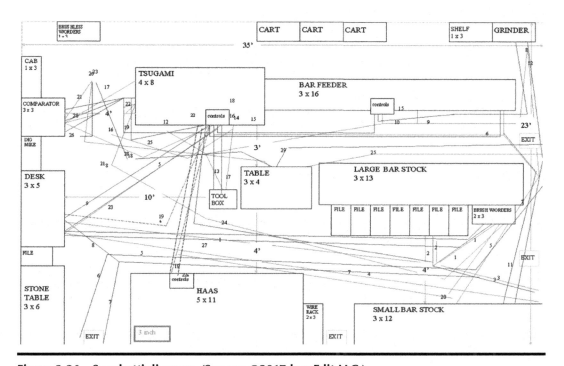

Figure 3.25 The summary screen web version. (Source: ©2017 leanEdit LLC.)

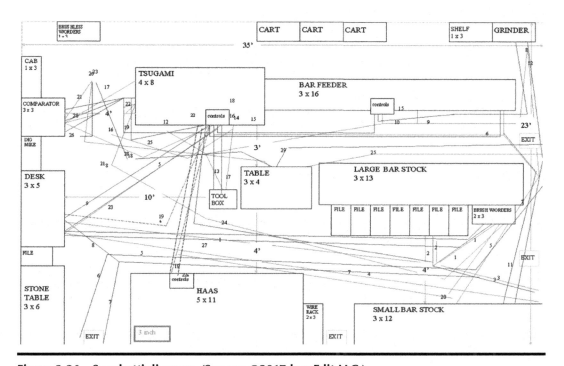

Figure 3.26 Spaghetti diagram. (Source: ©2017 leanEdit LLC.)

4. Some combination of assembly, machine, and/or transactional processes

In healthcare, they work with:

1. People
2. Machines in sterile processing department (SPD), robotics in surgery, and automation in the lab
3. Transactional
4. Some combination of people, machine, or transactional

Update the Process Block Diagram

Next, we need to review the list we put together during the WFA to determine what parts, equipment, jigs, tools, fixtures, tooling, etc., are required and list them out under each PFA step on the board. Note where and what type of electric is required, air (high or low pressure), other gases, safety checks, quality checks, etc., is needed.

Now we need to identify where SWIP will be required and how much. We then add the total labor time to each step. You can do a before-and-after process block diagram for comparison.

Part of the target condition is to make sure the product never goes backward in the flow. We need to identify, at this point, what additional tooling and equipment is desired and whether we have the funds and customer demand to justify its purchase.

Eighty percent of the time, we don't require additional funds or may require small expense dollars for tools or equipment but not large capital appropriations; however, there are exceptions. If a large-dollar purchase is required, we may have to implement the line in phases—that is, pre- and post-purchase of additional equipment.

Once the block diagram is completed, go back and review the PFA and WFA. Use the new block diagram to reorder the steps, eliminate the omitted steps, and create the new *to-be* PFA document.

The PFA spreadsheet will predict the improvement to be gained. Do the same for the WFA. Once the steps have been rearranged in the WFA, determine how much labor time will be required for each of the steps in the block diagram and note those times on the diagram. The WFA spreadsheet will predict the number of operators required based on the demand, which will become the basis for the standard work document and capacity analysis we will create later.

World Class

Our goal with Lean and the operator is to consistently measure and strive toward world-class benchmarks. While these may seemingly be unobtainable, they provide a guard against complacency and the impetus to drive toward continually improving the process.

Our goal should always be to reduce the number of operators in the process and yet continually develop them and move them to new positions. We must work to always use people wisely and safely throughout the company. We should always be working to reduce both direct and indirect labor and convert staff jobs to line jobs wherever possible and then stop distinguishing direct from indirect.

In machining, transactional, or service operations, world class should be:

- 3 × value-added

- The balance should be required work
- 0% idle

Automated lines:

- 0% value-added
  (Note: machine adds the value)
- 100% required work
- 0% idle

For transactional processes:

- 0% value-added (because the nature of transactional processes is non–value-added).
- 100% required work
- 0% idle

The operator analysis should yield a 20%–40% productivity improvement to your overall process when compared to a strictly batch environment. In addition to capturing the labor time, the distance traveled is also captured as a baseline and future state.

What We Get from the Operator Piece of Lean

Analyzing just the operator will provide the following pieces of the Lean implementation:

- TLT for one piece or small lot
- Percent value-added for the operator
- Percent required work for the operator
- Percent idle time for the operator
- Standard work for the supervisor
- Number of operators required
- Capacity planning when coupled with PFA analysis
- Scheduling flexibility/number of shifts and overtime required
- Operator walk patterns
- Operator buy-in and morale
- SWIP for the operators—total inventory required when coupled with PFA
- Paperwork required and how the paperwork travels in the cell
- Level loading
- Proper tool and material presentation
- Ergonomics/safety/fatigue opportunities
- Work standards
- Motion study
- 10-cycle analysis
- Operator work zones
- Baton zones (bumping)
- Job breakdown standard work for the operator
- Training golden videos

- Key points and reasons for key points for each step
- Operator cycle times for each step in the process
- Percent of overhead versus direct labor
- Mistake-proofing opportunities
- Opportunities to reduce variation

Motion Study

If you think you have improved all you can, let us provide you with a second thought. The tool to ultimately expose additional waste is Frank Gilbreth's motion study. Motion study involves analyzing what we do to the fraction of a second. This was all part of the scientific management movement of the Industrial Revolution in the early twentieth century. Gilbreth's Therbligs* are listed here (see Figures 3.27 and 3.28).

Class 1: The essence of an operation (highest value):

1. Assemble
2. Disassemble
3. Use

Class 2: Preparatory or follow-up motions

1. Transport empty
2. Grasp

Therbligs

Class	No.	Name	Symbol	Description
1	1	Assemble	‡‡	Shape of combined rods
	2	Disassemble	++	One rod removed from a combined shape
	3	Deform (use)	U	U for "use," or a cup placed upright
2	4	Transport empty (extending or retracting your hand)	⋃	Shape of palm opened up
	5	Grab	∩	Shape of hand grabbing
	6	Transport	⌣	Shape of object being transported with hand
	7	Release	⌢	Shape of object with hand facing down
3	8	Search	⌖	Symbol of searching eye
	9	Find	⊙	Symbol of eye having located object after search
	10	Select	→	Symbol of finger pointing at selected object
	11	Inspect	0	Shape of a lens
	12	Regrasp (reposition)	9	Symbol of regrasping object held by finger tips
	13	Hold	Ω	Shape of rod held with hand
	14*	Prepare	ß	Shape of a cuestick standing erect
4	15*	Think	ℙ	Shape of a thinking person with hand by head
	16*	Rest	ℛ	Shape of a person sitting on chair
	17	Unavoidable delay	⌒o	Shape of tripped person on ground
	18*	Avoidable delay	⌣o	Shape of person lying down

Note: An asterisk indicates a therblig that does not usually arise during normal tasks.

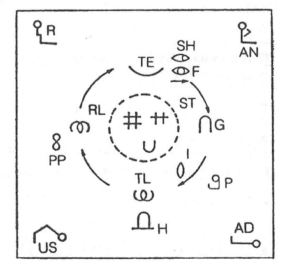

Figure 3.27 Gilbreth's Therbligs. (Source: Motion Study, Frank Gilbreth © 1911.)

---

* Therbligs is Gilbreth spelled backward.

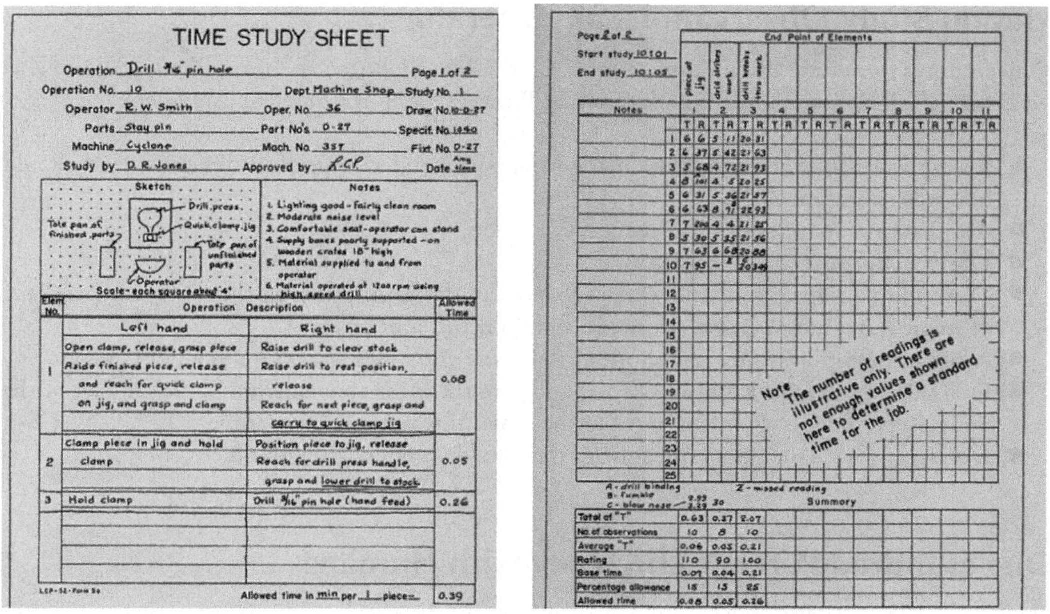

Figure 3.28 Time and motion study sheet. (Source: BIG Archives.)

3. Transport loaded
4. Release load

Class 3: Incidental motions:

1. Search
2. Find
3. Select
4. Inspect
5. Pre-position or reposition
6. Hold
7. Prepare

Class 4: These should be eliminated, if possible:

1. Think or plan
2. Rest for overcoming fatigue
3. Unavoidable delay
4. Avoidable delay

Notice that the only value-added Therbligs are assemble, use, and sometimes disassemble (i.e., re-manufacturer).

Motion Study Observations for Operator

Some findings from time and motion handbooks by Gilbreth, Ralph Barnes, Gilbreth's disciple, as well as conclusions noted in a master's thesis by Ranveer Singh Rathore are listed here:

- Motions of the hands should be made in opposite and symmetrical directions and should be made simultaneously.
- Avoid abrupt changes in the direction of motion.
- Use free, unconstrained motion.
- Direction and distance of movement do have a significant effect on the speed and accuracy of single-hand motions and two-hand simultaneous motions.
- Avoid unnatural postures and motions that raise and lower the body's center of gravity.
- Don't use the hands as fixtures. The hands are the most convenient and useful part of the body. Keep them both free to work at the same time as much as possible.
- Don't use your hands to perform work that could be done with your feet.

One Hundred Percent Efficiency with Humans

Looking at it from a very analytical, Lean, or motion study, purist point of view, only an operator who uses both hands and feet at the same time is 100% efficient (a piano player or a drummer is a good example). Normally, we look at use of both hands simultaneously as 100% efficient, but technically it is only 50% efficient since we are not using our feet.

People who use one hand as a fixture to hold something while the other hand is working on it are only 25% efficient and are also a common reason operations cannot be split between two persons.

Setup Reduction

The third analysis tool is analyzing the setup or changeover process.

Setup Analysis

SMED Definition

SMED (Single-minute exchange of dies) is a system for reducing the time to complete equipment changeovers. The principle of SMED is to convert setup or changeover steps from internal (when the machine is down) to external (performed while the equipment is running), and to simplify and streamline the remaining steps. The name SMED comes from Ritsuo Shingo, who coined the term for his father's, Shigeo Shingo's, golf score. He told his father anything under 10, or a single digit, is a good handicap. We now say the goal of reducing changeover times is to reduce it to single digits (i.e., less than 10 minutes).

Changeover Definition

Our definition for changeover is:

from the removal of the last good piece to the completion of the first good piece of the next lot.

This is a strict definition designed to drive the most improvement. This means, once you remove the last good piece, if there is paperwork you must do, turning off the machine, or moving the job in the MRP system, it all counts as part of the internal changeover time.

Clock Time versus Labor Time

In Lean changeovers, we make a distinction between *clock time* and *labor time*.

- Clock time is the internal time it takes for the changeover.
- Labor time is the total amount of labor involved in the changeover.

In a NASCAR pit stop for example, the clock time is 14.7 seconds (see Figure 3.29).

Labor Time

To calculate the total setup labor time, we need to review how many operators are involved before, during, and after the setup. If there are seven people doing the changeover, we would calculate the labor time by multiplying seven times the 14.7 seconds' clock time, which equals 109.3 seconds, but we need to add in the time for the steps done to prepare for the pit-stop changeover and what work was done after the car was back on the track. If you add people and can distribute the work accordingly, you can reduce the setup time. On YouTube® there is a video of a Formula One® pit stop that is 1.9 seconds with 22 people.

Successful Setup Characteristics

These are just a few of the characteristics that make the pit stop concept successful:

Figure 3.29   Pitstop. (Source: BIG Archives.)

- Everyone knows their job.
- Practice, practice, practice.
- They are dedicated to specific tasks.
- Multiple operators (pit crew).
- Doing job steps in parallel.
- Standard work for each person.
- Lots of training.
- 5S, which means everything in its place prior to, during, and after the changeover.
- A constant dissatisfaction with the current changeover time until it is zero!

Internal Time

Internal time is the time the machine is down. In the pit-stop example anything done while the car is in the pit is considered *internal time*. Examples would be changing the tires or refueling. In our machining operations, this translates into anything that can only be done when the machine is stopped.

External Time

Back to our pit-stop example … Anything we can do while the race car is going around the track is considered *external* time. For example, we can get the tires ready and properly located in the pit area ahead of time. For our machine, this means gathering all the tools ahead of time, dies are preset and/or preheated etc. so we basically should never leave the machine while setting it up.

Internal Time and Clock Time

So, if you think about it, the 14.7 seconds for the pit-stop is only a measure of the internal time and does not include the time driving to or from the pit stop area on pit row. It also does not include any external time. Why do we focus on internal time? Because this is the amount of time the machine, person, or asset is not available for use; that is, the car is not racing around the track or the machine is down. This means our SMED, or setup, in less than 10 minutes really refers only to the internal time.

Four Components of Setup

The next step needed for setup analysis is to break down each step into its component part or category. Dr. Shingo describes this in his book *A Revolution in Manufacturing: The SMED System*. The four components and codes we utilize for setup reduction are the following:

1. Preparation and organization (P)
2. Removing and mounting (R)
3. Calibration, centering, dimensioning, aligning, measurement, and testing (A)
4. Trial runs and adjustment (T)

SMED Process Steps (ICE)

The acronym we utilize for Dr. Shingo's setup methodology is *ICE*:

- *Identify* all steps as to whether they are performed on internal or external time. When first conducting setups almost all steps are not started until the machine is stopped.
- *Convert* as many steps as possible from internal to external.
- *Eliminate*, rearrange, simplify, or combine all remaining steps—the Omits process.

Steps for Setup Analysis

- Video the setup. This may require multiple cameras in order to follow each operator. Use the same video guidelines for filming the operator above. We must be able to see their hands all the times. Use a setup clock (see Figure 3.30).
- Watch the video together with the setup team and supervisor.
- Break down each step according to the codes and classify each with the code and times, internal or external, for that part of the setup.
- Use the SMED process (ICE) to convert as many steps as possible from internal to external.
- Give people roles to draw spaghetti maps, keep track of distances traveled, missing tools, or fixtures operators had to search for, keep a list of ideas, etc.

Figure 3.30 Setup clock with flipchart to capture improvement ideas. (Source: BIG Archives.)

Station	Area	Setup Type 1	Setup Type 2	Setup Type 3	Step # Mechanic	Operator or Mechanical	Step #	Description	Base Labor Time	Internal or External	Standard Work Times 1st pass	Actual from 1st Trial	Actual from 2nd trial	Goal 50%	Standard Work Completed	Comments
1	Area 1	X		X	1	Operator	1	Load and replace sensor	170	113	214	210	207	-22%	Yes	move sensor to exter
2	Area 1	X						Conveyor from Press - NA -never adjust								
4	Area 1	X						Gas flaming								estimate 600 sec - Hardly ever needed
5	Area 1	X		X	2	Operator	2	adjust conveyor	177	Internal	120	111	122	31%	Yes	
7	Area 1	X		X	4	Mechanic	12	adjust sensor	180	Internal	28	28	150	17%	Yes	
8	Area 1	X		X	6	Operator	4	press	91	Internal	25	34	35	62%	yes	
9	Area 1	X		X	5	Mechanic	13	test parts	235	Internal	120	120	120	49%	Yes	
27	Area 1	X		X	3	Operator	3	S - Fixture	160	Internal	81	80	93	42%	Yes	
13	Area 2	X		X	7	Operator	6	stamping machine	56	Internal	28	107	129	-130%	Yes	
14	Area 2	X	X	X		Operator	5	changed the paint	60	Internal		48		20%	Yes	
15	Area 2	X			8	Operator	8	3 each riveting	1270	Internal	471	107	0	100%	Yes	
15	Area 2	X			8	Mechanic	9	3 each rivet	220	Internal	314	314	399	-81%		
16	Area 2	X						conveyor unloading								never needs to adjust
17	Area 2	X						bar code reader - never adjust								never needs to adjust
18	Area 2	X		X	9	Mechanic	10	Move the grip	129	Internal	152	176	229	-78%	No	(future should be oper
21	Area 2	X				Mechanic		press the label								Don't do
24	Area 2	X		X	10	Operator	7	Rail - change the guide	996	Internal	410	309	765	23%	Yes	
24	Area 2	X		X	10	Mechanic	11	Rail - change the guide	996	Internal	841	841	330	67%	No	Operator can help
24	Area 2	X		X	10	Operator	13	Operator helps		Internal		359	330			Operator can help
3	Area 3	X						Drilling unit								
6	Area 3	X		X	15	Mechanic	5	R-fixture	199	Internal	54	104	87	56%	Yes	
28	Area 3	X		X		Mechanic	4	R- Plate	34	Internal	17	58	24	29%	Yes	
10	Area 3	X		X	14	Mechanic	3	C- Plate	118	Internal	35	51	72	39%	Yes	
22	Area 3	X		X	13	Mechanic	2	Mag Basket	420	Internal	79	77	92	78%	Yes	

Figure 3.31   Setup matrix example. (Source: BIG Archives.)

		Operation						
Step	Omit	Description	Type Code	As Is (I/E)	To Be (I/E)	Est	Each	
Total cumulative times:						372	372	
1		Remove back cover (see Figure A)	m	i		6	6	
2		Turned stroker knob to unlatched position	m	i		2	2	
3		Pull stroker arm all the way forward	m	i		2	2	
4		Grab 6 mm wrench	m	i		2	2	
5		Loosen mandril bolt	m	i		5	5	
6		Remove mandril by turning 90 degrees and pulling out and place on rack (see Figure B)	m	i		4	4	
7		Grab the next mandril	m	i		4	4	
8		Measure the stone length	m	i	e	3	3	
9		Pull the rear tab out of the mandril	m	i	e	2	2	
10		Insert the mandril at 3:00 horizontal position and crank clockwise to 6:00 so it locks in (see Figure C)	m	i		5	5	
11		Tighten 6 mm bolt	m	i		4	4	
12		Adjust stroke length (optional - see chart) to 95% of the stone length	m	i		15	15	
13		Place parts on mandril by turning stone feed knob clockwise to minimum position. Put parts on and then turn feed knob to expand and turn stone feed knob (see Figure D) counterclockwise until reads five lines above zero on the white meter indicator (see Figure E)	m	i		33	33	
14		Attach indicator (see Figure F) on stroker feed arm with the FC stamp facing up so it can be read by operator. Move indicator lever to release (from lock)	m	i		5	5	
15		Adjust indicator over the pieces of the part. Underneath there are two bumps over the parts	m	i		11	11	
16		Adjust indicator so that it reads zero by turning the knob marked A located on the left hand side of the indicator	m	i		1	1	
17		Adjust the conical movement of the mandril by loosening the high side indicator and tighten the forward set of set screws to 180 degrees on the other side with the 4 mm wrench. Keep loosening and tightening until the	m	i		28	28	

Figure A-Removing the cover

Figure B-Removing the mandrel

Figure C-Installing the mandrel

Figure D-Adjusting the stone feed

Figure 3.32   Honer setup standard work example. (Source: Courtesy of Ancon Gear.)

■ Develop the new process. Sometimes this may require listing all the steps on a board or creating a matrix to capture each step along with the times and then re-assigning them to each person to balance out the work (see Figure 3.31).
■ Create the standard work (see Figure 3.32).

Types of Changeover or Setup Improvement

There are six generally accepted types of setup improvement:

■ SMED
  – As stated before, SMED stands for single-minute exchange of dies. Single minutes is referring to the minute placeholder in the time-stamp designation _:__. This means the internal setup time takes 9 minutes 59 seconds or one can say less than ten minutes.
■ OTED
  – OTED stands for one-touch exchange of dies. The implication here is we can change-over in less than 100 seconds or we can change over multiple machines with the touch of one button.
■ NTED
  – NTED stands for no-touch exchange of dies. The process is totally automated without any human intervention.
■ Zero-Minute Setup
  – Zero setup is generally accepted to mean setups requiring three minutes or less. It should be equal to setups that take less than one minute
■ OSED/OCED
  – OSED stands for one-shot (cycle) exchange of dies. This means the entire cell is changed over within one cycle time externally, thus zero internal setup time.
■ Eliminate the Setup
  – Every setup reduction team and machine operator should not lose sight of the goal: to eliminate a setup completely. We have successfully accomplished these many times. Sometimes it takes some rather creative out-of-the-box thinking.

Why Reduce Setup/Changeover Times?

We find the clock time of almost every setup can be reduced by 50% or more the first time we analyze it and then implement improvements. By reducing setup times, we gain the ability to increase capacity in the operation and where the demand exists we gain the ability to produce multiple products in less time or what we call mixed-model cells or lines (see Figures 3.33 and 3.34).

For example, if our changeover time is 24 hours, we are going to want to run everything for the next week or maybe even next month that is scheduled. If we have five models (let's call them models A, B, C, D, and E) and run each model for one week, then it takes a five-week cycle to produce a set of parts for each customer. This means even if the customer only wants one model they have to wait until the week we run that model to get those parts. If they want a Model A and we just changed over from Model A to Model B and all of our Model As are allocated to other customers, then they are going to have to wait five weeks. Normally we run the lot, whether we need them or not, and we produce some extra just in case someone might order more or to have

Relationship between Setup Time and Lot Size—II					
Setup Time	Lot Size	Principal Operation Time per Item	Operation Time	Ratio (%)	Ratio (%)
8 hr	100	1 minute	$1\,\text{minute} + \dfrac{8 \cdot 60}{100} = 5.8\,\text{minute}$	100	
8 hr	1,000	1 minute	$1\,\text{minute} + \dfrac{8 \cdot 60}{1,000} = 1.48\,\text{minute}$	26	100
8 hr	10,000	1 minute	$1\,\text{minute} + \dfrac{8 \cdot 60}{10,000} = 1.048\,\text{minute}$	18	71
Source: Shingo, TPS from an Industrial Engineering Point of View, p. 35.					

Figure 3.33 Relationship between setup time and lot size—eight hours. (Source: *A Study of the Toyota Production System: From an Industrial Engineering Viewpoint*, Shigeo Shingo, 1989. Productivity Press: New York.)

Relationship between Setup Time and Lot Size—I					
Setup Time	Lot Size	Principal Operation Time per Item	Operation Time	Ratio (%)	Ratio (%)
4 hr	100	1 minute	$1\,\text{minute} + \dfrac{4 \cdot 60}{100} = 3.4\,\text{minute}$	100	
4 hr	1,000	1 minute	$1\,\text{minute} + \dfrac{4 \cdot 60}{1,000} = 1.24\,\text{minute}$	36	100
4 hr	10,000	1 minute	$1\,\text{minute} + \dfrac{4 \cdot 60}{10,000} = 1.024\,\text{minute}$	30	83
Source: Shingo, TPS from an Industrial Engineering Point of View, p. 35.					

Figure 3.34 Relationship between setups and time and lot size—four hours. (Source: *A Study of the Toyota Production System: From an Industrial Engineering Viewpoint*, Shigeo Shingo, 1989. Productivity Press: New York.)

some on hand until we can run that model again. This practice creates inventory, both finished goods and WIP, an inherent evil of batching.

This also means each run is going to encompass at least five weeks of demand and could be much more, meaning you are violating the *number one waste* which is *overproducing*. In this environment and all MRP environments, we were taught to use the economic order quantity model to determine how many parts to run for each lot. Most people think since we are spending all this time and money to setup the machine, any extra parts are essentially produced for *free*. If a customer wants a piece right away and is conditioned to the fact that these are long lead time parts and you just happen to have one in stock, you can charge that customer a premium to get them the part right way. The thinking is the customer is happy to get the part and the supplier is making more money on their overproduced parts. However, in reality, while this may occur some of the time, what normally happens is we end up with the following:

■ A rather large stockroom of many types of parts that have been sitting for months or years, sometimes decades!

- There was still labor, run time on the machine (capacity), wear and tear on the machine, and material required to produce those parts and these costs are lost in the parts until you can sell them.
- Customers may be happy to get the part, but no matter how happy they are, the buyer will always remember you over-charged them for those parts.
- Buyers have very long-term memories for these types of things.
- Many times there is an engineering change, which now makes all those free parts obsolete. This means they have to be scrapped and written off, which lowers your profit for the month.
- We spend labor to physically inventory the parts and make sure the counts reconcile.
- Some parts get damaged or lost when other parts are mixed in with them. Pretty soon it becomes easier to run more than to try to find the ones we ran previously.

So are they really *free* parts? This is a major mindset paradigm change we must get over in order to start to reduce setup times.

Let's say we can decrease our setup times in the previous example to two hours. The first argument we get is we are going to have to change the machine over more frequently. So, yes, we have more setups; but the setup time for all five models is now reduced from five days to 10 hours.

Now let's say we can reduce the setup time to less than 10 minutes and want to run each model even more frequently. What does that do for us? Yes, again, we have even more setups but the setups for five models only consume 50 minutes of the whole day versus what used to take five days. Now there is time during the day to run each of the five models every day. What does this do for our customers? They don't have to keep any large inventories or wait days to receive their parts.

We can then put a kanban of parts in our customer's facility and replace it every day or two. Where are they going to go for parts if your competitors' lead times are longer than yours? Can you get a higher price if you manage their inventory for them, by providing a value-added service? Advantages:

- You become much easier to do business with.
- You freed up more space and eliminated the stockroom, which can be used for more manufacturing.
- You have increased machine utilization and capacity for more business and customers.
- The overall cost of your parts has decreased and your profit increases.
- No excess inventory to count.
- No need for production control to keep track of the inventory since it no longer exists, or a fraction of it now exists.
- When the customer says they need to phase in an engineering change, you tell them there is no impact or cost to them for the change.
- You can now offer customers a price-break on their product(s).
- You've demonstrated the ability to meet customers' changing needs.

SETUP Example

Let's say we have to change a coffee-pot over from caffeinated to decaf. At first, all the steps are on internal time because the coffee-pot is down!

1. Empty out the pot—5 sec.
2. Refill the water reservoir—30 sec.
3. Place reservoir into coffee-pot—5 sec.
4. Empty the holder for the coffee into the trash—5 sec.
5. Clean the holder for the coffee—10 sec.
6. Get the paper filter—5 sec.
7. Put in the paper filter—5 sec.
8. Measure out the decaf coffee—5 sec.
9. Put decaf in filter—5 sec.
10. Close the holder—1 sec.
11. Start the coffee brewing—1 sec.
12. Wait for coffee to finish brewing —60 sec.

Which Steps Could Be External?

For sure, we could have the filter with the decaf coffee ready to go, savings 15 sec internal to external.

We could have a separate reservoir already filled with water, savings 30 sec.

We could even have a second coffee-pot and eliminate the changeover completely. Or we could switch to a Keurig and do one cup at a time. Now the entire changeover is eliminated.

Conduct the Omits Process—ERSC

We go through every step of the setup and look to see if it can be omitted, converted from internal to external, rearranged, simplified, or combined.

Once again, we can use leanEdit® to expedite the analysis (see Figure 3.35). The Setup Reduction tool gives us the ability to classify process steps as either Internal Activities (IA) or External Activities (EA). As described in this section, steps can be categorized as Preparation and Organization, Removing and Mounting, Centering and Aligning, or Trial Runs. The user can convert steps from internal to external, convert and improve steps, improve steps, and omit steps during the analysis. Graphical representations of current and future states develop real time and summary data is displayed for export.

External Checklist

The external checklist contains the steps we have identified as external in the analysis. We can then follow this checklist before and after the machine (setup) starts.

Dedicated Setup Teams

We find the use of a dedicated, knowledgeable setup person or teams can more than pay for themselves. At any typical company we increase their capacity by over 50% the first time we implement SMED. However, for this system to work, as in all new Lean systems, there must be a process and

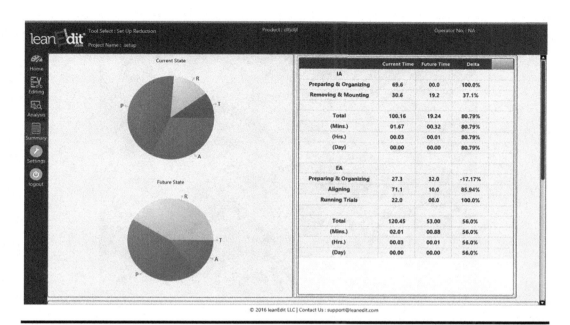

Figure 3.35 leanEdit® desktop setup reduction summary page. (Source: © 2017 leanEdit LLC.)

procedure behind it with metrics, discipline, and accountability and continuous improvement built into the process.

Setup Carts

Setup carts are an interim step to improvement (see Figure 3.36). The goal is to get all tools and fixtures at the point of use by the machine where it makes sense (see Figure 3.37).

A Couple of Other Points about Parts of a Setup

- ◾ The final optimized setup process should only be composed of external preparation and organization steps.
- ◾ as well as internal mounting and removing steps.

SMED, or less than 10-minute setups, only applies to the mounting and removing steps involved in the setup, which is only internal time. Keep in mind, the overall setup time includes the external steps. If it is not driven at the plant manager level, it will not sustain.

Are There More Setups than Just Machine Changeovers?

We often surprise people when we start to explain setup terminology and what constitutes a setup. Any time we load or unload anything or change from one to another in any process, whether man or machine, it should be considered a setup. In almost every workflow analysis there are steps where the concepts of internal and external work apply.

Figure 3.36 Setup cart. (Source: BIG Archives.)

Figure 3.37 Setup tooling at the point of use by the machine. (Source: Courtesy Ancon Gear.)

Consider the following example changing from one customer to the next in the grocery store. Have you ever stood in line waiting and waiting and then watched the cashier tell the person their total? Instead of being prepared, the person now gets out their pocketbook, searches for their wallet, gets out their credit card or phone.

Why couldn't they have been doing this on external time, i.e., when the cashier was scanning their items? Now the cashier and everyone in the whole line is down. How could we eliminate this setup time? In the future maybe we eliminate the cashier altogether and as we put our items in the cart they are automatically charged to our account.

What We Get from the Setup Analysis

Analyzing the setup/changeovers will provide the following pieces of the Lean implementation:

- Enabler for one-piece or one-patient flow or smaller batch sizes
- Immediately increases capacity
- Improves operator utilization
- Reduces labor costs
- Increases overall system reliability and predictability
- Enabler for chaku chaku
- Enabler for level loading
- Increases man-to-machine ratio
- Enabler for mixed model and ability to supply in sets
- Provides quick response to demand changes
- Less reliance on forecasting
- Capital asset utilization rate increases (if demand is there)
- Reduces material handling
- Reduces inventories
- Smaller layout footprint
- Results in standardization
- Improves operator safety
- Improves patient/product quality
- Integrates mistake-proofing

Total Process Optimization

When one obtains true one-piece flow the product and operator analysis become essentially the same. Take the following example: The operator reaches for a part, grabs and moves the part to the assembly and inserts it into the product, and repeats this pattern several times, slowly moving the product down the assembly line.

From the *product's* point of view, the TIPS analysis looks like this: see Figure 3.38.

B = Between-process storage while the operator is reaching, grabbing, and transporting the part to the unit should take no more than 12 seconds.

V = When the part is added to the unit (unit is having value added to it).

T = Transport—When the unit is moved to the next spot at the station (or to the next station). From the *operator's* point of view, the workflow analysis (WFA) is: see Figure 3.39.

P = Reaching for, grabbing the part, and moving it to the unit should take no more than 12 seconds.

Figure 3.38 From the product analysis.

| P | V | H | P | V | H | P | V | H |

Figure 3.39   From the operator analysis. (Source: BIG Archives.)

| B | V | T | B | V | T | B | V | T |
| P | V | H | P | V | H | P | V | H |

Figure 3.40   Comparing the product to the operator analysis in one-piece flow. Notice how the value-added steps align perfectly. (Source: BIG Archives.)

V = When the operator inserts the part in the unit (operator is adding value to the unit).
H = moving the unit to the next spot at the workstation (or to the next station).

So when placed on top of each other it looks like this … see Figure 3.40.

Notice the value-added steps align perfectly. Therefore, theoretically one can never get to 100% value-added.

Determining Potential Total Savings

Once we know which steps can be omitted or improved, we can take the labor time associated with those steps and convert it to dollars and develop a quick return on investment (ROI) to justify the improvement to management. In some cases, the improvements relate to safety and ergonomics and should just be implemented regardless of ROI. However, labor savings are not fully realized until the personnel are removed from the area and put to work on something else.

Improving setup times can, but doesn't necessarily, improve productivity, but does immediately increase capacity or the ability to perform more setups and deliver mixed models quicker and more efficiently.

Benefits from Analyzing Process, Operator, and Setup Separately

Some of our biggest opportunities lie in improving the process flow. For example, just improving the process flow and doing nothing to improve the workflow will reduce inventory and throughput time.

Improving the operator's workflow will reduce labor time regardless of the process flow. Most Lean practitioners don't realize that to improve any process, one must analyze and study each of the analysis components *separately* and then *solve them together as a network of operations* (see Figure 3.41).

PFA, WFA and Setup Analysis Results

Product Process Flow Analysis

	VA		NVA		Total
	Time	%	Time	%	Time
Valves	3,900	8%	42,925	92%	46,825
Hopper	65	2%	4,092	98%	4,156
Final Assy	5,943	28%	15,590	72%	21,533
Totals	9,908	14%	62,607	86%	72,514

Goal is 80% or more value added

Work Flow Analysis

	VA		NVA		Total
	Time	%	Time	%	Time
Dryer Bed	1014	34	1964	66	2978
Valve Assy	1414	32	2985	68	4399
MD50 Test	279	.7	87752	99.3	88031
Totals	2707	3%	92701	97%	95408

Goal is 80% or more value added

Setup Reduction Analysis (sec)

	Before		After		%
	Int.	Ext.	Int.	Ext	Improve
Weld bottle	423	0	25	0	94%
Punch press	491	0	95	25	81%
Press brake	428	0	148	0	65%

Goal is less than 10 minutes (SMED)

Projected results were obtained 100% increase in output with same census. Throughput time currently estimated at three (3) days or less for final assy. Value added can be increased to close to 80% for product and operators

Improvement identified and prioritized

Analysis is 100% complete

Source: BIG Archives.

Figure 3.41 Results of analysis—product, operator, and setup. (Source: BIG Archives.)

Chapter 4

BASICS Model:
Suggest Solutions (S)

The first S in our BASICS model stands for Suggest Solutions, and the goal of this chapter is to introduce the balance of the tools and how to proceed once the analysis is completed. There are many pieces to a Lean implementation and they are all interconnected (see Figure 4.1).

Update the Process Block Diagram

We use this process block diagram to help us determine the layout and workstation design (see Figure 4.2) for the line. On very simple lines, we can start implementing on the floor from just this process block diagram. On more complicated lines, we may draw up a layout with paper dolls or in CAD/Visio with rough workstation design, and on very complicated lines, we will design each workstation down to the part and tool locations and may use a simulation program (see Figure 4.3).

FMEA

The next step is to do a process failure-mode effects analysis (FMEA) to identify risks associated with the move, process changes, regulatory issues, safety, and environmental. After brainstorming this list we assess the severity and probability of what could go wrong and give it a rating. This rating then turns into a risk priority number (RPN). We then look for ways to reduce severity, risk, or probability and increase detection or poka yoke where possible (see Figure 4.4).

3P—Product Preparation Planning

We normally go to the area and use tape to outline the workstations and simulate building a part. You can also do a formal 3P event and use the actual scale along with 3-D cardboard cutouts to

SUGGEST SOLUTIONS
A. DESIGN / APPROVE LINE LAYOUT
Design Considerations:
- Operator safety & ergonomics
- Single point scheduling
- Sequential flow of product
- Operator work effort, geometric place of worker and part
- Easy access to tools and material
- Balanced distribution of work

Steps to approve new layout:
- Create before vs. after layout report card
- Create future state block diagram
- Draw scale diagram of cell
- Conduct FMEA on changes
- Draw Point to Point Diagrams of new product flows
- Draw operator walk patterns and baton zones
- Diagram inbound and outbound materials and tooling
- Follow the 10 step process for creating master layouts – if needed

MASTER THE FUNDAMENTALS OF PROCESS / INDUSTRIAL ENGINEERING AND MATERIALS MANAGEMENT

SUGGEST SOLUTIONS
B. DEVELOP STANDARD WORK
Define the order of process:
- Use process block diagram and group technology information

Define job steps, standard times and material location within each order of process:
- Use activity of operator analysis information

Define takt time:
- Use information from base line analysis

Establish line balance:
- Map combined walk patterns of all operators
- Identify baton zones
- Identify part production capacity information

Level load and smooth the schedule
- Combine part number, labor time, order quantity and calendar
- Setup heijunka scheduling box

STANDARD WORK DEFINES AND SUSTAINS THE INNOVATION

Figure 4.1   The BASICS six-step model for Lean implementation—suggest solutions. (Source: BIG Training Materials.)

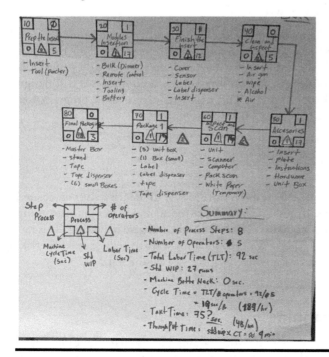
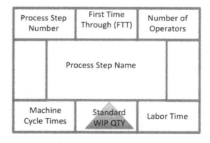

Figure 4.2   Completed process block diagram. (Source: BIG Archives and Andrew McDermott.)

Figure 4.3 Workstation design—two-bin system with parts and tools in correct order. (Source: BIG Archives.)

Component and Function	Potential Failure Mode	Potential Effect(s) of Failure	Severity Rating	Potential Cause(s) of Failure	Occurrence (probability) Rating	Current Preventioin Controls	Current Detection Controls	Detection Rating	RPN (severity x Occurence x Detection)	Action	Responsible	Target Completion Date

Figure 4.4 FMEA template. (Source: *The Basics of FMEA*, Robin E. McDermott, 2009. CRC Press: Boca Raton, FL.)

simulate equipment, parts, and station layouts and to check the flow as you layout the workstation (see Figure 4.5).

When implementing Lean lines, we want to create flexible layouts, with everything possible on wheels, as customers have changing needs and demands. Remember that layouts are a root cause for much of the waste we see in factories, government, health care, and offices.

The following items are required:

■ One-piece flow (or small-lot) production
■ Parts and tools and equipment in the order of the sequence of operations—right tool at right time to perform the task

Figure 4.5   3P layout planning for a hospital room. (Source: Bill Keen and BIG Archives.)

- Operators on the same side and inside the cell so materials can be replenished outside the cell
- Maximum flexibility for equipment, parts, and operators
- Separate human from machine work
- Implementation of new standard work methods
- Ability to balance work across operators
- Multi-process cross-trained operators
- Standing/walking moving operations
- SWIP identified with a quantity and always in place
- Visual controls

Create the Optimal Layout for the Process

Cell Layout Design

The shape of a cell is determined by the requirements of the process. There are many cell layouts possible. The advantage to the system kaizen approach over point kaizens is you don't have to change the layout 10 or 15 times over a year. At this stage, we can normally get the layout 90%–95% correct the first time, but over time, the layout will continue to evolve and change. Don't get hung up on trying to make the layout so perfect that it never gets implemented. Layouts can be in a U shape, L shape, C shape, or straight line. Make sure you involve HS&E to help create or review the layouts. Some guidelines include:

- Try to keep the working aisle width to 4–4.5 ft (1.37 m) and when not possible an absolute minimum width of 3 ft (0.914 m).
- Put machines as close together as humanly possible (don't worry about access panels; cut them in somewhere else, move control boxes, etc.).

- Get rid of excess space, workbenches, tool boxes, drawers, cabinets.
- Don't leave room for WIP. We are working on one piece at a time!
- Be sure to get anti-fatigue mats* or shoe insoles† for the people working the new line.

Whenever possible, incorporate the building of subassemblies into the line.

Office Layouts

The physical office changes brought on by Lean may not be popular with your staff. For example, most offices are full of five or six-foot high partitions, which were sold as efficiency improvements, but, in the end, block line of sight and reduce or eliminate crucial communication flow and create isolated islands for all your employees. Lean offices have either no or very low partitions (Figure 4.6). In addition, many people are moved to the shop floor with stand-up desks to be co-located with their value-stream team or focus factory. This speeds up communication and accelerates the problem-solving process.

Figure 4.6 Lean Office Layout No 5 foot walls, open conference room and offices. (Source: BIG Archives.)

---

* http://www.smartcellsusa.com/. These are the best anti-fatigue mats we have found to date. We are not affiliated with this company.
† http://www.aline.com/. These are the best insoles we have found. I, Charlie Protzman, have been wearing them for six years. We are not affiliated with this company.

Avoid Isolated Islands

The most important thing to avoid in any layout is *isolated islands*. Isolated islands are created when operators are positioned in such a way they are boxed in or are so far away from each other they cannot flex and help each other out. This leads to the creation of fractional labor.

Fractional labor occurs where we have a stranded operator whose cycle time is less than the TT. We lose the time difference between the TT and the isolated operator's labor or cycle time. Some lines have the operators on the outside of the line surrounded by equipment or materials.

In the layouts pictured in Figures 4.7A and B, what do you observe? This person works only at this station all day long. He is basically stuck there by himself. If his cycle time is longer than the takt time, he will create a bottleneck because the station's layout will not work with two people. If his cycle time is quicker than the takt time, he will be idle part of the time or if he keeps working, his parts will back up at the next station.

This is an example of an isolated island (see Figure 4.8). Traditional electronics assembly, offline subassembly operations, and office layouts normally contain isolated islands.

The next layout is called the bird-cage layout (see Figure 4.9). We see this often in machining environments where the operator is trapped inside the equipment layout like a bird in a cage. The operator moves from machine to machine and generally has a bunch of idle time. Each machine is producing different batches of parts that may or may not be in router sequence.

We also see this with monument-type machines (see Figure 4.10). Monument machines are very large, very difficult to move, normally requiring concrete foundations or pits. These can be wave solder machines, large presses, etc.

The layout pictured in Figure 4.11 shows a traditional fishbone layout. This layout was taught as a Demand Flow Technology® (DFT) layout and has been very successful at many companies.

Figure 4.7A   Isolated Island. In most restaurants the greeter or hostess is stuck on an isolated island. We pay them for their idle time waiting for someone to arrive.

Figure 4.7B   Isolated Islands result in fractional labor. (Source: BIG Archives.)

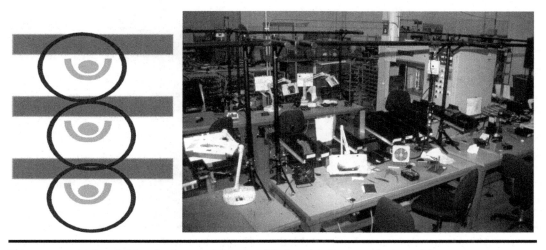

Figure 4.8   Isolated Islands electronics assembly layout. (Source: BIG Archives.)

It is mainly used when there are a lot of subassemblies to a product (or many mixed models where the entire unit is built by each operator). The subassemblies are built on feeders to the main line which looks like a fishbone. The subassembly is then added to the main unit, which progresses down the center of the line.

This type of line still yields a great improvement over traditional batch lines because it gets the "product" piece of Lean right, but not the entire operator piece because each feeder becomes

Figure 4.9 Isolated islands—bird-cage layout this operator is stuck running four machines, has idle time, and can't get out. (Source: BIG Archives.)

Figure 4.10 Monument—huge horizontal lathe with pit, steps, walkway, and railing. (Source: BIG Archives.)

an isolated island. Therefore, the operators can't flex and it can never realize the true productivity possible unless it is perfectly station balanced.

Lean layouts should promote flexible workspace design. Layout redesigns should result in a decrease in overall space and travel distance needed to perform a task and eliminate/minimize fractional labor.

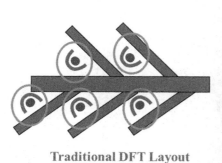

Figure 4.11 Traditional DFT Fishbone layout. (Source: BIG Archives.)

U-Shaped Layout

The U-shaped layout has some advantages over other shapes (see Figure 4.12). The main benefit is the ability to share resources. The staff is better able to help each other should the need arise. Communication among the staff is easier, especially between the beginning and end of the process or part of the process you are trying to improve. Walking distances are shorter, and the person can work while they are standing and moving. The staff will be more productive yet potentially feel less fatigued.

This layout maximizes the ability to flex the staff across operations. It can be run with one person or multiple persons (see Figure 4.13). If, for example, the line is station balanced, and it is run with three people, one person could do stations 1, 5, and 6 or 1, 2, and 3. If one person runs 1, 5, and 6, then that person controls the input and output of the area, so we can never start more

Figure 4.12 U-shape layout point-to-point drawing. The problem in this U-shape layout is that operators are sitting and should be standing. The last station is an isolated island. (Source: BIG Archives.)

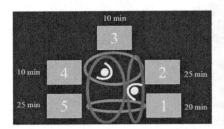 

Figure 4.13 U-shape layout—maximum flexibility for operations. Notice now that the operators are standing and walking and there are no isolated islands. (Source: BIG Archives.)

than we finish (a pull system). Materials and supplies are replenished from the outside so there is no interruption to those working inside the area.

Disadvantages of U-shaped cells are that the corners of the U can be difficult to flex and the outside corner of the workstations may not be reachable by the operators. U shapes may be impractical, or the workstation that makes the U may be the handoff point for the next cell for long lines with many subassemblies.

One sees this in chaku–chaku cells, which we will explain later; however, this tends to make the cell more of a parallel line versus a U shape. Cell layouts should be based on what makes sense for the product and for the master layout as well.

Straight-Line Layouts

Straight lines (see Figure 4.14) or linear layouts allow workers to move down the line sequentially for the process. Staff can still flex in a straight line, but the flexing is limited to the operator immediately before, or after. The drawback to this layout is that, with one team member, the travel distance is longer from operation one to operation six; however, the process generally dictates the layout, and often, straight lines work best for the master layout. Most car-assembly lines are straight-line layouts.

Parallel Layouts

Parallel-line layouts are designed with the staff on the inside to facilitate resource sharing, as staff can move across to the other parallel line or down the same line (Figure 4.15). Materials and supplies are replenished from outside the work area or cell to minimize interruptions. This layout works well in a high-mix, low-volume environment. Operators can still flex as if they were in a U-shaped layout, which works well for lines that have multiple subassemblies.

Layout and workstation considerations should include baton zones or flex spaces in between work process zones. These areas are located before or after standard work zones (see Figure 4.16) in which operators can flex to absorb minor variations in time.

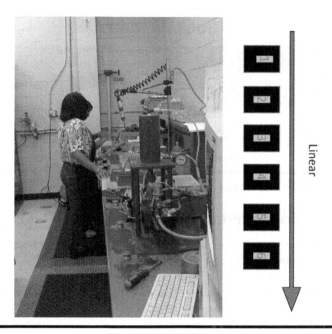

Figure 4.14   Straight-line layout—walk pattern. (Source: BIG Archives.)

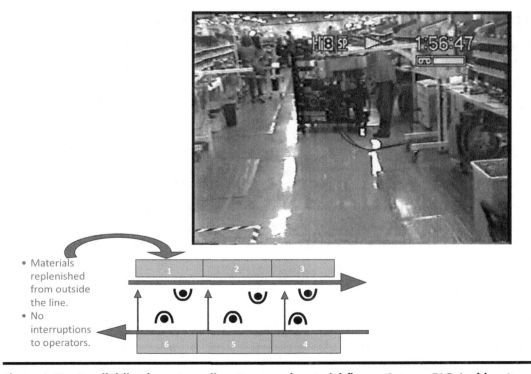

Figure 4.15   Parallel-line layout—walk patterns and material flows. (Source: BIG Archives.)

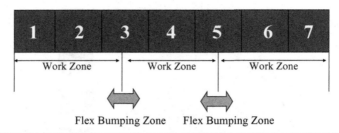

Figure 4.16   Operator flex (bumping) zones. (Source: BIG Files.)

Chaku–Chaku and Hanedashi

A chaku–chaku cell is called a place–place or load–load cell. The operator picks up and loads the finished part from one machine to the next as they proceed through the entire cycle. The equipment uses a tool called hanedashi, designed into the machine so it loads and unloads itself. A hanedashi device (see Figure 4.17) is used for automatic unloading of a workpiece, which provides proper state and orientation for the next operation.

The chaku–chaku line is about the farthest one can go with semi-automation prior to completely automating a cell. In addition, simple rotating wheels are used for SWIP where necessary for cooling or drying (i.e., epoxy).

How Do We Know When the Layout Is Right?

This is a difficult question to answer, but we find it to be both qualitative and quantitative. Many times, you just know when you get it right. The true test is when point-to-point diagrams work for

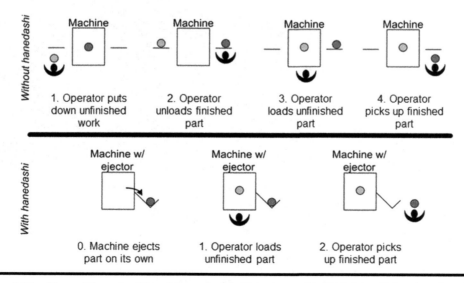

Figure 4.17   Line with and without hanedashi. (Courtesy of Jeff Hajek—Velaction Continuous Improvement at www.Velaction.com.)

MASTER LAYOUT TARGETS:	Line 1	Line 2	Line 3	Line 4	Line 5	Line 6
ONE PIECE FLOW	Y	N	Y	Y	Y	Y
WIP REDUCTION - 90%	Y	N	Y	Y	Y	N (50%)
EFFICIENCY INCREASE +50%	55%	N	33%	100%	50%	50%
FTE Reduction	2	1	0	0	0	4
SPACE REDUCTION	Y	N	N	Y	Y	Y
TRAVEL DIST FOR PRODUCT REDUCTION	50%	80%	90%	75%	80%	85%
NUMBER OF TOUCHES REDUCTION	Y	N	N	Y	Y	Y
TPT (THRU PUT TIME) REDUCTION	90%	85%	90%	90%	80%	90%
MAN TO MACHINE RATIO REDUCTION	3	5	4	6	4	TBD
MATERIAL FURNISHED OUTSIDE LINE	Y	Y	Y	Y	Y	Y
INCREASE FREQUENCY OF DELIVERIES	Y	Y	Y	Y	Y	Y
ISOLATED ISLANDS REDUCTION	Y	Y	Y	Y	Y	Y
CRANES REDUCTION	Y	N	Y	N	Y	N/A
FORKLIFTS REDUCTION	Y	Y	Y	Y	Y	N/A
HAMMERS REDUCTION	Y	Y	Y	Y	Y	Y

Figure 4.18 Before versus after layout report card. (Source: BIG Archives.)

each model and the overall metrics of reduced space, travel distance, number of operators, inventory, percentage of fractional labor, etc., support it (see Figure 4.18). When the product flows, operator travel is minimized, changeover can be performed quickly, and there is room for expansion; we know the layout is close to being correct. Keep in mind that, as we continue to implement improvements or expand capacity, the layout may need to change.

Therefore, walls are never in the right place and it is important to have workstations and equipment on wheels with quick disconnects to facilitate easy and ongoing layout changes. Tools and materials should be laid out close to the employees and positioned so they can be easily picked up. Determine locations and keep the tools and materials in their designated locations to maintain the cycle time.

Avoid Moving Parts Vertically and Move Parts Horizontally.

Moving parts vertically (up and down) requires extra effort and in time is a potential ergonomic issue. To avoid waste of energy, align the heights of the machines so parts can be moved horizontally. Many examples of this principle are visible in factories. Chutes are used to roll products down; sloping part-shelves along the assembly lines help to slide boxes into positions. The advantage is low cost or no cost; gravity is your friend.

Make sure you have good lighting. Important factors to consider when choosing lighting include strength, contrast, glare, and color. In all cases, lighting should be arranged so that it shines on the work, not directly in the worker's eyes—especially important for paint and inspection.

Many times, in almost every country, government assistance can be obtained for improving and installing more energy-efficient lighting in the workplace.

The 10-Step Process for Creating Master Layouts

Major planning phases include:

1. Future requirements analysis
2. Issues and problem statement
3. Group-tech matrix (if needed)
4. Point-to-point diagram of current or proposed future layout and findings (see Figure 4.19)
5. Ideal layout piece flow from start to finish with capital wish list
6. Assumptions and options
7. Block diagram future-state master layout
8. Detail layout
9. Review with health, safety, and environment (HS&E) and facilities
10. Implementation planning: Did we fix all the issues and problems?

If you want a Lean layout, hire a Lean architect or use your internal or external Lean practitioners *before* you start the layout process.

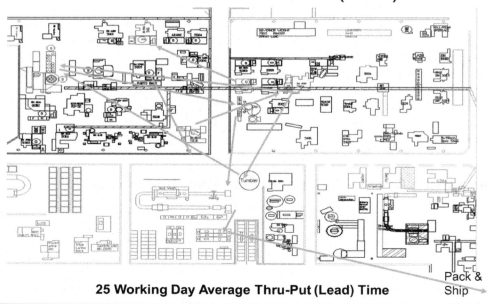

Figure 4.19 **Master layout baseline with point-to-point diagram. (Source: BIG Archives.)**

Future Requirements Analysis

The first question we ask is, will this new master layout support your future requirements over the next five to 10 years (Figure 4.20)? Normally, the answer is yes. The next question we ask is, what problems are you trying to solve? Normally, we get a blank stare and then we get "We need more space for capacity." We ask, what metrics have you evaluated in terms of the layout? What is the minimum and maximum number of people it will handle? How much space have you reduced? Does it reduce cost per square foot in operations? Does it reduce travel distance? Have you eliminated isolated islands? Will it support one-piece flow? Does the product ever travel backward?

Point-to-Point Diagram

We have them do a point-to-point diagram of their current state or planned future-state master layout (see Figure 4.21). The point-to-point diagram follows the major products through the

Master Layout

Available Time		370								
Future Years	Line A	TT	Line B	TT	Line C	TT	Total Line A & B	TT	Total Overall	TT
2013	37,144	2.39	64,489	1.38	16,640	5.34	81,129	1.09	118,273	0.75
2014	38,952	2.28	67,254	1.32	30,240	2.94	97,494	0.91	136,446	0.65
2015	40,773	2.18	74,899	1.19	42,720	2.08	117,619	0.75	158,392	0.56

Figure 4.20   Future requirements analysis. (Source: BIG Archives.)

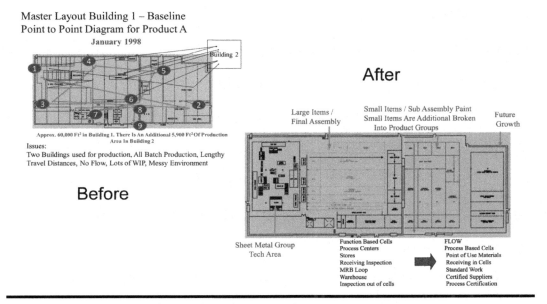

Figure 4.21   Master layout point-to-point before. (Source: BIG Archives.)

master layout. Most times, it is very telling, and virtually every time, it's a mess. There will always be the 20% or so (Pareto rule) that will not fit the flow. We call these parts misfits.

Ideal Layout

Now we need to put an ideal layout together. The ideal layout means we have the new technology we need and all the money in the world, and if it was your business, how would you lay this out to make money? In addition, it means we would be able to move the product one-piece flow from beginning to end. This entails creative thinking and brainstorming.

The ideal layout will in most cases not be practical right away, therefore we need to list out what our assumptions will be for our new layout as well as any barriers (see Figure 4.22). Generally, we can develop 10–15 different layout options before we select the right one. Paper dolls (see Figure 4.23) or CAD layout options are good tools for this and we project the CAD drawing to a whiteboard and use the whiteboard (see Figure 4.24) to review different options.

Block Layout Draft

The next step is to construct five or 10 different options at a high level and avoid agreeing on the first layout attempt. The block layout (see Figure 4.25) is designed to house the entire product line or parts of product lines, machine shops, materials locations, offices, etc. The layout should have an "in" location for RMs and supplies and an "out" location for FG. It is best if these are separated but adjacent where staff can be shared. This is not always possible. The overall material (and information) should flow throughout the plant and never go backward.

Detail Layout

The next step is to create the detailed layout for each block. This means we lay in all the workstations and material racks required to support the line. Again, do a point-to-point diagram for each

- Why do we use ovens for temperature soak?
- Is cycle test at high-temp necessary?
- What are customer change requirements? What do they control and what types of changes do we need to communicate?
- Tolerance stackups
- DIRFT- Repeatable processes
- Silicone temperature bath
- Traceability
- Source Inspection
- Acceptance of tolerances requiring high-tolerance capability
- Belleville sorting & tweaking
- OP
- Perceived lack of engineering resources
- Engineering – Why fix it if it works?

Figure 4.22   Issues and barriers. (Source: BIG Archives.)

Figure 4.23 **Paper dolls are cutouts from the CAD drawings and then positioned by hand. (Source: BIG Archives.)**

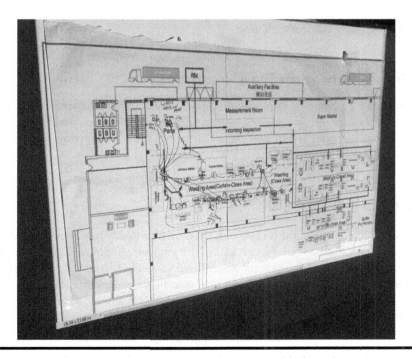

Figure 4.24 **Layout planning projecting the CAD layout on whiteboard. (Source: BIG Archives.)**

Figure 4.25   Block diagram for master layout. (Source: BIG Archives.)

line to ensure a smooth flow. At this point, it is probable that there is no layout for much of the line, in which case, we will need to leave these areas in the block form until we are able to implement Lean on those lines. We have covered the detail layout earlier in the book.

Phased Implementation Plan

We should construct a phased-in implementation plan with projected costs after the detail layout is complete. This plan should be reviewed by engineering, maintenance, and HS&E, who should be involved during the entire layout process. For master layouts, we develop a phased-in plan for the overall layout (see Figure 4.26).

ROI Analysis

In some cases, especially if capital is involved, there will probably be a requirement for a return on investment (ROI) analysis (see Figure 4.27). The analysis should include all the investment costs in terms of expense and capital. We generally don't include internal maintenance labor as an expense, as we pay for it as part of doing business; however, external labor and subcontractors should be included in the analysis and budget. The ROI should contain a savings section with payback analysis. A payback of one or two years is required at most companies; however, we should do the change, as it is the right thing to do, but we do need to have the budget, if necessary, to pay for it.

You know you are well down the Lean path when ROIs take a back seat to doing what's right by the Lean principles as well as ergonomics and safety.

1. Demo / Clear out area A - includes moving cell 50
2. put in office in area A
3. Setup First Flexible Cell 20 lines in Area A – Dec 2010
   - With Plan to run line starting Jan 2011
   - Setup up Capsule Assy area and Kanban rack
   - Setup 2nd Flexible Cell 20 lines in Area A – Jan 2010
   - With Plan to run line starting Feb 2011
4. Overlay Cell 50 on existing cell 20 lean line #1
   - Overlay Cell 50 on existing cell 20 lean line #2
   - Demo Wall and inside Door only
   - Move lean lines cell 50 #1 & 2 to new location
   - Move Capsules and electricals to new location
5. Demo Weld Area and Spring Room
   Move Cell 40 and electricals to Demo'd Area
   Move Spring Room to Machining Area across hall?
6. Move the cell 20 lean lines to the area vacated by cell 40 and electricals
   Demo Wire Storage Room
   Setup capsule and electricals area
7. Setup Cell 50 Line #3
8. Setup Cell 40 Lines #1,#2 & #3 and electrical and capsules in Area A
   Move Cell 40 Lines to old Spring Room Weld Area
9. Setup Cell 20 Line #4 and #5

Master Layout Phases – Phase I

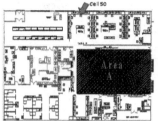

1. Demo / Clear out area A - includes moving cell 50 to south of existing lean lines

Phase II

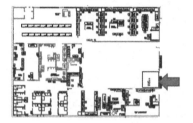

2. put in office in area A

Figure 4.26 Phased implementation plan. (Source: BIG Archives.)

Centralized versus Decentralized

The great debate is as follows: Do we buy one big centralized printer/copier/fax/scanner or do we put one on each person's desk? Information systems will always vote to centralize. They will argue economies of scale. However, what it really means is less work for them, that is, one cable drop and one router location and one machine for maintenance. The drawback is when that one machine goes down or someone ties it up with a larger printing job, everyone else is stuck; dead in the water. In addition, everyone must now walk to that printer, which generates conversations with everyone on the way. Sometimes lines may even form at the printer.

We have found it much more productive to have the right type of office equipment at the desk of the person doing the job.

The batch logic drives centralizing. When transport gets centralized in hospitals it seems like it's the right thing to do but once it's centralized it becomes an isolated island and has to have a process owner, its own metrics, etc. It results in everyone having to schedule it.

It is not unusual to see a transporter nearby doing nothing; yet, when the call is made to scheduling, they send someone else. When we converted from centralized scheduling for clinics to each having control over their own schedule, they became much more efficient and the patients were seen faster.

There are some things it makes sense to centralize, i.e., paychecks. But most other things generally are better off decentralized. It all comes down to the ROI. Normally what is not included in the ROI is all hidden waste embodied in centralization and supposed economies of scale.

ROI Analysis

Capital					
Qty	**Equipment**	**Price per Unit**	**Totals**		
7	Welders	$ 48,000	$ 336,000		
3	Leak Check	$ 20,000	$ 60,000		
10	Link Gages ($8.k ea., qty 10)	$ 8,100	$ 81,000		
2	Laser Markers	$ 100,000	$ 200,000		
5	Test Equipment	$ 40,000	$ 200,000		
1	Re-vamp Cell 60 Flow Bench Estimate	$ 15,000	$ 15,000		
Sub Total Capital			$ 892,000		
Demo and Construction					
Qty	**Area**	**Price**	**Total**		
1	Switch Assy Offices	$ 23,000	$23,000		
1	Final Inspection Offices	$ 10,000	$10,000		
1	Welding/ Spring Room	$ 33,000	$33,000		
Sub Total Demo and Construction			$66,000		
Grand Total Capital			$958,000		

Expense

12	Lean Line Setups				
No. Per Lean Line	**Total for 14 Lines**	**Equipment**	**Price Per Unit**	**Per Cell**	**Total all Cells**
8	84	Workbenches	$ 435	$ 3,480	$ 36,540
5	55	Ovens	$ 420	$ 2,100	$ 23,100
5	60	Regulators	$ 400	$ 2,000	$ 24,000
5	60	Swagelock Fittings	$ 900	$ 4,500	$ 54,000
1	14	Grainger/ Home Depot/ etc MISC	$ 1,500	$ 1,500	$ 21,000
1	14	Misc. Electrical Drops	$ 2,500	$ 2,500	$ 35,000
Sub Total Expense				$ 16,080	$ 193,640

Grand Totals Capital and Expense			$ 1,151,640
		savings per yea	$ 404,982.75
		payback	$ 2.84

Figure 4.27 ROI analysis. (Source: BIG Archives.)

Overarching Guidelines to Layout Redesign

- No isolated islands.
- No, or limited use of, doors, drawers, walls, and partitions.
- Maximum flexibility.
- Review layout and workstation design for travel distance and "ergonomics," limit reaching, and implement standing/walking operations.
- Oba gauge (line of sight—4–5 feet high).

- Staff should be located on the inside of the work cell and replenishment should be from the outside.
- The layout should be designed with flow and visual controls in mind.
- Co-locate executives and office staff on or near the floor or areas with their products.
- Don't plan rework inside a cell.
- Develop a master layout early in the project.
- Layout approval. Make sure someone with extremely good Lean knowledge reviews the layout prior to implementing.
- Incorporate housekeeping and 5S.

Workstation Design

We recommend that team members, consisting of frontline staff and supervisor, plan the workstation and locate all supplies and needs on the drawing. Workstations should be designed to the product flow and not the individual operator's time. The team needs to decide on quantity and location for inventory and buffer or backup supplies and discuss the replenishment or restocking of supplies to determine the impact to workstation design. It is recommended that, if multi-shifts and staffs are sharing work areas, each person on each shift can review the workstation redesign and process and there are standards and audits put in place to ensure compliance.

Workstations should be constructed at stand-up height, generally 38–40 inches, approximately one meter, for jobs done with the hands. Even though we are all at different heights, our arms are generally within 1.3 inches or 38 cm of each other (see Figure 4.28). However, for workstations that have microscopes or are eye- or height-dependent, the workstation or object on the workstation will have to be set up so the height is adjustable.

Figure 4.28   Great difference in height but small difference with arm working height. (Source: BIG Archives.)

There are all different types of workstations. One can buy erector set-style workstations (see Figure 4.29), which can be expensive, or one can fabricate one's own rather cheaply. Each workstation should be on wheels where possible, with air and other utilities designed to be as flexible as possible.

A good operator will show you how their workstation should be setup as shown during review of the videos. It is important to notice where they move their eyes, and where they place their hands, parts, and tools during their operations.

As discussed earlier, we will normally run a pilot or mock up (3P Cardboard Exercise) with the operator or office person when setting up the new workstation. We literally go step by step, following the block diagram as we go, lining up their materials (see Figure 4.30) and supplies in the proper sequence as they are building or processing the parts to minimize reaching and excess motions. We draw an outline around it (or use tape) and label it. This is a very time-consuming process that requires much patience by the person we are working with and the Lean team or supervisor.

Figure 4.29   Erector set–style workstations. (Source: BIG Archives.)

(a)   (b)

Figure 4.30   Workstation design. (a) Creativity Based Holder and Standard WIP Location Label; (b) Mixed Model Cell—Parts tools and epoxy lined up in order of use. 2nd bin (behind first bin) is for next model build. (Source: BIG Archives.)

Once we get everything in place, we have the operator run the workstation in a pilot and we make adjustments on the spot as needed (see Figure 4.31).

When we are comfortable that everything is set up correctly and they have practiced it, we will video them and review the video. After reviewing the video, we will make other improvements or adjustments as necessary. At this point we can start to think about creating the standard work.

Once we are satisfied the lines and flow are running well, we will perform a formal redesign of all the workstations. Simple stand-up workstations on wheels with lights are very flexible and allow for easy improvements or adjustments (see Figures 4.32 and 4.33). Batching fixtures need to be modified to support one-piece flow (see Figure 4.34), which is an example of mistake-proofing.

Figure 4.31   5S Workstation design. (Source: BIG Archives.)

Figure 4.32   Flexible workstation. (Source: BIG Archives.)

Before	After

Figure 4.33 Workstation design. What's wrong with the "before" workstation? First, it is sit down; second materials cannot be fed from behind, meaning either the operator gets their own materials or we have to interrupt the operator in order to replenish the materials. The "after" is now standup and materials can be fed from behind and it is half the width of before. What else does the "after" workstation need? (Source: BIG Archives.)

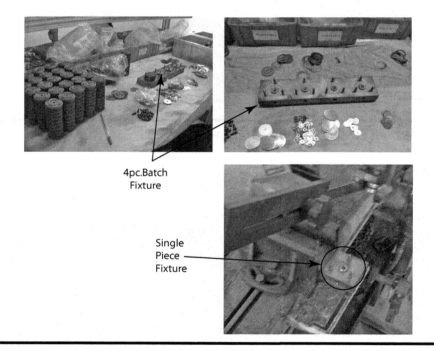

4pc.Batch
Fixture

Single
Piece
Fixture

Figure 4.34 Batching fixtures need to be modified to support one-piece flow. Sustain—we came back the next day only to find they had welded the pieces back together again. So we moved the other three pieces to the maintenance room. (Source: BIG Archives.)

As the Lean practitioner, you must stay with the line for several days, if not weeks, to make sure it runs correctly. This means to continuously watch what is going on and coaching the operators all the time until they start to Figure it out.

OBA Gauge

The story is that a 4-foot-tall Japanese Lean sensei named Mr. Oba was notorious for insisting nothing in the factory be taller than his eye level. This resulted in the Oba gauge for a visual workplace (see Figure 4.35). The idea is to avoid creating view blockers in your workplace whenever possible. It is also called the 4-foot rule or 1.3-meter rule. Six-foot-high cubicle walls and doors create isolated islands or silos in office and work environments. Cubicle walls should be no more than 3–4 feet high to encourage line-of-sight management. Many times in the United States, we adjust the Oba gauge to 5 feet (1.525 m) high.

Tool Boxes Are Bad

Why do we say this? As an example, try searching in a toolbox for a ½ inch wrench or #3 screwdriver. Most tool boxes are unorganized and a mess; even organized tool boxes are wasteful, as operators are always searching for a tool. The biggest problem, however, is having operators bring in their own personal tools. For instance, when a team member comes up with a great idea and designs and modifies a tool to do the job and then leaves, the tool goes with them.

Figure 4.35   OBA gauge—notice there is clear line of site in this retail store layout. (Source: BIG Archives.)

Point-to-Point Diagram After

The best way to check any new workstation, cell, or master layout design is with a point-to-point diagram to make sure the parts and products flow (see Figure 4.36). When you install a rack, and have parts at three to four levels high, it is important to have the parts run vertically up or down the rack versus horizontally. If they run horizontally, the operator will have to continuously move left to right and it will tie them up at that station. See the Lean storyboard pictured in Figure 4.37.

Designing the Layout Based on the Number of Operators

A deeply misunderstood concept is that workstations must be designed to meet the number of operators. This is not necessary if the operators can flex across the stations and "bump." The problem with designing stations to TT is that the TT or number of operators may change or there may be a lot of variation in the process. In order to station-balance the line, we are faced with having to change the workstations or part of the workstations every time the TT changes. So, we potentially lose the product-flow to balance the line.

Sitting versus Standing and Walking Operations

Any good ergonomics and safety person will confirm that moving and walking is better for you than sitting all day. Sitting creates many health problems and standing in one place is also bad for

Baseline

1st Iteration

2nd Iteration

Figure 4.36   Getting tools and materials in proper order takes several trials. This one was complicated by multiple models and low volumes but very successful—30%–40% increase in productivity with two new operators. (Source: BIG Archives.)

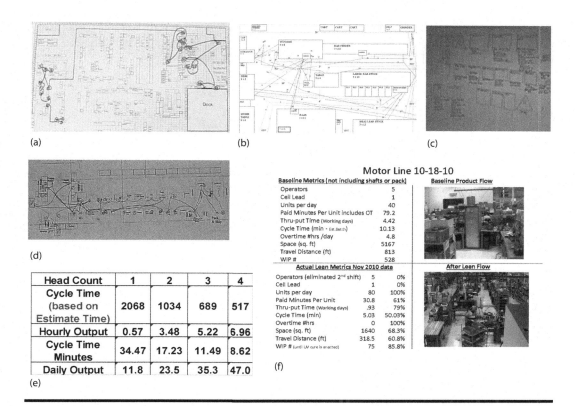

Head Count	1	2	3	4
Cycle Time (based on Estimate Time)	2068	1034	689	517
Hourly Output	0.57	3.48	5.22	6.96
Cycle Time Minutes	34.47	17.23	11.49	8.62
Daily Output	11.8	23.5	35.3	47.0

(a) (b) (c) (d) (e)

Motor Line 10-18-10

Baseline Metrics (not including shafts or pack)	
Operators	5
Cell Lead	1
Units per day	40
Paid Minutes Per Unit includes OT	79.2
Thru-put Time (Working days)	4.42
Cycle Time (min - Est.Batch)	10.13
Overtime #hrs /day	4.8
Space (sq. ft)	5167
Travel Distance (ft)	813
WIP #	528

Actual Lean Metrics Nov 2010 data		
Operators (eliminated 2nd shift)	5	0%
Cell Lead	1	0%
Units per day	80	100%
Paid Minutes Per Unit	30.8	61%
Thru-put Time (Working days)	.93	79%
Cycle Time (min)	5.03	50.03%
Overtime #hrs	0	100%
Space (sq. ft)	1640	68.3%
Travel Distance (ft)	318.5	60.8%
WIP # (until UV cure is enacted)	75	85.8%

(f)

Figure 4.37 Storyboard—61% increase in productivity. (a) Point to Point (Product) Before; (b) Spaghetti (operator) Before; (c) Block Diagram; (d) Point to Point (Product) After; (e) Capacity Analysis (based on FWA); (f) Baseline and Result. (Source: BIG Archives.)

Figure 4.38 Stand-up office desk. (Source: BIG Archives.)

you. Standing/moving operations also promote operator and/or office staff flexibility and health (see Figure 4.38). Sitting can lead to back problems and obesity, which can eventually lead to the possibility of early health problems.

Fit Up

We use the term fit up to designate what actions need to be taken to get utilities to the line, install new equipment, increase power to an area, or anything else needed to support the installation of the line. We have normally noted these ahead of time in the block diagram. The next step is to meet with the physical plant/maintenance manager and HS&E and physically go to the floor or office area and check to see what will be required to get the line up and running.

Chapter 5

BASICS Model: Implementation (I)

The I in our BASICS model stands for Implementation (see Figure 5.1). An important aspect for the team to realize is that some tasks are "just do it" in nature and can be implemented quickly, or at latest the next day. However, many improvements require the action of work done by an improvement team. Many times, this will be done with sub-projects and will take time and resources to complete.

Implement the New Process, Use Pilots, and Test It out Using Scrum

We have been one of the first consulting firms to use the Scrum approach to Lean implementation. This was a challenge given to us by our Scrum sensei Nigel Thurlow, former internationally renowned consultant and now a V.P. at Toyota. This approach utilizes one-week sprints with the Lean team. The team includes a part-time product owner and full-time scrum master (one of our consultants) to do the scrum coaching for the team. Scrum has allowed us to implement the process much quicker, but it relies on having the right people on the team that can carry out all the stories. We use a simple board to keep track of our progress (see Figure 5.2). The board contains the backlog of stories for the entire implementation, a "To Do" column for the sprint week, "In Process" for the one or two stories being worked, and "Complete" for the stories that are finished.

The team meets in the morning to discuss their activities for the day and in the evening to debrief the day and suggest improvements (see new Figure 5.3). The board contains the stickies from a 10-minute meeting, with key learnings, accomplishments, to do's, and challenges, which is where escalation may be necessary.

This process has almost doubled our implementation speed and keeps the team focused, and there is never a question about what they should be working on or what they have completed.

Once it is complete, the story must get added to the chrono file. This way we have a record, similar to an ongoing kaizen newspaper, of what has been accomplished and key bottom-line savings.

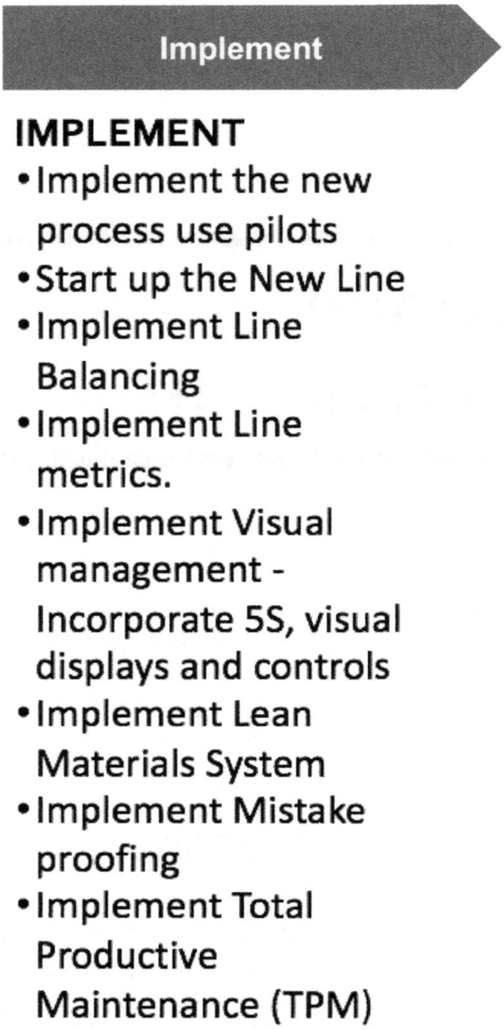

Implement

IMPLEMENT
- Implement the new process use pilots
- Start up the New Line
- Implement Line Balancing
- Implement Line metrics.
- Implement Visual management - Incorporate 5S, visual displays and controls
- Implement Lean Materials System
- Implement Mistake proofing
- Implement Total Productive Maintenance (TPM)

Figure 5.1 **The BASICS six-step model for Lean implementation—implement. (Source: BIG Archives.)**

Parallel Implementation

Production is near and dear to all our hearts. We work diligently to keep this in mind whenever we implement a new line. As stated earlier, the best implementation is where one can execute pilots and still have the main line running. Many times, this option is viable.

What Is the Difference between Apparent and True Efficiency?

By reducing batching with its extra steps and complexity, we reduce the opportunity for defects in the process. This is extremely important. Behind this are the wastes of overproduction and over-processing. While this may sound very simple, it is violated all the time.

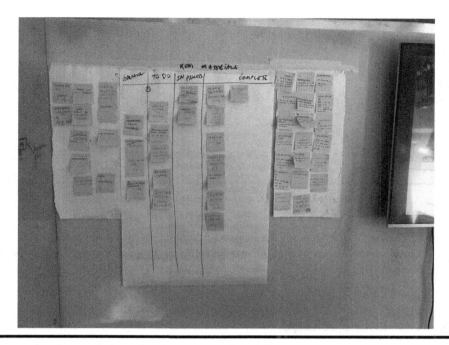

Figure 5.2   Simple Scrum board to keep track of our progress. (Source: BIG Archives.)

Figure 5.3   The team meets in the morning to discuss their activities for the day and in the evening to debrief the day and suggest improvements. (Source: BIG Archives.)

Stats	Base	Kaizen #1	Kaizen #2
Units Produced	480	545	480
Workers	10	10	9
Hours per shift	8	8	8
Total Man Hours	80	80	72
Hours per unit	.17	.15	.15

Demand Is 480 Units Per 8 hour Shift.
Which Example Is True Efficiency? Why?

Figure 5.4   Apparent versus true efficiency. (Source: Toyota Training Manual.)

Toyota differentiates this by highlighting the difference between apparent versus true efficiency. True efficiency occurs only when we increase efficiency without overproducing or overprocessing (see Figure 5.4).

Create Lean Line Package

Next, we create what we call the Lean line package. It is made up of several starting documents required to bring up the line. We have the supervisor own this document, which is a team collaboration. This package includes the following:

- Role of the operator.
- Guidelines for running the line.
- Team leader duties (first level of supervision, working line leader, supervisor, etc.), group leader duties (manager)—this is the beginning of leader standard work and quality's duties.
- Pre- and post-shift checklists.
- Guidelines for water spider and water-spider duties.
- Guidelines for safety, TPM, and 5S.
- Role of day-by-hour chart.
- Standard job sheet (layout with walk pattern by number of operators).

Starting up the New Line

When implementing the line, we start with the Lean practitioner running the line. We then coach the team leader how to run the line and then hand it back to them. A team leader must not only understand the line but must also be able to perform all the processes (functions) on the line for which they are responsible.

As the name implies, they are leaders and a leader leads by example. The ability for the team leader to do all processes on the line helps develop respect as well.

When you first start up the line you must have discipline and make the operators or staff accountable to follow the standard work. If you just let the team members go at it, you will find that despite their training class on how to work in the new line, they revert to their old jobs and behaviors in the brand-new line. Some are naturally excited to start working and some of course are probably not as enthusiastic. They will start to create WIP everywhere because they want to keep busy and will think you want them to rush, even though you have repeatedly told them this is not the case.

We also suggest creating a quick-response team. This team should be at the line, prior to its starting, to ensure the line launch is smooth. We will discuss this more later.

The team leaders must stay on the line 100% of the time. This is one of the most difficult issues to resolve. Normally, the team leader is called to many meetings or has other tasks or sometimes other lines to run. In this system, the team leader needs to be available 100% of the time for cross-training, filling in on the line when a team member has to use the facilities or experiences some type of problem.

Prior to starting up the line, we always ask if everyone is cross-trained. "Oh yes," is the normal response. Then the first problem we seem to run into is that they are not all cross-trained. It becomes obvious as soon as we ask each person to run the line by themselves.

This creates all kinds of problems bringing up the line. Suddenly, one operator can only do one job. Now they are at one station the entire time and then they want a chair! It also leads to some operators having to work around others. This then makes standard work impossible. One thing the Lean practitioner can do, starting immediately before the pilot even begins, is to promote cross-training on all lines, especially the pilot.

Quick-Response Team

Prior to implementing the line, we need to designate a quick-response team. This team should be composed of maintenance, process engineering (with design on call), quality materials, HS&E, and the Lean team members.

This team should be on hand initially for the first few hours the line is running to be able to immediately react to problems. After, the team should be on call so in the event of a problem, the team leader can call them. When first bringing up the line, have a flipchart and markers ready on the floor (or office) to capture any problems or ideas that are found. The LP should work with the team leader to assign actions and due dates to work on the problems or implement the ideas.

Create Standard Work—Why Are Standards Important?

Imagine a world without standards. How would one measure an inch or a cm? How could you make any recipe without a cup or liter? What if a dollar was worth 90 cents to one store and $1.10 to another?

Without standards, we have nothing to consistently measure our progress or our results. In effect, we have no quality. This leads us to standard work. Without standard work, there can be no real improvement, flexibility, or guarantee of quality. Standard work must be the foundation and definition of every process throughout the organization to create a continuous improvement environment.

Standard Work Definition

Standard work is defined by Ohno as three items:

1. *Work sequence*: Each operator must be trained and must execute the process steps in proper order for each operation the same way, every time. This does not mean that the operators are robots; however, it does mean that the operators will get into a rhythm as they perform standard work. Standard work is a very inflexible yet flexible system. It is inflexible in that we want everyone to always follow the standard and do the work the same way; yet, it is flexible in that we want everyone to constantly think about how to improve the process and then experiment with the improvements. This step includes capturing the key points and reasons for key points for each step. This foundation came from TWI Job Instruction (JI) training.
2. *Cycle time*: The next component of standard work is cycle time. Cycle time is the time it takes to do each step in the sequence of operations. It is important to differentiate cycle time from TT. Standard work must be based on cycle time because to run to TT may not always be feasible.
3. *Standard work in process (SWIP)*: Inventory is the amount of inventory necessary to meet the cycle time and perform the job safely.

Job Breakdown for the Operator

In the BASICS approach, standard work comes from the job breakdown. We break down the job to the second, as part of the workflow analysis (WFA). Included in the analysis are minor steps, key points for each step (how you do the work), and reasons for key points (why you do the work). Key points include quality, safety, ergonomics, and sometimes PPE (personal protective equipment).

We combine this document with a video of the operation and use it to train the operator. We call the video depicting the operator standard, the *golden unit video*. This becomes the foundation for our cross-training program which then leads to creating a certification program for all the operators and staff in an office setting.

How to Create Standard Work

We wait until the line is up and running to create the formal standard work. This is because there are many improvements we normally find and implement once we get the line up and running. Once we have stabilized the line then we start to work on creating the standard work and standard work audits.

Standard Work Combination Sheet/Operations Routine Sheet*

This sheet combines the PFA (product steps) and WFA (operator steps) generally at higher-level time increments (see Figure 5.5). We tend to use it the most when humans are interacting with

---

* Standard work combination sheet used with permission—RAYAMA Corporation, February 2017. Mr. Tadashi Mori, a senior consultant at the TPS training center, explains the standard work combination sheet.

Figure 5.5 Mr. Tadashi Mori, the senior consultant at the TPS training center, explains standard work combination sheet (SWCS). (Source: BIG Archives—used with permission—HIRAYAMA Corporation. February 2017.)

machines. It can be used for assembly operations, but we find assembly standard work sheets are better for this purpose.

The SWCS is the primary sheet used by Toyota. The purpose of the sheet is to graphically depict the operator steps against the operational or physical machining steps that may be in a different sequence depending on how the work is split up between the operators. It is also used to highlight waste in the process.

In the left-hand column of the SWCS is the sequence of operator steps, manual time, machine time, and walking time. A straight line is shown for manual work, a dotted line for the machine work (to show how long the machine runs), and a squiggly line for walk time. A red line is drawn vertically on the page to show the takt time. Very quickly one can see waste and determine if the operator has more work than the overall cycle time (or takt time) or if a machine runs longer than the cycle time or TT.

Standard Work in Process (SWIP)

We can approximate the calculation of SWIP in the process using Little's Law, which is:

$$\text{Throughput time} \div \text{cycle time} = \text{SWIP}$$

When calculating SWIP, we need to include the piece the operator has in their hands and then any inventory necessary for the machines or equipment in the process. For machines which the operator can leave unattended, we would keep one piece in the machine all the time. If the machine is a manual machine, then the piece in the machine and the operator piece would be the same.

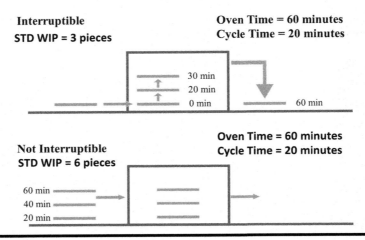

Figure 5.6 Standard WIP for interruptible = 3 pieces versus standard WIP for non-interruptible oven = 6 pieces. (Source: BIG Archives.)

We then need to determine if the equipment is interruptible or uninterruptible. If it is interruptible, it means we can unload a piece and then load a piece and start the machine one-piece flow. If it is uninterruptible, then we consider it a *batch* machine, which means we can't interrupt the machine cycle until it is completed.

Example: an interruptible oven would be a conveyor-type oven or oven where we can open the door each cycle. To calculate the quantity we need in an oven: take the oven time and divide it by the cycle time. If the oven takes 60 minutes and we are running 20-minute cycles, then we would have to have three pieces in the oven at all times (60 minutes per piece ÷ 20 minutes per piece = 3 pieces) (see Figure 5.6).

An example of an oven that is uninterruptible or a batch oven is one where we cannot open the door for the entire 60 minutes until the thermal cycle is completed. This means we must have three pieces in the oven always. In addition, we must build up an extra three pieces while the three pieces are in the oven because we cannot open it. These three pieces are needed to replace the three that will be removed from the oven after the thermal cycle. So, we need a total of six pieces to manage the oven.

Wetting versus Drying up the Line

Wetting the line means we have all the SWIP in place prior to starting the line. Drying out the line means we have used up all the SWIP prior to leaving the line.

What happens if we dry out the line at the end of each day? Assuming we are running the same parts the next day, we are now going to have to wait to wet the line again and we will lose the output during the first hour.

True Standardized Work

Some make a distinction between true standardized work and standard work. You can only have true standardized work if the operation is repeatable without variation. True standardized work is visible only in the results and can initially be sustained through standard work audits. True standardized work can be very difficult to obtain in some processes owing to the variation that exists.

Work Standards

In almost all operations, we encounter substantial variation. Very seldom do we get a line where everyone has exactly, to the second, the same amount of work. Variation generally leads to overproduction, which is batching and excess inventory.

So, in many cases, we must first implement work standards (Figure 5.7) instead of, in addition to, or as part of standard work. Work standards are different from standard work and are designed around jobs that do not repeat or only repeat every so often. In some cases, the work standard may have no cycle times for each step or may have a range of times for each step because there is so much variation in the process.

Advantages of Standardizing Work

As we standardize work and activities, we can now see opportunities to semi-automate or completely automate tasks. This concept, especially in the United States, is met with resistance. Yet, this is the nature of processes, equipment, and technology. Think about how fast technology is moving. Our experience is jobs can be semi-automated (i.e., in its simplest form by just using a power screwdriver vs. a manual screwdriver) and realize 80% of the improvement for about 20%

WORK STANDARD			Date	Sheet No. ___ of ___	
	Product		Prepared By		
	Area		Approved By	Dept.	Date
	Machine No.#				
	Operation Name				

#	Work Elements	Key Point	Sketch/Drawing/Picture
1	Fill in the **Plant, Product, Location, & Processing Information**	1.1 Location refers to the specific area within the plant. Process refers to specific line or work center within the area.	
2	Fill out Operator ___ of ___.	2.1 Represents total # of operators in the cell or work area.	
3	Fill out Takt Time and Cycle time. Go to Engineering or Lean area for information	3.1 For Takt Time, P.C. or Eng. Can supply this # 3.2 Cycle time refers to elapsed time from completed part to completed part.	
4	List Major Operational Steps, including sequence and QC checks.	4.1 Seq. No. is simply the numbering of steps. 4.2 BNC and QC are identified by diamonds and should be strictly adhered too.	
5	Fill in Manual,Auto, Wait, and Walk times.	5.1 These times are calculated from the PPF or Eng.	
6	Fill in Total times at the bottom of each column.	6.1 Fill out total times at the bottom of each column.	
7	Sketch, draw, or insert a picture describing the work sequence in the space provided.	7.1 Show work sequence and SWIP. 7.2 Refer to legend for symbols used.	
8	Must fill out the "last Updated" section.	8.1 Make sure to place the name of the person who does the update and the date on which the update was done.	
9	Get approval signatures and submit a copy to the QS document control person.	9.1 Must be signed by the group leader/supervisor and Eng. 9.2 Must have appropriate QS verification.	

Figure 5.7 Work standard template. (Source: BIG Archives.)

of the cost. It normally takes the other 80% of the cost to get 20% remaining improvement by fully automating tasks.

Assembly Standard Work Form

The assembly standard work form is derived from the WFA we did earlier. After documenting the operator steps, key points, and reasons for key points, we go back and look for items to omit or items where we can save time through the improvements brainstormed during the omits process, that is, eliminate, rearrange, simplify, or combine. The steps not omitted are then rearranged into the proper sequence and become the basis for how to do the job. This becomes the basis for the operator standard work. Figure 5.8 shows a standard work form.

The standard work form is primarily designed for the operators and supervisor or anyone else observing the line. It is constructed at a higher level than the WFA (job breakdown).

We have added columns for key points and reasons for key points, which were derived from TWI.

We have also merged the capacity by headcount and what is called a standard job sheet, which depicts a layout of the area. The standard job sheet is used to show the operator walk patterns and denote safety items, WIP storage, and number of operators, quality checks, and utility (electric, air, water, gas, etc.) locations.

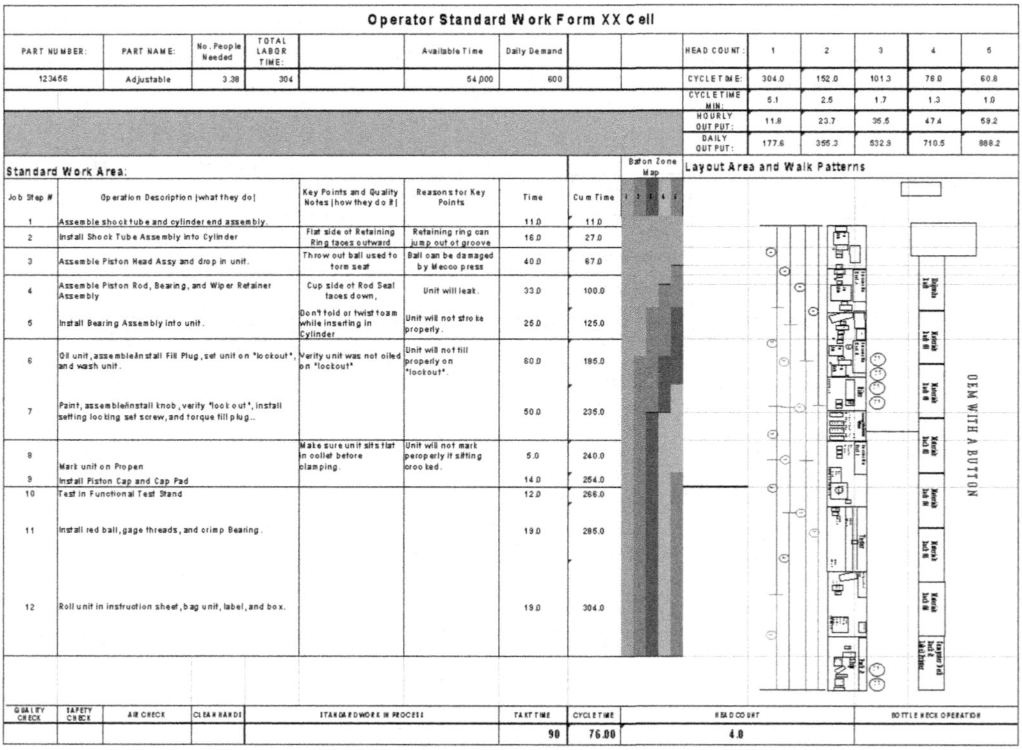

Operator Standard Work Form XX Cell

PART NUMBER:	PART NAME:	No. People Needed	TOTAL LABOR TIME:		Available Time	Daily Demand
123456	Adjustable	3.38	304		54,000	600

HEAD COUNT:	1	2	3	4	5
CYCLE TIME:	304.0	152.0	101.3	76.0	60.8
CYCLE TIME MIN:	5.1	2.5	1.7	1.3	1.0
HOURLY OUTPUT:	11.8	23.7	35.5	47.4	59.2
DAILY OUTPUT:	177.6	355.3	532.9	710.5	888.2

Standard Work Area:

Job Step #	Operation Description (what they do)	Key Points and Quality Notes (how they do it)	Reasons for Key Points	Time	Cum Time
1	Assemble shock tube and cylinder end assembly.			11.0	11.0
2	Install Shock Tube Assembly into Cylinder	Flat side of Retaining Ring faces outward	Retaining ring can jump out of groove	16.0	27.0
3	Assemble Piston Head Assy and drop in unit.	Throw out ball used to form seat	Ball can be damaged by Mecco press	40.0	67.0
4	Assemble Piston Rod, Bearing, and Wiper Retainer Assembly	Cup side of Rod Seal faces down,	Unit will leak.	33.0	100.0
5	Install Bearing Assembly into unit.	Don't fold or twist foam while inserting in Cylinder	Unit will not stroke properly.	25.0	125.0
6	Oil unit, assemble/install Fill Plug, set unit on "lookout", and wash unit.	Verify unit was not oiled on "lookout"	Unit will not fill properly on "lookout".	60.0	185.0
7	Paint, assemble/install knob, verify "look out", install setting locking set screw, and torque fill plug..			50.0	235.0
8	Mark unit on Propen	Make sure unit sits flat in collet before clamping.	Unit will not mark peroperly if sitting crooked.	5.0	240.0
9	Install Piston Cap and Cap Pad			14.0	254.0
10	Test in Functional Test Stand			12.0	266.0
11	Install red ball, gage threads, and crimp Bearing.			19.0	285.0
12	Roll unit in instruction sheet, bag unit, label, and box.			19.0	304.0

Baton Zone Map

Layout Area and Walk Patterns

QUALITY CHECK	SAFETY CHECK	AIR CHECK	CLEAN HANDS	STANDARD WORK IN PROCESS	TAKT TIME	CYCLE TIME	HEAD COUNT	BOTTLENECK OPERATION
					90	76.00	4.0	

Figure 5.8 Standard work form. (Source: BIG Archives.)

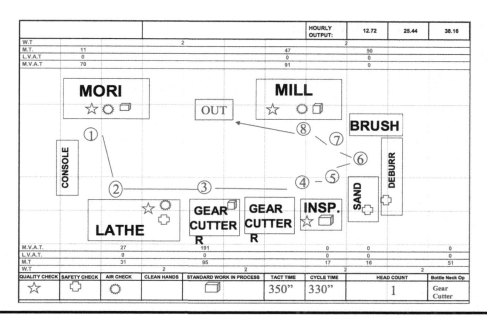

Figure 5.9 Standard job sheet. (Source: Courtesy of Ancon Gear.)

This form can be adapted to any area. We normally create standard job sheets to cover running the line with plus or minus one or two operators, so the supervisor can run the process short or with additional staff (see Figure 5.9).

Separate Man from Machine

It is important, during analysis, when operators interact with machines, to separate the work performed by the machine from the person. We have run into several situations where people perform the work better than robots, and others where the robots perform better than people.

Robots and machines have their place, as they are good for repetitive tasks, dangerous tasks, and for total automation; however, if the robots continue to operate and batch up parts, they are not very useful for Lean. Robots should do one-piece flow, just like people.

There are many cases where we have removed robots to ensure one-piece flow. We apply all the same Lean tools to analyze robots and machines as we do with people. We break out machine time into value-added and non–value-added. With the respect for humanity principle, human work should include the following:

- *Creativity*: The joy of thinking
- *Physical activity*: The joy of working with sweat on the forehead
- *Sociality*: The joy of sharing pleasure and pain with colleagues
- Leadership implementation of total company-wide quality management (TCWQM)

People need to be used wisely, have challenging work, and be taught to constantly identify problems and make improvements.

Determine the Capacity and Labor Requirements

Part Production Capacity Sheet (PPCS)

Lean has a tool we used called the part production capacity sheet (PPCS) (Figure 5.10). This form is easy to create and gives the supervisor or line leader most of the knowledge they need to know about capacity in order to staff their line properly to meet the required cycle time.

How to Create the PPCS

The PFA is captured in the description of process boxes and listed in the proper sequence on the left-hand side and the labor times come from the sequence of operations on the WFA sheet. Setup times are also factored in the middle of the sheet and amortized based on the lot size across each part. The next two columns are for labor value-added and labor non–value-added time. These two columns add up to TLT.

The next two columns are for machine value-added and machine non–value-added time (a new column we created back in the mid-1990s). These two columns sum up to total machine time. This is where we separate operator (person) from machine.

The next column is complete time. This column adds the labor and machine columns together to get the total time necessary for each step for one piece.

The next column is called tool exchange time. This is where changeover information is entered if applicable.

There are different ways to use this form and it can be modified to suit the project application. The tool exchange time contains a column for the lot or batch size utilized and the setup time column has the amount of time required for the changeover.

The form then divides the setup time by the number of products run (lot size), which will amortize the runtime per piece. This is then added to the complete time for that step.

PART PRODUCTION CAPACITY SHEET

Part No	Gear #12345	Hours/ Day	SECONDS/ DAY:		Total Labor Time	Takt Time (sec):				Head Count	1	2	3	4	5
Part Name	Gear	7.3	26,280		283	275				Cycle Time	283	142	94	71	57
Desc.	Gear				TIME DISTRIBUTION					Output Hourly	12.72	14.12	14.12	14.12	14.12
Job Step	Process Step	Labor Non Value Added	Labor Value Added	Machine Non Value Added	Machine Value Added	Complete Time	Bottle Neck	Tool Exchange Time		Output Daily	92.86	103.06	103.06	103.06	103.06
		(sec)	(sec)	(sec)	(sec)	(sec)		Units	Sec	Time Allocated	Prod Cap (units/day)	Comments			
	Cumulative Times:	283	0	0	383	666									
1	Mori	11			70	81					324.44				
2	Lathe	27			31	58					453.10				
3	Gear Cutter	64			191	255					103.06				
4	Inspection	17				17					1545.88				
5	Sand	50				50					525.60				
6	Deburr Lathe	51				51					515.29				
7	Brush	16				16					1642.50				
8	Mill	47			91	138					190.43				

Figure 5.10 Part production capacity sheet (PPCS). (Source: BIG Archives—and with permission from Ancon Gear.)

The next column is capacity. But before we get to that, let's discuss the top lines.

On the top is customer demand and available time. Once these are filled out, the form calculates the TT. There is also a block for factory demand (or transactional area demand) and once we have this number, we can calculate the cycle time we need to use. The next block is TLT. This block is the total of value-added and non–value-added labor time. If we divide it by the cycle time, it tells us how many operators we need based on the demand we are going to run through the process versus the customer demand.

Now, back to the capacity column. Once we have the available time, we can divide it by complete time to determine our capacity. The lowest capacity number represents the bottleneck. Again, a bottleneck should never be a person because we can always add people. The longest complete time driven by a machine is the bottleneck operation (but keep in mind it may not be a true bottleneck). If there is a machine, we need to SWIP the machine, which means that the machine always has a piece to work on while the operator is running the rest of the cell. The next step is to calculate headcount.

The cycle time with one person is always equal to the TLT with one person unless there is a machine with a longer run time. The cycle time with two people would be half the cycle time with one person and so on. This assumes that the work is or can be balanced.

The output per hour is determined by dividing the cycle time into one hour or 60 minutes; however, the output per day is determined by dividing the cycle time into the available time per day.

Remember that this form was originally designed for manufacturing but it is a powerful form. It can be used for any process from banking, insurance, emergency rooms, to landscaping.

This is a phenomenal tool for the supervisor of an area to have at their disposal. Now, they have data with which to answer any question thrown at them from upper management at their fingertips.

Staffing Analysis and Plan

To staff the line, we take the TLT that comes from the WFA and divide it by the TT or cycle time we wish to run. In a machining line, this same formula will work if there is not a machine that runs longer than the cycle time in which case the operator will be idle at that machine. The capacity is then determined by how many people run the line and the cycle time of the machines.

Every time there is a change in demand, a change in products or services offered, a change in process, or new machinery introduced, it necessitates updating the standard work and recalculating all the numbers on the PPCS. World-class companies see these changes as opportunities to improve and eliminate even more waste in the process.

Types of Improvement

The term process improvement can be misleading. When reading Ohno and Dr. Shingo's books, one will find that their approach to improvement is prioritized in the order listed below.

Work Improvement

The improvement starts with the work itself first. The reason is if one starts with equipment improvement, we may find as we improve the work, the equipment is not needed, or it has too many features or the tooling needs to be modified.

Equipment/Machine Improvement

This is about improving the machines. The first step is to make sure your machines are back to "like new" condition. Then we work to speed up the machines, programs, or speeds and feeds.

You must have the ability to tinker and improve the machines you have. If you buy the latest high-tech machines and use unskilled workers who become slaves to the machines, then you lose the sight of what will keep costs down.

Process Improvement

Refers to improvement of processes. For this we utilize the BASICS tool we have been discussing throughout the book.

Facilities/Information Systems Improvement

This involves looking at the entire facility layout and potential improvements. This is normally the costliest. There is a hierarchical approach to doing improvement. It is important to do work improvement first, then equipment improvement, process improvement, facility improvement, and information system improvement. Following this order will save money in the long run as otherwise you can end up doing lots of rework or automating waste.

True Bottlenecks

A true bottleneck is defined as a machine that runs 24 hours a day and cannot meet TT. One has to manage a true bottleneck differently than an ordinary bottleneck. This means a true bottleneck should run over breaks, lunch, shift changes, etc. It should be optimized for setup times. It must be assigned an owner to manage it. If it runs on its own, it should be connected to a system that can text a message to someone before it goes down.

Make and Approve Recommendations

When you have completed the analysis, and new layout and workstation planning, we call a meeting to review it with management. Prior to this all the operators/workforce should have been either involved or updated in preparation of the new system. If management is far down the Lean maturity path then they will already be aware of the Lean progress, and approval is probably a formality.

Training

Prior to implementing the line, we must run all the operators through at a minimum two to eight hours' Lean course. This includes a Lean overview, which they should already have had, and a batch versus flow exercise where we teach them baton-zone/bumping handoffs. This training is very important to gain buy-in and to prepare them for what is coming. We cover a simple overview of what Lean is and do a before-and-after Lean exercise. We all know that learning by doing is an effective learning methodology.

TWI Training

TWI stands for Training Within Industry and was a US government program launched during World War II. It was initially composed of three parts.

1. JI—Job instruction—taught how to break down the job into steps and add the key points and reasons for key points to each step. It is the foundation for standard work today.
2. JM—Job methods—taught how to continuously improve the job.
3. JR—Job relations—taught how the supervisor should react to various problems in the workplace. This became the foundation for respect for people.

Since then JS and PD—job safety and program development programs—have been added.

Roles and Responsibilities (R&R) Matrix

We use a roles and responsibilities sheet to define owners and accountabilities across functional lines. Some people call this a RACI chart. The R&R makes it very clear as to who owns what in the organization (Figure 5.11). The rule is there can only be one owner or person responsible for a decision. There can be shared owners, as well as people consulted, informed, or needed to approve, but only one owner. The format for this chart (see Figure 5.12) comes from a book called *Designing Organizations* by Jay Gailbraith.

146 DESIGNING ORGANIZATIONS

EXHIBIT 9.1. Responsibility Chart for a Financial Services Organization.

Decisions \ Roles	Sales	Segment marketing	Insurance	Mutrual funds	Marketing council	CEO	Finance	Human resources	Regional team
Product price									
Package design									
Package price									
Forecast	A	R	C	C	C	I	I	X	X
Product design									

R = Responsible
A = Approve
C = Consult
I = Inform
X = No Formal Role

Figure 5.11   Roles and responsibilities matrix. (Source: *Designing Organizations*, Jay Galbraith, 2002. John Wiley and Sons.)

Tasks / Authorities **R**esponsible *(Can only have one owner!)* **A**pprove **C**onsult **I**nform **S**hares responsibility **X** - None of the above	Focus Factory Mgr	Buyer Planner Scheduler	Shipping and Receiving	Stategic Acquisition Manager	Water Spiders	Eng.	Shop Floor Team Members	Site Lead	Acctng.	Customer Service	Q.A.	Sales \ Product \ Project Manager	Shipping
1 Develop Supplier Statement of Work	C	C		R		C		A			C		
2 Create Customer RFQ				C		C				C		R	
3 Take the Sales Order										C		R	
4 Enter the Sales Order				I				I		R		I	
5 Field Customer Inquiries	C	C				C		I		R		C	
6 Develop Vendor Managed Inventory Agreeement	C	C		R		C		A	I				
7 Develop Long Term Agreements	C	C		R		C		A	I				
8 Negotiate Blanket PO	A			R				A	I				
9 Enter Blankets /VMI / LTA into system	I			R				I			I		
10 Udate approved supplier list		R		A				I	I			C	
11 Release against blankets		R							I				

Figure 5.12 Roles and responsibilities matrix example. (Source: BIG Archives.)

How to Construct a Cross-Training Matrix

A cross-training matrix (see Figure 5.13) is one of our tools that comes from the JI module of TWI. It provides the training status for each member of a work cell and lists the skills and associated training for each member. This matrix lists all the employees in the cell/area/company and the skills they have acquired to date.

The matrix should be posted in the work area for all members to review and should be used to help staff the cell as well as to develop the training plan for the cell.

The team lead should oversee and manage the matrix and ensure the maximum amount of team members are trained to offer both flexibility and to ensure staff is available as customer demand changes occur. Each staff member that works in the area is rated based on a set of objective measures one to four. These ratings should be continually monitored and revised. This requires the staff to be trained on the latest developments and standard work in the area. The levels vary by company but generally follow:

1. In training
2. Can follow the standard at 50% of the cycle time
3. Can follow the standard and hit the cycle times and suggest improvement ideas.
4. Qualified as a TWI trainer

The team leader is responsible to create and update the cross-training plan each year (see Figure 5.14).

Implementing Line Balancing—Bumping versus Station Balancing

If we have a process in which there are 30 minutes of total labor time per unit and six people working on the line, how much work should be done by each person?

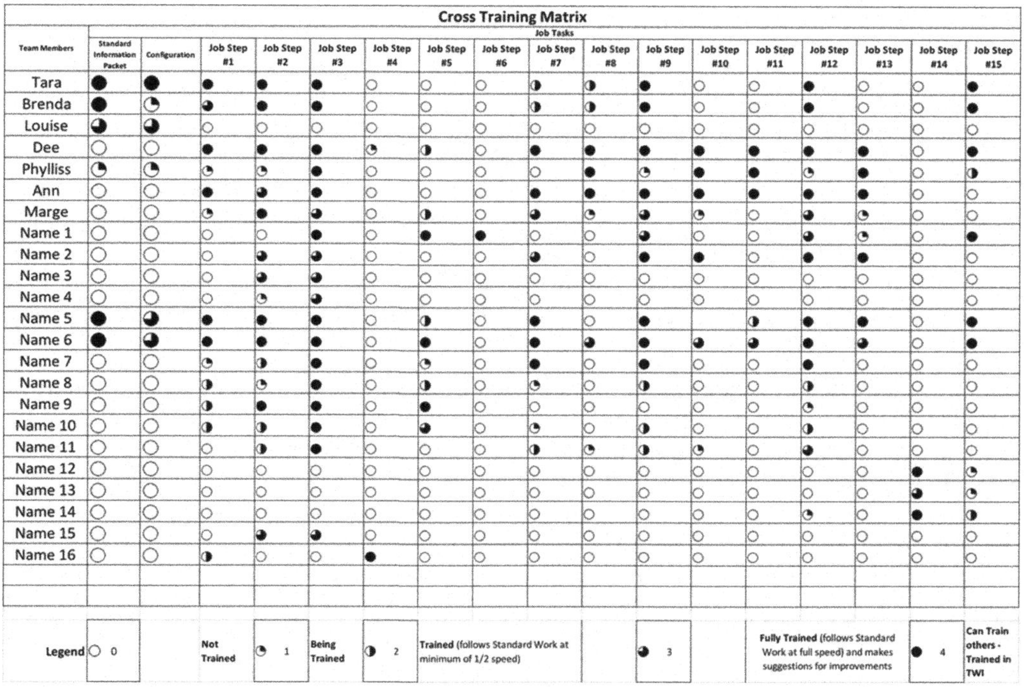

Cross Training Matrix

Team Members	Standard Information Packet	Configuration	Job Step #1	Job Step #2	Job Step #3	Job Step #4	Job Step #5	Job Step #6	Job Step #7	Job Step #8	Job Step #9	Job Step #10	Job Step #11	Job Step #12	Job Step #13	Job Step #14	Job Step #15
Tara																	
Brenda																	
Louise																	
Dee																	
Phylliss																	
Ann																	
Marge																	
Name 1																	
Name 2																	
Name 3																	
Name 4																	
Name 5																	
Name 6																	
Name 7																	
Name 8																	
Name 9																	
Name 10																	
Name 11																	
Name 12																	
Name 13																	
Name 14																	
Name 15																	
Name 16																	

Legend: 0 — Not Trained | 1 — Being Trained | 2 — Trained (follows Standard Work at minimum of 1/2 speed) | 3 — Fully Trained (follows Standard Work at full speed) and makes suggestions for improvements | 4 — Can Train others - Trained in TWI

Figure 5.13 Cross-training matrix example. 1 = in training, 2 = can follow standard work at 50% speed, 3 = can follow standard work at 100% speed, 4 = can train others/suggests improvement ideas. (Source: BIG Archives.)

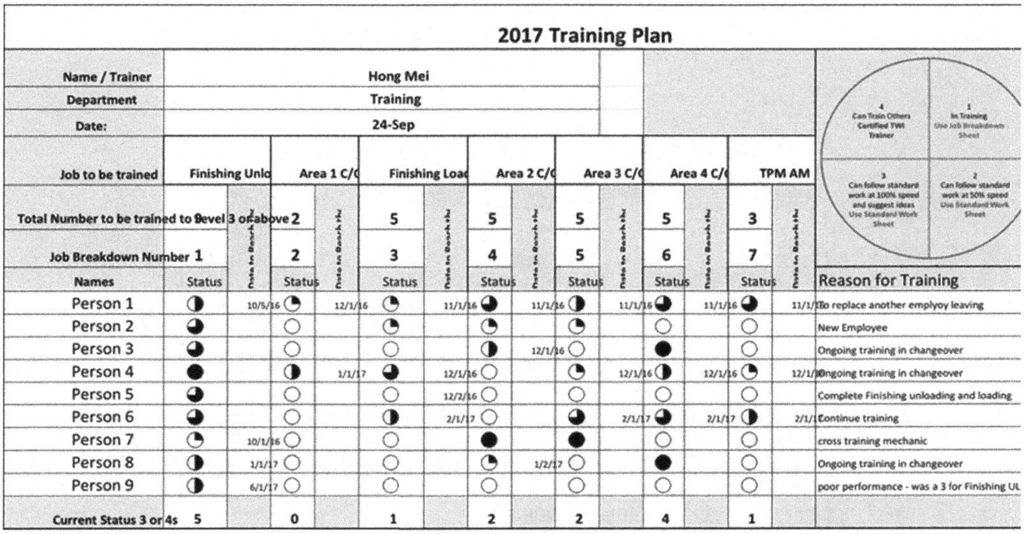

2017 Training Plan

Name / Trainer	Hong Mei
Department	Training
Date:	24-Sep

Legend: 4 Can Train Others Certified TWI Trainer | 1 In Training Use Job Breakdown Sheet | 3 Can follow standard work at 100% speed Use Standard Work Sheet | 2 Can follow standard work at 50% speed Use Standard Work Sheet

Job to be trained	Finishing Unlo		Area 1 C/O		Finishing Load		Area 2 C/O		Area 3 C/O		Area 4 C/O		TPM AM		
Total Number to be trained to level 3 or above	2		2		5		5		5		5		3		
Job Breakdown Number	1		2		3		4		5		6		7		
Names	Status		Status		Status		Status		Status		Status		Status		Reason for Training
Person 1		10/5/16		12/1/16		11/1/16		11/1/16		11/1/16		11/1/16			11/1/	To replace another emplyoy leaving
Person 2															New Employee
Person 3								12/1/16							Ongoing training in changeover
Person 4				1/1/17		12/1/16				12/1/16		12/1/16			12/1/	Ongoing training in changeover
Person 5						12/2/16									Complete Finishing unloading and loading
Person 6						2/1/17				2/1/17		2/1/17			2/1/	Continue training
Person 7		10/1/16													cross training mechanic
Person 8		1/1/17						1/2/17							Ongoing training in changeover
Person 9		6/1/17													poor performance - was a 3 for Finishing UL
Current Status 3 or 4s	5		0		1		2		2		4		1		

Figure 5.14 TWI cross-training plan example. (Source: BIG Archives.)

The answer is 30 minutes ÷ (6 people equals 5 minutes/person)

This requires each person to be given exactly the same amount (five minutes of work) and each person, in turn, must *do* his or her fair share of the five minutes' worth of work.

To accomplish this, we need to consider the skill-set of the operators or staff performing the tasks or activities. This works well if everyone in the line can do the same work at the same speed. It is important that each person has the appropriate cross-training to enable flexibility between tasks, processes, and equipment.

The true test of Lean is found by examining and looking for two items on your lines or in the office process. These are: excess inventory and idle time. If there is excess inventory, it means either the line is not balanced or there is a piece of equipment not functioning properly (downtime), has a lot of variation, or is not process capable.

People should never be the reason for imbalance if the line is set up with bumping/baton-zone balancing. Does anyone in the line have idle time? It is important to look closely and be objective. However, not all problems necessarily manifest themselves as excess inventory or idle time. Excess inventory always covers up some type of problem. This is an example of what we referred to earlier as hidden waste.

When balancing the line, the Lean layout should never change. Proper batons zone-balancing layouts can run with one person or ten people. This is the most difficult concept for people to get in Lean training. They always want to move the product steps around to balance the labor at each station.

Station Balancing

Most cellular models we see today date back to 1983 when Hewlett Packard created an instructional road-show video demonstrating stockless production or how to move from batch to small-lot flow to one-piece flow manufacturing. In the HP video, they showed how they could "pull 3 or pull 1." This is a system with WIP caps or what we call the lazy-man's balance (see Figure 5.15). In effect, the line is being balanced by the WIP present between the operators. Remember, excess

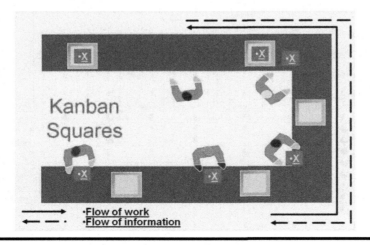

Figure 5.15 Lazy-man's balance. (Source: BIG Training Materials.)

inventory and idle time hide problems. With this kanban-square system in between each operator, we encounter both idle time (when we fill up the square to the WIP cap quantity) and the fact that the inventory in the kanban is and of itself by definition *excess*. The excess materials in the kanban squares hide the fact that the line is imbalanced (if you have not learned how to "read the WIP").

The other problem we have witnessed is that even if the WIP caps are labeled with the maximum amount allowed in the squares (which in many cases are bins or trays), the operators that don't have enough work will inevitably fill them with more than the maximum and in many cases as much as will physically fit in the area. Lines that utilize this model have the following characteristics:

- They are sit-down lines.
- They were originally balanced based on a station approach with the goal of equal work at each station.
- There are spaces or kanban squares (WIP) in between each operator.

Station balancing consists of simply trying to divide [the total labor required to build one product produced by the cell] by [the number of operators in the cells] (see Figure 5.16). Ohno described the material handoffs in the pull 1 HP-type of assembly kanban system as swimming relay handoffs. In a swimming relay, the swimmer cannot leave the starting block until the prior swimmer has touched the wall. In a cell, the next operator cannot start an operation until the prior operator completes the work at their station and moves their part(s) into the kanban square. The kanban squares (see Figure 5.17) have rules:

- The rule is that you can't start working on a part unless there is one in your kanban square.
- You must stop working on it once you have filled your downstream kanban square.

Station Balancing

Total Labor = 3 minutes
Number of Stations/Operators = 3

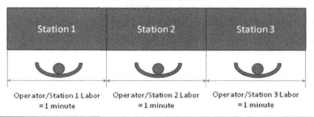

Figure 5.16   Station balancing. (Source: BIG Training Materials.)

- Total WIP in the system = 9
- 1 pc at each station and 3 pc between each station.

Figure 5.17   A pull 3—kanban squares have rules.

Problems with Station Balancing

- People are not robots and we all work and improve at different rates.
- If the line needs to run more than one model or style of product, it is difficult to keep the labor balanced
- Because station balancing was designed based on a set number of operators, if an operator is missing, it creates problems.
- Most station-balanced lines are sit-down lines, where the product flow is normally lost, and are 10%–30% less efficient than stand-up and walking lines.
- The operators tend to dry out the line (use up all the SWIP) going from one product to another.
- If we have a fast worker in a station-balanced line, he/she will finish the work and sit idle. With a slower worker or worker that has too much labor assigned, the WIP will pile up before them.
- Where a line is balanced to takt time (customer demand) instead of cycle time.
- When the total labor changes due to a different product or even sometimes a slower operator.

Because of these problems, we end up with either idle time, excess WIP inventory between stations, or both. When we station-balance a line, we must allow enough time for the operators to perform each task. An industry standard taught in every Lean class is to create man-loading or station-loading charts (see Figure 5.18). The problem with operator load charts is that they are symptomatic of station-balanced lines and while they should, they seldom drive waste elimination. In addition, most practitioners will pad the labor times and allow a 5% or more variation in the cycle times for each operator in order to make them feel good. This immediately creates imbalance in the line.

Rabbit Chase

The rabbit-chase line-balancing methodology has each operator make their own parts by working around the entire cell every cycle. So instead of one operator bumping back to another, each operator is continuously circling the cell working on making a complete product from start to finish.

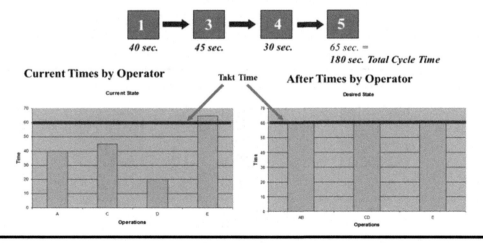

Figure 5.18   Traditional man/station-loading chart. (Source: BIG Training Materials.)

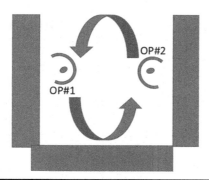

Figure 5.19 Rabbit chase. You can only go as fast as your slowest person or have the slower person stop while the other moves around them. Kind of like playing through in golf. (Source: BIG Archives.)

The rabbit chase (see Figure 5.19) is generally less productive. You lose the time pressure that exists when working on a team and bumping.

However, there are times when this approach may be optimal. For example, we had a forced isolated island in a layout. The operators would open bags of material and dump them into a mixer. In order to speed up the process, while one operator was dumping the other was getting the next bag cut and ready to dump. It was faster to do rabbit chase than to try to hand off an open bag of material.

One-Piece Flow and Baton-Zone Line-Balancing (Bumping)

To facilitate work balancing, we utilize a concept Ohno referred to as baton zones, or flex zones, which are areas where handoffs occur between operators (Figure 5.20). In this system, the operators or assemblers are spread out on the line to work just like runners in a relay race. Like the

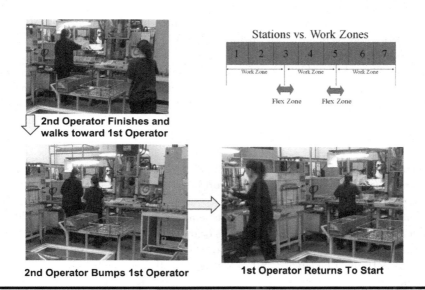

Figure 5.20 Stations versus work zones with flexing (bumping). (Source: BIG Training Materials.)

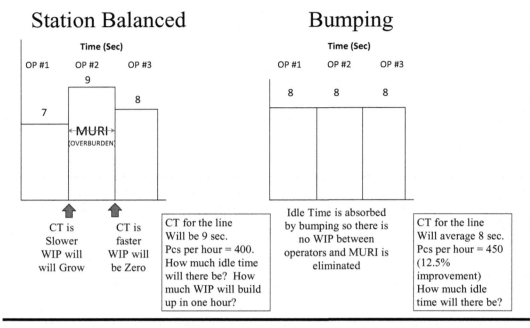

Figure 5.21 Bumping versus station balancing. (Source: BIG Training Materials.)

baton handoff in the relay race, the operators hand off the product to the operator after them and then bump to the operator before them. This bumping process continues until the first operator is reached, who goes to the beginning of the line and starts a new part (see Figure 5.21).

Bumping eliminates the kanban squares, results in zero WIP between the operators, and automatically balances the operators across stations. We tell the operators: You no longer have stations, and the work zones are guidelines only! This would be equal to the pull 1 in the HP model that was said in the video to be impossible.

The bumping rule is you must continue to build until the operator at the station after yours pulls the part from you. When the last operator (closest to the end of the line, i.e., pack and ship) completes a unit, they then walk back to the operator before them and *bump* that operator by taking their part from them wherever they may be in the process. The bumped operator communicates where they are in the process and then goes and *bumps* the operator before them and so on until the first operator in line starts a new part.

This system requires the operators to flex. Some of the major differences with this approach are as follows:

■ The stations must be stand-up height and redesigned with the parts sequenced in the order of assembly (the basis for true standard work).
■ Everyone must be cross-trained.
■ Operators must stand, move, and bump as required to maintain continuous flow.
■ May have to duplicate some tools, fixtures or materials.
■ Operators should rotate several times a day.
■ Standard WIP must be labeled and maintained at all times.
■ The line works best when the fastest person is last, at the end, as they create the pull. However, this should not be an excuse for slow people not to have to speed up.

- You cannot bump forward … only backward.
- Do not bump to the standard WIP (SWIP); you must bump to the person.
- Operators should never have to wait on a machine. SWIP the machine, and it takes the machine out of the equation.
- On mixed-model lines, since several orders could be running down the line at the same time, one has to figure out how to handle the paperwork. Normally, the paperwork travels with the first unit.
- When balancing the cell, start with the bottleneck. Assuming there is demand, the bottleneck should never be idle. You can only go as fast as your slowest machine. The bottleneck should never be a person, only a machine.
- There should be a training progression path for the operators within each line and lines across the plant.
- Don't tie workers to a station (i.e., with a piece of test equipment).
- Major variation should be removed wherever possible.
- Day-by-hour charts must be in place so operators and team leaders catch problems in real time as they occur.
- Operators must follow the guidelines for running the cell (see Figure 5.22).
- First person only drops their piece of WIP and bumps if they can't advance or if the other person will bump back on top of them. If rework is a big problem, some extra stations may have to be added to handle the repair or allow extra time to rework the units. Obviously, the goal is to eliminate the rework but in the real world this does not always happen. Someone must own the rework and fix it so it doesn't come back.

The main difference from station balancing is all the operators in this type of line are not waiting for the person before them to hand them the product (or the baton) like in a push-type station-balanced system. Instead they are literally pulling the part from the operator before them, even if the operator before them are not finished their station's work.

Once the operators see the bumping in action, they will be self-balancing and figuring out how and when to bump. Eventually with some experimenting you will learn how to introduce people

- Have QDIP meeting once a day
- Record day by hour chart and month by day chart
- Do not run orders if they are short ANY parts
- Operators should never wait for a machine! Do not stand at machines while they are running. Bump and take the part from the person in front of you.
- Do not bump to the WIP bump to the person
- You may rotate positions any time
- Run the line one piece flow
- Need batch of 20 to wash, batch of 20 cooling and batch of 20 working from between both sides –standard WIP
- Do not run 2 small orders in a row unless they use the same parts fill
- Check all orders for today and lookout next two days for parts shortages
- Rework on line for quick fixes and take off line for major tear downs or test failures
- Cell lead must support line first before working on reworking or repairing units
- Parts should not go on back shelf unless they are washed and ready
- Test should pace the line. The goal should be to keep the tester running as much as possible (this will be based on takt time)

Figure 5.22 Guidelines for running the cell. (Source: BIG Training Materials.)

to the line and remove them from the line and keep the line running. In some cases, if people must be added you may have to add stations. The goal is to have people moving and walking, not standing in one place on the line.

Bumping Results

By implementing bumping we increase the output and corresponding productivity by up to 60% and pieces per person per hour by 150% (see Figure 5.23).

Line balancing is always controlled by the number of people or the SWIP. There are two types of bumping scenarios. One is as described above where the operators do the bumping. The other is where the operators remain at their stations and the SWIP moves to them. This means they must have all the tools and materials at every station necessary to complete the product.

Advantages of Bumping

Aside from the obvious elimination or reduction of some of the wastes mentioned earlier in this chapter, there are more obvious advantages of the baton handoff-style line. They are the following:

- Maximizing team member's efficiency.
- Maximizing output of the line by using the fastest person to create the pull.
- Minimizing the effect of absenteeism.
- The line does not have to be U shaped.
- Drive cross-training.
- Ability to easily measure output.
- Quality improvements and mistake-proofing opportunities surface from breaking the operations into small steps.
- Incorporation of subassemblies or other operations being performed off-line.
- Eliminates idle time (assuming SWIP is in place).
- Line is not dried out each shift or after each product model change.

Baseline Metrics – 2pc flow

Operators	4
Units Per Hour	26
DL mins per unit	9.2
Thru-put Time (min)	33
Cycle Time (Est.Batch min.)	2.3
Space	

Demonstrated Lean After Metrics 1 pc flow

Operators	2	-50%
Units Per Hour	32.5	+ 20%
DL mins per unit	3.75	- 60%
Thru-put Time (min)	3.75	- 94%
Cycle Time (min)	1.875	- 18%
Space	freed up 2/3 of conveyor	

Figure 5.23   Results from a finishing area in a foundry show implementing baton zone bumping increased the output 60%. (Source: BIG Archives.)

- Variation with options or mixed model is easy to handle.
- It is easy for operators to rotate in and out of the line.
- It is easy for operators to rotate to a different position in the line.

Failure Modes of Baton Handoff Lines

- Most people want to bump to the SWIP, not the person.
- They are not cross-trained and cannot bump.
- Equipment is off the line, requiring operators to leave the line, disrupting the flow.
- Line is not stand-up and walking.
- Team leader or supervisor doesn't understand how to run the line.
- SWIP is dried up or not maintained in the line.
- All components for the product being built are not available when the order is released.

Line Operations/Pre-Assembly

One common mistake people make in implementing Lean is that people want to keep certain operations offline. We are not sure why this is but it is commonplace and widespread. Generally keeping off-line operations in a separate area results in batching and huge waste.

For instance, one must figure out how to link the area up to the line that it is feeding. This means that there needs to be an inventory buffer between the lines or, if not, the final line cannot start until all the subassemblies are available. Keep in mind pre-assembly is batching even if we are doing it one-piece flow. Any defects found are likely to be contained in the whole batch that is pre-assembled.

For some reason, as human beings, we are literally compelled to want to keep subassemblies offline, as if this gives them some type of advantage over the process. They still require labor; the labor is sporadic and inefficient and normally ends up holding up the line.

Job Rotation

Job rotating (see Figure 5.24) can be done each hour, after breaks, or after lunch, based on whatever makes sense for the business. Job rotation also gives the workers a sense of accomplishment, and by learning new skills, they become more marketable. Additionally, it can break down silos and provide a better understanding of the whole process.

Implement Line Metrics

Day-by-Hour Chart

The day-by-hour chart (see Figure 5.25) displays the planned production for each hour, considering breaks, meetings or huddles, and exercise times. There are many variations of this chart depending on the line or area in which it is utilized. Each hour, the team lead or one of the operators enters the actual amount of product (or paperwork) produced.

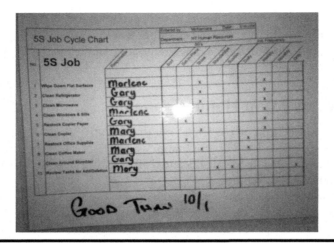

Figure 5.24   Job rotation chart. (Source: Joe McNamara, president of Ttarp Industries, and BIG Training Materials.)

Figure 5.25   Day-by-hour board. (Source: BIG Archives.)

If there is a variance for the hour, the team lead or operator enters in the variance and the explanation for the variance and whether any containment actions or countermeasures were required. The real value in the chart is twofold.

■ First, it shows the team members how they are doing against the plan (which originally comes from the workflow analysis [WFA] and subsequent standard work).
■ The second is to assess and fix the root cause(s) for the variance so it never comes back.

There should be some type of action taken by the team lead or supervisor to begin to root-cause and take countermeasures to correct the variance. If the problem can be corrected right away, that is noted on the sheet. If it cannot be corrected right away, it should go to the +QDIP board under the appropriate heading and then root-caused by the team or supervisor. The key is to flush out all the problems in the line. If the variance is positive we need to understand why? Maybe we can update the standard times?

The day-by-hour chart will also give the operators something to shoot for each hour since they know from sitting in the analysis sessions these times are more than achievable. When we first set up the line, we normally don't require the supervisor to put in the plan, but we do get them used to recording the actuals each hour. The reason for this is, when we put the plan up immediately, the team members (operators) think we want them to rush to meet the numbers. Nothing could be farther from the truth. We let them get used to the line and work our way down the learning curve, and normally a week later, we will start entering the plan by hour.

Some plants will set the targets at 80% or less of what could be achieved. This is wrong. It is important to set the plan to align with the results supported by the video analysis. Making the plan numbers easy to achieve or to make the employees happy does not drive continuous improvement, and is not fair to the employees, as it allows supporting functions to slack off, but still hit the plan.

Takt Time Board and Line Counters

It helps to install line counters to support day-by-hour charts (see Figure 5.26). With standards in place and line counters, it is easy to determine if you are ahead or behind schedule.

Introduction to + QDIP

The acronym +QDIP stands for:

- Plus (+) stands for 6S (safety + 5S)
- Q = quality (typically first-pass yield but rolled throughput yield has been used also)
- D = OTD
- I = inventory
- P = productivity

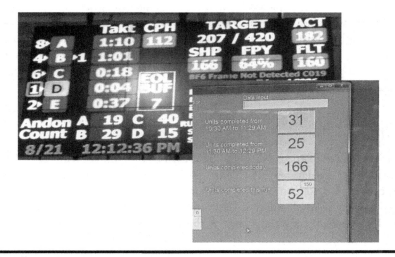

Figure 5.26   Takt time versus actual real-time status.

Figure 5.27 QDIP meeting being run by Tom Turton, focus factory manager Xylem Corp. Tom is also a Master BlackBelt and Master Lean Practitioner. (Source: Joe McNamara, president of Ttarp Industries, and BIG Archives.)

Companies use other acronyms, such as QCD, SQDP, and SQDIP, where QCD stands for quality, cost, and delivery; SQDP substitutes S for safety instead of + for 6S and does not include inventory; and SQDIP includes inventory as well (see Figure 5.27).

Plus (+) = Safety/5S*

Plus (+) stood for our 5S, plus safety metrics of severity and frequency were agreed to and the team focused on the metrics. A highly visual, daily 5S standard work board exists in each value stream, noting that any safety incidents that resulted in lost time had to be reported directly to the president of the division.

If all the 5S tasks were completed from the day before and there were no injuries or near misses, then the day was colored green. If there had been a near miss or a 5S task was not completed, then the frontline leader switched markers real time in the meeting and colored the day's box red within the "+" month. The day would be colored blue when the cell or value stream was not working due to a planned shutdown. If the shutdown was not planned (i.e., equipment down or short components needed for an order), blue would not be used.

Q = Quality

Quality was the measure of the quality for the area. For a manufacturing cell, if there were no quality issues that day, the day would be colored green during the meeting. If there was a quality issue that was caused by a nonconforming component or an assembly/machining error in the cell/area, the day would be colored yellow if the commitments for the day were still met despite the issue, and red if commitments weren't met. A shop floor nontraditional definition was used for

---

* The +QDIP section was contributed by Joe McNamara, president of Ttarp Industries. He developed this system over several years at ITT Heat Transfer, now Xylem.

quality for +QDIP boards in support areas or departments. If all drawings and bills of material engineering produced and delivered to the shop floor were correct without errors, then the day was colored green for the engineering board. If not, the day was colored in red.

D = Delivery

Delivery was a measure of the delivery from that area against their schedule. For example, the receiving inspection +QDIP board would be green only if their inspections were all completed correctly and on time for the day, which allowed parts to go to the cells on time.

Inventory

This metric changed from the number of inventory turns to a shop floor–based metric if all parts that were supposed to be available were available. If a work order was found to be short while building an order, or short such that an order could not be started, the day would be colored red. If a part was not the right revision letter or had quality issues (missed by receiving inspection), it would be coded red. If a part was missing in the bill of material (BOM) list, it was coded red. If a component inventory level was below the expected level in the cell but no orders were required, and the parts were being built, the day would be colored yellow.

Productivity

The productivity definition evolved rapidly going from standard versus actual hours to a shop-floor metric of:

■ Any unplanned machine downtime
■ Issues that caused the machine to operate at a slower speed
■ Any missing tools

If any of these items impacted the cell the day prior it would be colored red. Daily counters and the day-by-hour charts also fed into this metric. The color code is as follows: If the plan on the day-by-hour chart was met with no problems, then the day was colored green; if the plan was met but we had any of the issues noted earlier, it was yellow; and if the targeted plan output was not met on the day-by-hour chart, then productivity on the +QDIP board for the day was colored red.

KPI (Key Performance Indicator) Board

The KPI board*—and other value stream–related metrics (i.e., bookings, sales numbers, customer feedback) posted at the cell—is another template that can be used as an alternative to the +QDIP template. It emphasizes root-cause analysis through its Pareto sheets, which is advantageous from

---

* Some are now referred to as KBI or Key Business Indicator.

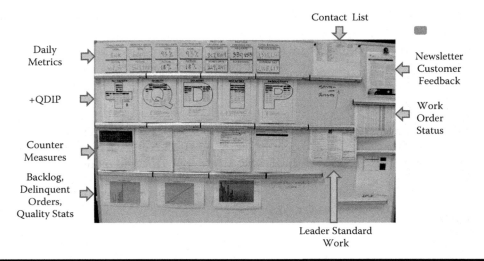

Figure 5.28 QDIP board and daily cell metrics and goals. (Source: BIG Archives.)

a Toyota Kata (coaching) standpoint when indoctrinating the concept of root-cause analysis (i.e., 5 Whys) into your culture.

In addition to the +QDIP letters and countermeasures sheets that are below the QDIP letters, we also include the daily orders, delinquent backlog, and backlog (see Figure 5.28), which, in some cases, we simply wrote on a whiteboard daily during the huddle. It is important to share a quick high-level view of the health of the business to every employee.

The equivalent KPI board modified for the focus-factory or value-stream level is shown in Figures 5.29 and 5.30. Sample cell metric calculations are shown in Figure 5.31, and should be adjusted to align with your businesses' exact need and strategic goal deployment. The productivity

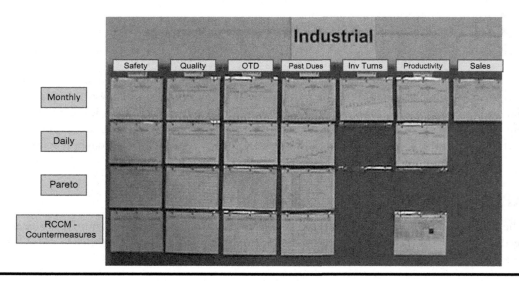

Figure 5.29 Alternative KPI metric board for focus-factory level. (Source: Joe McNamara, president of Ttarp Industries, and BIG Archives.)

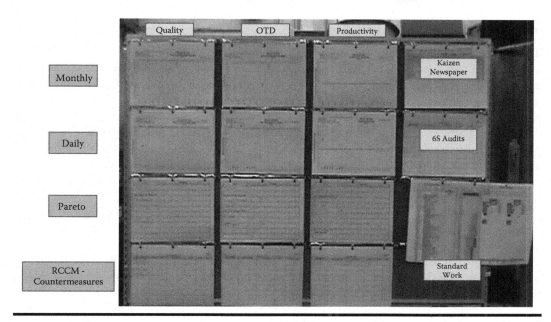

Figure 5.30 Alternative KPI metric board for work-cell level. (Source: Joe McNamara, president of Ttarp Industries, and BIG Archives.)

	Safety	Quality	Delivery		Cost	
			OTD	Past Dues	Inventory	Productivity
Metric	OSHA Recordable Incidents	Total Yield	On Time Delivery to Customer Request Date	Past Dues	Turns	Productivity %
Calculation	Data - Tracked	Total Acceptable Units / Total Units Produced	Lines shipped OT to CRD / Total lines shipped	Data - Tracked	COS / Total Inventory	Total Conversion Cost (*less materials*) / Total Sales
Data Required	Recorded incidents	Daily Defects	Lines Shipped OT to CRD	Number of Lines Past Due	Total Cost of Sales	Total Conversion Cost (*less materials*)
		Daily Total Units Produced	Daily Total Lines Shipped	Total Past Due $	Total Inventory	Total Sales
Goal	0	98%	98%	0	4.5	TBD (lower)

Daily

Weekly or Monthly

Figure 5.31 Cell metric calculations. (Source: BIG Archives.)

and inventory turns are typically weekly or monthly at the focus-factory level. This is particularly applicable if it is an engineered-to-order or large-dollar build-to-order business model as day-to-day measurement is too variable and thus not meaningful. To the extent that productivity can be meaningfully measured daily at the focus-factory level, that is clearly preferred.

+QDIP Boards/Meetings

The +QDIP board is generally created for each assembly and machining cell to record problems and to encourage root-cause analysis and corrective action to fix the problem. The team that is assigned to the board—to include supervisor, manufacturing engineer, quality engineer, buyer, and planner—would be responsible to check the board and assign their name as the owner of the issue for their functional area.

Support staffs, such as engineering, sales, and HR, are in attendance to provide needed support and feedback to ensure the operations run smoothly, providing quality, affordable products and services to customers. The employees from all the different cells in a focus factory may all attend the same huddle in the morning, but they may each have their own +QDIP board for their individual cells.

Metric development should be evolutionary and focus on what the business needs and must be measurable when the metric is introduced. The metrics must ultimately be tied to customers, such as customer demand, quality, delivery, and affordability.

This approach brings accountability into the organization at all levels. It also is the beginning of developing a Hoshin environment where everyone on the shop floor saw how they contributed to the strategic goals of the business.

Visual Management—Incorporate 5S, Visual Displays, and Controls

Visual management is made up of three activities: 5S, visual displays, and visual controls (see Figure 5.32). Visual management is a work area that is

1. Self-explaining
2. Self-regulating
3. Self-improving

where what is supposed to happen does happen, on time, every time.

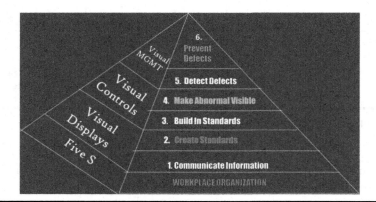

Figure 5.32 Visual management pyramid. (Source: BIG Archives.)

5S—Housekeeping and Discipline

As we make changes to the layout and workstations, we implement 5S as we go. While some organizations add an S for safety and call this 6S, and others add a seventh S for Satisfaction (employee), many use 3S. It's a simpler way to start. Safety is really a part of each of the 5Ss. The 5Ss are:

Seiri: Proper arrangement, sort, cleanup, clearing up, or organization. The first step is to separate and consolidate those items necessary for the proper functioning of the work area (i.e., tools, fixtures, work instructions, parts, or office supplies) from the unnecessary items. Get rid of those unnecessary items.

Seiton: Arrange, put in order, and store, set in order, order, orderliness, organize logical order, or neatness. Arrange items so they can be retrieved immediately in the order required. Make a place for all the necessary items and put them in their place. Identify their appropriate place by outlining the area and/or labeling the space.

Seiso: Neat, tidy, sweep, shine, cleanliness, cleaning, or pick up. Operators clean the work area daily, sweep the floors, wipe off the machines, and keep a sanitary work area. Make sure everything is neatly in its place. This concept is often misinterpreted and misunderstood.

Seiketsu: Cleanliness, standardize, neatness, or maintaining a spotless workplace. Find ways to keep the overall environment neat and clean. The white-glove test is very applicable here. Are there ways to reduce dust, dirt, and debris that make the cleanup easier? How are old documents purged from the area? Are minimums and maximums identified and visible in storage? This makes visual management easier to maintain. Can we eliminate safety hazards? Make sure standard procedures and work standards are created to document the 5S process, including how 5S tasks are to be completed and visual photographs of what the area should look like when it is completed.

Shitsuke: Discipline, sustain, conduct, changing work habits, or training. Discipline and training. The most important step of all is to maintain/sustain the area once it has been created. Everyone must follow and update the standardized procedures for cleaning and organizing. Continue to look at the whole area, not just your workspace.

This is the most difficult S of all. To sustain, the 5S program must become part of the documented procedures of the company, monitored, and audited (see Figure 5.33).

5S must be led by every executive, manager, group leader, and team leader. Management must provide the training and resources to ensure 5S succeeds.

If you walk by a piece of trash you should pick it up. Lead by example and let others see your back. If you see someone not put a tool back and don't say anything, you have just rewarded that person's behavior. Many area teams audit themselves regularly to track their improvement. The area team uses the audit results to focus their improvement efforts and increase their score on the next audit.

We prefer the 5S audit not have a score. This keeps the focus on improvement and takes the pressure away from "gaming the system" to just increase the 5S score.

Since the audits are conducted with the team leader, they get real-time feedback on the opportunities. In summary, 5S has two major components—housekeeping and discipline. Housekeeping is about the old saying, "a place for everything and everything in its place," but it is also about discipline.

Discipline is putting things back in their place, which is the most difficult part of 5S. We all need to be part of setting the standard at the highest levels if we are to be considered world class.

5 S Daily Inspection

Rank
A = Perfect Score = 4 points
B = 1 or 2 Problems = 2 points
C = 3 or more problems = 1 points
Maximum score in each category = 20 points

Category	Item	A	B	C	Comments
Sort (Organization)	Distinguish between what is needed and not needed				
	Are things posted on a Visual Display board uniformly?				
	Have all unnecessary items been removed?				
	Is it clear why unauthorized items are present?				
	Are materials inside cabinets neatly organized?				
	Are passage ways and work areas clearly outlined?				
	Are hose and cords properly arranged?				
Stabilize (Orderliness)	A place for everything and everything in it place				
	Is everything kept in its own place?				
	Are things put away after use?				
	Are work areas uncluttered?				
	Is everything fastened down that needs to be?				
	Are shelves, tables and cleaning implements orderly?				
	Are all machine guards in their place?				
Shine (Cleanliness)	Clean and looking for ways to keep it clean				
	Is clothing neat and clean?				
	Are exhaust and ventilation adequate?				
	Are work areas clean?				
	Are machinery, equipment, fixtures and drains kept clean?				
Standardize (Adherence)	Maintain and monitor the first three S's				
	Is the area free of trash and dust?				
	Have all machines and equipment been cleaned?				
	Has the floor been cleaned?				
	Are clean-up responsibilities assigned?				
	Are all tools and gages within calibration dates?				
(Self Discipline)	Stick to the rules, scrupulously				
	Are smoking areas observed?				
	Are private belongings put away?				
	Does everyone refrain from eating, drinking and smoking in the workplace?				
	Sub Total	0	0	0	
	Total	0			

Figure 5.33 5S audit sheet. We prefer to have non-scoring audits; otherwise, it becomes more about the score than 5S. (Source: BIG Archives.)

Benefits of 5S

- A cleaner workplace is a safer workplace.
- Contributes to how we feel about, and the pride we take in, our product, process, our company, and ourselves.
- Customers love it.
- Product quality and especially contaminant levels will improve.
- Cleaning typically reveals problems and areas that need repair.
- Efficiency will increase.
- Good program to get everyone in the organization involved.
- Demonstrates an enterprise commitment to the Lean/5S program.

Red-Tag Strategy

Using red tags are helpful when establishing the 5Ss. Continuous improvement teams use red tags to mark unneeded items for removal. The red-tag strategy helps identify and separate out needed items from unneeded items. Items tagged are placed in a cordoned-off area to be dispositioned later. The red-tag strategy helps lay the foundation for improvement by making obvious which items are not needed for daily production activities.

The 5S Board

5S boards (see Figure 5.34) can have the employee name or picture at the top and the days (and sometimes week, month, or quarter) on the side. The boards can be set up several different ways. Every employee is assigned a short five-minutes-or-less task each day to complete.

This can be expanded to include safety and TPM tasks as well. When the task is completed, its tag is turned over to show the complete side. These boards can be expanded to incorporate TPM and Lean audit-type tasks as well. The advantages of these boards are that they get all the employees in the area involved in the care and maintenance of the area and they are also useful to maintain audit compliance.

A 5S board, if it covers all the 5S points, becomes self-auditing. If the person does not do their task, everyone else knows in real time. A simple walk around the area to inspect the tasks provides the audit function.

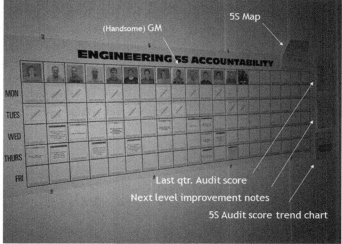

Figure 5.34 5S board for engineering department—each person gets a daily five-minute 5S task. When it is complete, they turn the magnet over. (Source: Joe McNamara, president of Ttarp Industries, and BIG Archives.)

Visual Displays

Visual displays communicate important information (see Figure 5.35) but do not necessarily control what people or machines do. Visual displays such as signs and bulletin boards do not suggest or enforce any action. They only communicate the name of an area, machine, or some other type of information.

The 5/20 Rule

We use the 5/20 rule for visual boards. Within 5 ft of the board, you should only need 20 seconds to see the current state of the cell/process and determine if it is in control. It is also useful to use red/orange/green color coding to show the immediate status of an item. At Toyota they have a standard green circle, yellow triangle, and red box to show the immediate status on boards, electronic displays, and even on A3 actions.

If you can't read the board from 5 ft away, then the information is too small and no one will read it.

Visual Controls

- Communicate information in a way that helps everyone identify or prevent a problem.
- Build in standards and make defects (abnormalities) obvious.

The analogy for visual controls is the human body. When the body has a problem, it lets you know. It may be in the form of a fever, pain, bleeding, blister, etc. Once your body signals a problem, it needs to be taken care of right away or it tends to get worse. The goal is to make every problem immediately visible, so it can be fixed right away. This sounds easy to do but is very difficult.

As you walk around an area, the factory or office should *talk to you* and communicate its condition as you walk around it. Think about an airport. Everything is visual, even the tarmac. Sign boards communicate the status of the flights; each gate is labeled and contains a signboard of which flights are leaving the gate and when. Restrooms, handicap areas, safety issues concerning strollers on escalators, and a speaker above saying "caution, the moving walkway is ending" are all visuals and *talk to you* as you walk through. You immediately know the status of your flight and

Figure 5.35   Visual display example. (Source: BIG Archives.)

Figure 5.36 Visual controls on the tarmac. (Source: BIG Archives.)

Figure 5.37 Visual controls—red light, stop sign, and RR signal. (Source: BIG Archives.)

what is going on around you. Does your factory communicate to you the same way the airport does (see Figure 5.36)?

Visual controls are different than visual displays because they go a step further to suggest some action be taken or they help remind us to do something but usually can't force certain actions to be taken. For instance, a red light, stop sign, and RR signal (see Figure 5.37) are visual controls versus displays because they tell the driver to stop, but can't force the driver to stop. We can still go through the red light, RR crossing, or stop sign with some risk to ourselves and others. The driver stops because they know if they continue, there may be some negative consequence, like an accident or a ticket.

Advantages of a Visual Factory (see Figures 5.38 and 5.39)

- Surfaces problems quickly, indicates non-conformances and when help is needed, reduces search time by 50%
- Improves safety, increases audit compliance for HS&E, and increases productivity
- Management by sight

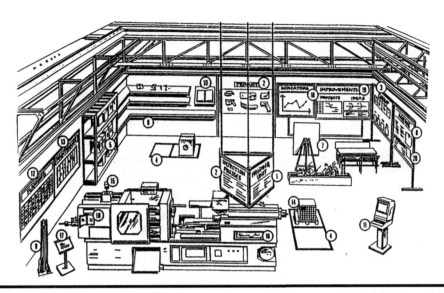

Figure 5.38 Visual workplace example. (Source: *Five Pillars of the Visual Workplace*, **Hiroyuki Hirano** © **1995, Taylor & Francis.)**

The Team's Territory

1. Identification of territory
2. Identification of activities, resources, and products
3. Identification of the team
4. Markings on the floor
5. Markings of tools and racks
6. Technical area
7. Communication area and rest area
8. Information and instructions
9. Neatness (broom)

Visual Documentation

10. Manufacturing instructions and technical procedurest

Visual Production Control

11. Computer terminal
12. Production schedule
13. Maintenance schedule
14. Identification of inventories and work-in-process

Visual Quality Control

15. Monitoring signals for machines
16. Statistical process control (SPC)
17. Record of problems

Displaying Indicators

18. Objectives, results, and differences

Rendering Progress Visible

19. Improvement activities
20. Company project and mission statement

Figure 5.39 Visual workplace description. (Source: *Five Pillars of the Visual Workplace*, **Hiroyuki Hirano** © **1995, Taylor & Francis.)**

- No technical knowledge of area is needed to assess the current condition
- Can sometimes lower insurance rates
- Enabler for high-performance work teams
- Reduces meetings to discuss work issues
- Shows if you are on target to meet requirements
- Identifies flow, roadblocks, and controls inventory
- Communicates real-time feedback to everyone
- Can positively influence the behavior and attitude of team members
- Customers love it
- Shows everything has a place and everything is in its place

Gemba Walks

The term gemba walk has many meanings today. There are books written on them, but everyone has their own opinion. In our case if you go to the floor (or office) it is a walk to the gemba. Gemba is where the action is going on. The common three aspects are to see, to eliminate waste, and to learn.

We conduct different types of walks. These include waste walks where we look for waste, process walks where we look at each workstation along with the tools used to see what could go wrong and how to mistake-proof. There are daily management walks where the manager should be able to look at the visual board and know immediately if there is a problem. Depending on the severity of the problem, the manager may leave a note to be answered by the team leader or supervisor (to see if they are managing the board) or they may use an urgent problem/gap on the board as a coaching moment to further develop their team leader's thinking.

Mike Rother suggests in addition to the three common aspects above that the gemba walk should focus on how people are working. This means "… focusing on their pattern of thinking or acting which they utilize as they improve and strive for their goals." This involves four steps:

1. It should be used system-wide
2. It should be suitable for any goal or problem
3. It should be based on the scientific method
4. It should include structured practice routines for beginners

This approach is described in detail in his books and videos which can be found on his Kata website.

The bottom line on it all is the gemba walk should be focused on teaching and driving ongoing improvement toward your targets. This means you need to understand the gaps between where you are now and your target and then experiment using small PDSA cycles to overcome the gaps.

Typical gemba-walk questions encourage problem-solving. The first question we always ask is: what is the standard? If there is no standard then we have an immediate problem and it means we need to do a job breakdown and develop the standard work. If there is a standard then we should be looking to see the actual condition. Are we meeting the standard? Are we ahead or behind? Both are problems. If we are behind, we need to understand why and remember the problem is not the person. If we are ahead we need to understand if we are following the standard. If we are, and have figured out a way to better it, then we need to update the standard work to include the improvement.

Another question we can ask is what improvements the team is working on now. Then we need to understand how and where they are in the problem-solving process. We need to understand the target they are shooting for compared to the baseline and if they have identified the root cause. The most important thing is to make sure they are not just throwing solutions at the problem.

You can't manage the floor or office area or fix a problem without going to the gemba, floor, or office, to determine what is really going on.

Ritsuo Shingo,* when he was president of Toyota in China, personally walked the entire property, prior to building their new facility, in order to root-cause a problem with a stream and related drainage that would have seriously impacted the plant. If he hadn't walked the property he would have never discovered the problem. You cannot manage a plant from your office.

---

* Ritsuo Shingo taught at the Lean Leadership Institute (LLI) conference, August 2017, hosted by George Trachillis in Santorini, Greece.

Dashboard

Some companies create a dashboard of commonly tracked metrics. These may appear electronically or via manual charts tracked at the cell or in the office each day.

Most companies will use electronic dashboards and they can be useful when managing multi-sites or remotely. We caution you against only using electronic systems though. We have found a great deal of value in using manual tracking systems. They force the first-line leaders to acknowledge abnormal conditions and thus react to them. It also requires leaders to understand the formulas for the metrics for which they are responsible.

Process- versus Results-Focused Metrics

We tell companies to focus on the process and the results will take care of themselves. This is a very difficult "leap" for most executives to take since there is so much pressure on short-term results. Seeing and eliminating waste becomes how everyone in the organization does business.

Lean and Productivity, Efficiency, and Effectiveness

What to Do When There Is Rework or Scrap?

One-piece flow will bring every problem that has ever existed immediately to the surface. Initially there will probably be scrap and rework issues. We must figure out how to deal with it. This is a difficult point in the project.

The Lean answer would be to shut down the line and fix the problem so it never comes back. However, we have never worked with an organization that is even remotely at the Lean maturity level to deal with this. If the stop-the-line strategy is employed at this stage, the line probably won't run for a week, month, or even a year.

The initial answer is to develop a countermeasure and work to figure out the root cause. The obvious danger is that once you work around the problem, the pressure to determine the root cause and fix the problem is now gone. We call this drive-thru parking.

Implement the Lean Material System

Kanbans

Kanban literally means "watch over board for a period." Kanbans facilitate inventory management by providing a trigger i.e., sign or signal for replenishment. According to Taiichi Ohno, kanban is a means through which JIT is achieved. Ohno believed the goal for kanbans should be no more than five pieces of inventory with a goal of zero inventory. This would mean the prior process would produce the parts needed for the next process JIT. The purpose of a kanban system is to control the flow of material by providing inventory as a buffer to synchronize two disconnected processes.

Kanban is a visual management tool to help curb overproduction—the number one waste—and for detecting delays in the process, or when processes are producing ahead of schedule (a pacemaker to prevent overproduction i.e., produce only what is ordered, when ordered, and quantity ordered).

Kanbans are inventory, which is waste, thus we must constantly work to minimize the amount of materials. A kanban trigger or signal can be an empty space, an empty bin, a piece of paper, an electronic signal (lights, EDI), or an icon (e.g., rolling golf balls down a tube). The term kanban can initially be very confusing because the term kanban itself is used in several ways.

Kanban Replenishment: Constant Time or Constant Quantity

Kanbans can be replenished in two ways:

■ *Constant time* means they are replenished the same time each day or several times a day. This is referred to as breadman-type replenishment, which is like grocery store shelves being restocked each night.
■ *Constant quantity* is like the two-bin system. It may empty out at any time, and we refill it with the same quantity every time.

There are several types of kanbans, as explained in the first six chapters of Monden's book entitled *The Toyota Production System*. The two main types are:

■ *Withdrawal*: Toyota refers to this as retrieval
■ *Production*: Toyota refers to this as informative

Two-Bin Systems

The simplest type of kanban is called a two-bin system (see Figure 5.40). A two-bin system is a constant quantity system, which can be used for withdrawal or production kanbans. It is composed of two separate bins containing the same parts, with one bin placed behind the other. When the first bin empties, the next full bin slides down.

The empty bin becomes the kanban signal or trigger visually indicating that the bin needs to be replenished. The empty bins are then collected, taken to the stockroom (or sent back to the supplier), and refilled. The new bin of materials is then returned to the original location in the area. This is called a withdrawal-kanban system.

Kanban systems regulate the inventory in a production system as the volume or rate of the process changes. The kanban system can be a one-bin system as well if the parts are replenished every day. Normally in a one-bin system, the bins are refilled to the top, or a water level, as one might refill bread in a store.

In some areas, parts are scanned into a bar-code terminal as the quantity of supplies is taken. This information is passed immediately to the stockroom or supplier as data for replenishment. This is called a point-of-sale system.

Kanban systems can also utilize card systems. Kanban cards are normally paper-based cards in clear vinyl envelopes. They are used to disseminate three types of information.

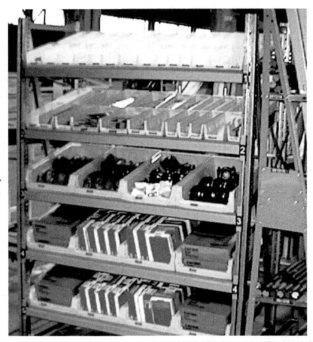

The operator draws from first bin then 2nd bin slides down. First binis signal to replenish. Operators could still draw from second bin but this bin setup is more clear. (vs. a work order or request) by the area to replace the parts in the bin.

Figure 5.40 Two-bin system. (Source: BIG Archives.)

1. Pickup information
2. Transfer directive information
3. Production directive information

This is the same when using bins. The back of the bins show the pickup information, the front of the bins show the production information.

In this system, the card is taken from the empty bin and placed in a holder (to be ordered). This is called a kanban post. At certain frequencies during the day, the team leader, material handler, or water spider comes and collects the cards in the post. The cards are used to reorder the parts from the supplier. Once the material is ordered, the card is placed back in the kanban post in the *ordered* slot (see Figure 5.41).

When the new bin of materials arrives, the card from the reordered slot is placed on the arriving bin of materials. The new bin of materials is returned to the original location in the area. This is called a withdrawal-kanban system.

Some jobs have non-common parts. For these jobs, we must create a special-order kanban card. These cards are typically generated once for a work order.

Kanban systems have two major failure modes:

1. First, the kanban system was originally designed in the plan for every part (PFEP) to support a certain maximum volume or customer demand. If this volume is exceeded, there will be parts shortages.
2. Second, if kanban cards are lost, inventory will not be replaced. If there are too many cards in the system to begin with, it will create excess inventory.

Figure 5.41   Kanban post. (Source: BIG Archives.)

Every book has a different formula for calculating the size and number of kanban (see Figure 5.42). The simplest way to consider sizing a kanban is to think about a two-bin system. When the first bin empties out, the second one slides down to replace it. How much material do we need in the second bin? The answer is as much material as it takes to replenish the first bin and place it back behind the second bin. In addition, we need a small buffer of material to cover us in the event something goes wrong and the bin does not get replenished right away, which we define as buffer stock.

We also carry some extra parts just in case there are quality issues, which is called safety stock. It is normal to carry a small percentage of the overall quantity (up to 10%) to cover safety and buffer stock. The goal of initial kanban systems should be 12–20 inventory turns the first year and 40–60 by the third year.

How Do You Know If It Should Be a Kanban Part?

The simplest way is to consider any part for kanban which has a consistent demand over a user-defined period and will not be obsoleted. This may be daily, weekly, monthly, or sometimes even quarterly. Parts that are considered special orders or ordered only once a year are not good candidates. For parts that repeat frequently we use average daily demand to divide into the lead time plus safety/buffer stock and for parts used infrequently we use peak demand. While this is a broad generalization, in order to minimize inventory and reduce stock-outs, we look at the cost of each part and each part as a separate case to determine what and how much to keep in stock.

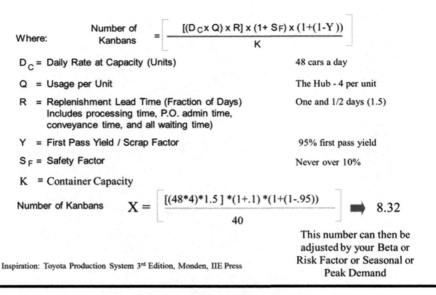

Figure 5.42   Sizing kanbans—kanban calculations. (Source: BIG Archives.)

Transition to Lineside Materials

Lineside materials are generally in two-bin containers or in slotted sequence to the line. In an office, this includes any tools needed to do the job at that station, such as a stapler, a three-hole punch, or a two-bin stack of blank paper. Lineside inventory can be sized differently for different applications, but the normal rule of thumb is to start out with a day's worth of product in each lineside bin. For large or bulky parts, this may require replenishing every hour or sometimes even every cycle (assuming longer cycle times). For mixed-model lines, we may have parts for each model on a different row of shelves, or we may have shelves that roll up to the line. The goal is to determine what will work best for your situation and to make the operator's job easy.

The material warehouse or supermarket on the shop floor is composed of parts kept next to or near the line to feed the lineside materials. The end goal is to eliminate these parts and have the vendor supply right to the line (vendor-managed products). Ideally, these would be flow-thru racks like the lineside racks, but this is not always possible.

There are two main strategies for the warehouse. It can be next to the line or in a centralized area off the line. Each strategy has pros and cons.

1. If the warehouse is next to the line, it is easier for the team leader or group leader to see all their materials. The disadvantage is that it does add space to the cells, so that each cell has a space for the warehouse in between the lines.
2. If the warehouse is centralized, it allows the cells to be placed closer together, but it is a longer walk for the water spider and team or group leader to check on their parts. Many times it requires the purchase of a train or small parts truck (see Figure 5.43).

Our next step during implementation is to set up and label the warehouse materials. Labeling of supplies and where they are placed, such as shelves and bins, is important because our goal is

Figure 5.43 Supermarket parts train. (Source: BIG Archives.)

to never search for a part or tool. Labeling shelves should include a designation for the rack, shelf row, and position on the shelf row. In the example in see Figures 5.44 through 5.46, the location for the top left box is A1A, that is, rack A shelf, row 1, in position A on the shelf.

Labeling the bins is important. The front bin location should match the shelf location. This is true whether they are for the material warehouse or the lineside materials. The back of the bin tells how or where the bin is resupplied.

Labeling is an important part of visual controls and is a critical component when implementing Lean initiatives to help eliminate the waste of searching. Some racks are not conducive to lineside inventory.

This type of hanging rack (see Figure 5.47) cannot be easily replenished from behind, which requires us to interrupt the operators to replenish the materials.

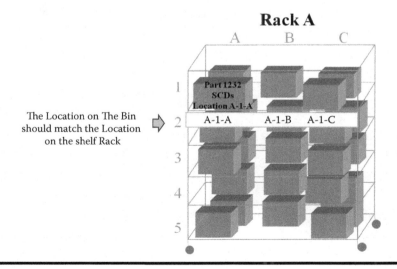

Figure 5.44 Material warehouse rack labeling (racks can be labeled from the top or the bottom). (Source: BIG Archives.)

Figure 5.45 Front-bin labeling "to address." The location on the bin should match the location on the rack whether it is lineside or warehouse. (Source: BIG Archives.)

Figure 5.46 Back-of-bin labeling is the "from address." This tells you where to replenish it from the warehouse. Notice the warehouse location normally starts with a "W" for warehouse. (Source: BIG Archives.)

Figure 5.47 The problem with this type of shelves is that bins cannot be replenished from behind and are difficult to setup as two-bin systems. (Source: BIG Archives.)

Figure 5.48 Mistake-proofing elements help point out metric parts versus English unit parts. (Source: BIG Archives.)

Mistake-proofing elements can also be incorporated into bin labeling, for example, highlight metric versus English measurement systems or color codes (labels or bins or both) with geometric shapes (for color blindness) for common parts, or different model types (see Figure 5.48).

Water-Spider Process

A non-starter in manufacturing is to use your assemblers or machinists to get their own parts or tools. We must keep operators operating, thus we add material handlers or water spiders.

The water spiders (see Figure 5.49) replenish the parts when the bin is empty or when triggered by a kanban card. This means the operators can continue to work on the product and not have to worry about replenishing their own stock. Some hospitals, such as ACMH in Kittanning, Pennsylvania, use friendly, constantly monitored AGV (automatic guided vehicles) robots (see

Figure 5.49 Water spider replenishes parts, checks on BOM "special" parts availability and other jobs as needed. (Source: BIG Archives.)

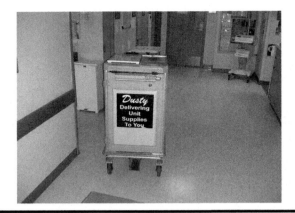

Figure 5.50   Dusty the AGV at ACMH hospital in Kittanning, Pennsylvania. (Source: BIG Archives.)

Figure 5.50) as water spiders to make deliveries. The goal is to enable staff members not to be interrupted or inconvenienced by having to search for supplies; this increases productivity and efficiency in the area.

Toyota uses AGVs to automatically load and unload lineside racks. This is part of their SPS system established several years ago. We have seen this system in operation at Toyota in Japan.

In assembly, water spiders are used to replenish lineside materials from the materials warehouse. They are also used to sometimes perform offline tasks or to relieve for restroom breaks. They can be used to print out labels for orders and used to help with changeovers on assembly lines.

They can also be used to make sure incoming jobs (kits) have all the proper parts and quantities and stage those parts on the line where required. Water spiders can be a skilled or unskilled position.

Types of Containers

There are various categories of containers. They are:

■ Recycle (grind up and reuse)
■ Reuse (use the same container repeatedly)
■ Re-Purpose (figure out how to use the container in a totally different way or application)

Reusable containers make sense (see Figure 5.51) and are more than just friendly to the environment. The reusable containers eliminate all the packaging, which used to come with the parts.

Think of how much time and money is wasted each year, packaging up parts in bags, then small boxes, and then larger final shipping boxes. The receiving company also wastes time unpackaging the parts. Many times, the parts end up on the line in the plastic bags in which they were shipped. What does this do to efficiency? The first thing the operator must do is remove the parts from the bag and dispose of the bag. They will normally batch this task versus doing it in a one-piece flow, so the line shuts down. There are companies that now have zero landfill waste. Lean is green!

**Figure 5.51 Reusable containers—no packaging to remove—Lean has always been "green."
There are three types of containers: reuse, recycle, repurpose. (Source: BIG Archives.)**

Breadman Systems

Breadman is a term normally applied to parts consigned or vendor-managed and centralized in one or several locations within the plant. These parts are normally replenished by the water spiders/material handlers.

Vendor-Managed Inventory

This inventory is in the manufacturer's or customer's facility but still owned by the supplier or manufacturer, respectively. The difference between this and consigned inventory is this inventory level is physically managed by the supplier.

Plan for Every Part (PFEP)

For an example of PFEP, see Figure 5.52. This term was first coined in 2003 in the book *Making Materials Flow*. The basic idea is to literally plan each part in terms of usage, locations, replenishment quantities, container sizes, and supplier information, and in many companies, we add how the part is planned if it is in MRP.

We only utilize the data necessary for the implementation. The vision for the PFEP is to create a pull system from the customer through the supply chain where we have the following:

- Level-loaded demand
- All parts vendor-managed and at POU
- Shop-floor control system removed from MRP
- All material triggers come from kanban

Part #	Number used to identify the material in the facility	Find
Description	Material name (e.g., frame, bolt, nut, yoke)	plan
Daily Usage	Average amount of material used in a day	
Usage Location	Process/areas where the material is used (e.g., Cell 14)	▶ R
Storage Location	Address (location) where the material is stored	
Order Frequency	Frequency that the material is ordered from the supplier (e.g., daily, weekly, monthly, as required)	
Supplier	Name of the material supplier	
Supplier City	City where the supplier is located	
Supplier State	State, province, region, or district where the supplier is located	
Supplier Country	Country where the supplier is located	
Container Type	Type of the container (e.g., expendable, returnable)	
Container Weight	Weight of an empty container	
1 Part Weight	Weight of 1 unit of material	
Total Package Weight	Weight of a full container of material	
Container Length	Length or depth of the container	
Container Width	Width of the container	
Container Height	Height of the container	
Usage Per Assembly	Number of parts required for 1 finished product	
Hourly Usage	Maximum number of pieces used per hour	
Standard Container Quantity	Piece count of material in 1 container	
Containers Used Per Hour	Maximum number of containers required per hour	
Shipment Size	Size of a standard shipment in days (1 week shipment = 5 days)	
Carrier	Company providing parts-transportation services	
Transit Time	Travel time required from the supplier to the facility (in days)	
# of Cards in Loop	Number of pull signals that are in the system	
Supplier Performance	Supplier performance rating that includes on-time delivery, quality, etc.	

Figure 5.52 PFEP example. (Source: *Making Materials Flow*, Rick Harris, Chris Harris, Earl Wilson, LEI, © 2003.)

There will always be some parts that do not fit this vision and still must be managed by MRP. We are literally looking at each part to determine the triggering strategy whether it be: Kanban, MRP, min-max, or other.

It is a tool that gets all the information about each part in one spreadsheet on one row. In the past, a multitude of screens or reports had to be run to glean the same data we now have in one row on the PFEP.

The PFEP provides a mechanism to track and determine the parts needed, the current demand, and the current-state inventory information. We need to know where they are located, how many will be replenished, and have a buffer plan to ensure that supplies will be available to meet peak demand.

Peak demand is extremely important to consider especially if your sales teams have promotions or large-lot discounts, etc.—all the things that get in the way of level loading.

Our experience is it is better to err on the side of too much inventory in the beginning and then to wean yourself off it rather than trying to cut the turns so low that you run out. If the kanban runs out, the "I told you so"s will surface and the effort may fail. Until you can get rid of the peaks, you must consider them in the demand and kanban sizing. We generally add a small buffer of supplies, called safety stock, to cover this risk (see Figure 5.53).

Developing the PFEP is very time-consuming but so worth the effort. One can have IT set it up to feed monthly or more frequently by MRP system. We utilize the PFEP to integrate the kanban information for each line as well as highlighting where adjustments are required due to changes at the master-schedule level or in customer demand.

It is important to have an owner assigned to the PFEP updating process to ensure the kanban sizes are adjusted based on changes in mix or demand. The goals/benefits of the PFEP are to:

■ Decrease lead times by 80% or more
■ Set up pull-type production, ordering Kanban systems for finished goods
■ Decrease inventory throughout the plant and significantly increase inventory turns
■ Free up warehouse space and cash, but this can impact short-term profitability

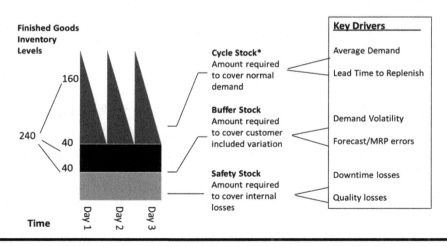

Figure 5.53   Buffer and safety stock. (Source: BIG Archives.)

Measuring Inventory and Cash Flow

Most companies track inventory dollars; however, it is typically not very accurate even though they think it is. Many times, inventory is not truly based on earliest due date (EDD) or FIFO; much is obsolete; some is damaged, mislabeled, or stocked in the wrong location; and many times, the amount you have is not what the system says you have.

Days of Supply (DOS)

To determine a day's worth of inventory, we must calculate the inventory used over a specified period and divide it by the number of days in the period. For example, if a department has $6 million in RM inventory and they use an average of $1.2 million per month, we would take $1.2 million per month and divide by 30 calendar days per month:

- $1,200,000 ÷ 30 calendar days = $40,000 average per calendar day. If we take the $6,000,000 supply inventory on hand,
- $6,000,000 ÷ $40,000/day = 150 calendar days of supply (DOS). Once we have DOS, we can calculate inventory turns:

Inventory turns = calendar or annual working days ÷ DOS. For example,

365 days in the year ÷ 150 DOS = 2.43 turns per year.

In the PFEP, we will use the most recent pricing and multiply by average daily part usage to determine a day's worth of supply. Using the formulas previously, we can determine a true day's worth of usage for any product line or program.

ABC Classification

Parts can be classified into various types, which is called ABC stratification. Companies have different definitions for ABC classifications. Experience has proven over and again that the Pareto rule applies to parts classification. We have found that typically 20% of parts account for 80% of inventory dollars, usage, and suppliers.

By examining and understanding this distribution, we can implement phased-in strategies to manage and lower our inventory costs. ABC analysis can be performed using either dollars or usage as a criterion or a combination.

We normally build both usage and dollar analysis into the PFEP. Parts are generally classified in two ways: either by individual part-dollar value or overall part usage by volume or by total dollar value.

We start out managing "A" parts down to the week with a goal to manage them down to the day or hour. This is easy to do as it is relatively few parts and suppliers. We start managing "B" parts to two weeks with a goal to move toward one week and then days (and eventually hours).

We like to look at "C" parts as parts initially at the one-month level and move toward weeks, and then days. We then work toward moving the "C" parts from capital to expense, which removes the "C" parts from MRP pick lists and treats them as floor stock or expense parts. The parts still appear on the router. The "C" parts are normally screws, fasteners, wire connectors, etc., and are prime candidates for breadman and later-material warehouse or lineside VMI.

True Partnering with Suppliers

The goal is to move suppliers from the typical antagonistic environment to one where the supplier becomes a true partner or an extension of your facility. The goal with Lean is to develop and nurture a partnering supply base, which means the supplier literally becomes an extension of your company, like any internal manufacturing or transactional area.

True partnered suppliers do not cut margins but work with their customers to reduce their costs. The goal is to keep your partners as viable sources by maintaining reasonable profit margins. Partnered suppliers will respond immediately to production problems. They work together to secure and maintain the business of the end customer.

Long-Term Agreements (LTAs)

LTAs are annual or multiple-year contracts with partnering suppliers. The goal is to lock in the best pricing with a long-term quantity and quality commitment but only take material as it is needed. LTA may have any of the following components:

- Can range from 1–5 years.
- A fixed price is the norm; however, time and material contracts can work for some services but as a last resort.
- Some escalation factor built in, that is, price of precious metals pegged to an index, with rebates if certain thresholds are met and there are options for pricing for additional years.
- Continuous improvement requirements.
- Lean assessment components.
- Flex fences.
- EDI and Logistics terms.

LTAs should have built-in quality requirements with the goal of zero defects. Suppliers should have ongoing requirements/challenges to reduce the cost of the product, whether it is through design or taking waste out of their processes.

It is important to make sure your suppliers are financially viable. Electronic data interchange (EDI) refers to the ability of supplier and customer computer systems to talk to each other. It eliminates the need for paper purchase orders or other paper-based transactions. EDI systems will allow the supplier to see the customer's part usage. There are also electronic and internet-based kanban systems, i.e., Nocturne, available in the market today.

Flex Fences

Flex fences is a concept that provides flexibility to an LTA. Flex fences examine the overall horizon of the agreement and add in risk mitigation plans in the event the projected volume was to increase by 10%–30% or reduce by 10%–30%. For example, we may pay the supplier to keep extra raw

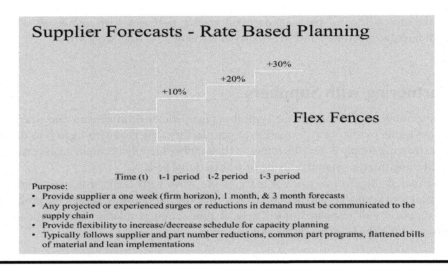

Figure 5.54 Flex fences. (Source: BIG Archives.)

materials on hand so we can increase our volume by 30% over a specified period. We may arrange with our supplier to have 10% of the material just about completed all the time in case our volume increases rapidly (see Figure 5.54).

Supply Sequencing

Part of LTAs may involve sequencing of parts to fit the supplier's assembly line. This typically involves loading the parts in reverse order, so when they are offloaded, they are in the correct order. Supplier sequencing is generally supplying to the automotive industry where delivery is measured to the hour.

Forecasts

Forecasts are a necessary component of any materials system. However, we always say an accurate forecast is an oxymoron.

The problem with forecasts is the longer the forecast horizon, the less accurate it usually is. The goal of just in time (JIT) is to reduce the cycle time to allow a forecast in days or weeks versus months.

Early Supplier Involvement (ESI)

Engaging suppliers early in any of your Lean initiatives, with the goal to decrease inventory, can save significant dollars and should be a part of the overall materials cost-reduction strategies. Once suppliers are engaged and partnering with your facility, they should receive feedback (sometimes in the form of report cards) on their progress for quality, cost, delivery, and service (QCDS) improvements.

This process involves the supplier very early on but generally after the concept phase. These suppliers are true partners working with design-to criteria, with cost and value engineering targets set by their customer.

Certified Supplier Program

Certified suppliers generally have met the quality, production, and financial criteria necessary to support bypassing receiving and incoming inspection and can deliver directly to the floor using a breadman stock, kanban warehouses, or lineside material process.

Risk Mitigation Plans

These plans are paramount in the event there is an unforeseen problem with a supplier's order. This is especially true at a strategic team, commodity team, or LTA level. The supplier should have this as part of their agreement. Another term for this is developing a failure modes and effects analysis (FMEA). This tool looks at all the things that could go wrong and the likelihood of it going wrong and the severity or impact if it does go wrong, and what corrective actions can be put in place in the event the unexpected happens.

Implement Mistake-Proofing

Six Sigma tools are designed to measure, highlight, and eliminate defects with a focus on reducing errors to Six Sigma or 3.4 defects per million. Many organizations use statistical process control (SPC); however, SPC will not ensure zero defects, since the defects are usually detected after they are made (historical data). SPC should be used as a preventive tool to identify patterns before an out-of-control condition happens. In a truly Lean environment, abnormalities should be clearly and immediately visible in the workplace and fixed in real time. Lean requires defect-free processes to support a just in time (JIT) system, thus the goal of Lean is 100% defect prevention at the source. If this is not the case, then the system breaks down and delays occur.

Mistake-proofing, also known as poka yoke in Japanese, is a critical component of Lean and provides a mechanism to eliminate the errors so defects won't occur.

The only way to prevent defects from escaping to the customer is to inspect 100% of the parts at each operation by machine, not human, which leads to the concept of jidoka.

The only way to obtain zero defects is to eliminate the error before it occurs. Therefore, it is important to understand the difference between an error and a defect. An error is a mistake that is made; a defect is a problem that occurs because of the error. Dr. Shingo often referred to this as the importance of separating cause from effect. An example would be as follows:

■ (Cause) Error—leaving the lights on in the car
■ (Effect) Defect—the car battery died.

There are basically three types of defects:

■ Materials
■ Processing
■ Design

When dealing with cause and effect, it is important to understand the difference between common-cause and special-cause variation. For example, if one were to drop a penny on the table, it will end up in one spot. If you drop it again from the same location, it will end up in another spot. This is an example of common-cause variation. The penny is going to land within some range of different spots.

If, however, we move the drop location, it will land in a different spot. This is a special-cause action. Many times, in a process, we will see a result that is not the norm and assume it is a special cause when in fact it is within the normal range of variation. If we then take a special-cause action, we will probably upset the norm.

If Six Sigma Is 3.4 Defects per Million, What Sigma Level Are Humans?

Errors and mistakes cost all of us money and, more importantly, the reputation of our companies. We must take caution if humans are doing any job, since humans are at best one to three sigma. Three-sigma quality (with the 1 1/2 sigma shift) is approximately 66,000 mistakes per million opportunities. As long as the process depends on a human, the system will probably never get better than two or three sigma because humans make mistakes. To mistake-proof or foolproof processes, we need a way to take the humans out of the equation. Mistakes and errors not only cause human tragedy but also add expensive hidden costs to our manufacturing systems.

Process Capability (CPk)

Process capability is the measure of the ability of a process, product, or service to consistently meet specifications (customer specifications or company tolerance limits). The most widely adopted results for process capability are as follows:

- CPk > 2.0 means the company has good control over their process but still not zero defects.
- CPk > 1.67 as minimum standard most companies use. Still need 100% automated visual inspection.
- CPk > 1.33 = minimum acceptable with goal to continuously improve. Still need 100% automated visual inspection.
- CPk ≤ 1.33 but > 1.00 = inadequate—must be continuously monitored. Still need 100% automated visual inspection.
- CPk = 1.0 just meets specifications.
- CPk ≤ 0.67 = totally inadequate as a supplier or process.

The goal of jidoka is to stop the machine before it crashes or makes a mistake and, worst case, *after* it makes a mistake. If the equipment is not able to meet and exceed the machine specifications, then jidoka may not help improve quality other than shutting the machine down constantly for parts that don't meet the spec.

Poka Yoke and Baka Yoke

See Figure 5.55.

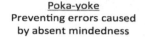

Poka-yoke
Preventing errors caused
by absent mindedness

Baka-yoke
Preventing errors when the standard is
beyond human ability

Figure 5.55 Poka yoke versus baka yoke. (Source: https://www.linkedin.com/pulse/re-translating-lean-from-its-origin-jun-nakamuro#a11y-content.)

Baka yoke means preventing errors when the standard is beyond human ability or mistake-proofing. Poka yoke means preventing errors caused by absent mindedness of foolproofing. A poka yoke is any mechanism in a Lean process that helps your team members avoid mistakes. Its purpose is to eliminate product defects by preventing, correcting, or drawing attention to errors as they occur (see Figure 5.56). In the example, Figure 5.57, when the cotter pin is removed, the shadow of it remains.

Poka yoke can be applied to any process, whether shop-floor or transactional. The first step to poka yoke is self-inspection. This is where each operator inspects his or her own work.

The second step is successive-check inspection, where each operator inspects the work of the previous operators in addition to his or her own work.

The next level is 100%-inspection at the source by machine, and the last step is to mistake-proof the operation. Listed below are the steps to implement poka yoke:

(Plan)

Describe the defect or *potential* defect.

Figure 5.56 Mistake-proofing device for assembly to make sure consumable bottles are placed in correct holes in tray. (Source: BIG Archives.)

Figure 5.57 Painted cotter-pin example. When the cotter pin is removed you see the shadow of the cotter pin. (Source: BIG Archives.)

- Use observation, video, or statistics (i.e., Pareto chart) to identify the opportunity for a defect or, more important, for the cause (error) to occur.
- Show the defect rate.
- Identify the operation where defect is or can be discovered.
- Identify where the defect is made and what is the standard.
- Run the gap through the 5 Whys.
- Become the thing in the process. Detail the sequence of events documented in the standard. Watch the operation being done and detail the steps that differ from the standard. Understand the ways a process or a machine can fail.
- Brainstorm solutions; involve everyone.
- Decide the right poka-yoke approach. Identify the mistake-proof device required to prevent the error or defect.
  - Control device (prevent an error)
  - Warning device (highlight an error was made)

A poka yoke can be electrical, mechanical, procedural, visual, human, or any other form that highlights or prevents errors during a process step.

(Do)

Train the operator if necessary and implement the poka yoke.

(Check)

To make sure it is working.

(Act)

Update the standard work (if necessary) or process documentation.

Depending on the device, determine if any preventive or predictive maintenance is required and add to the total productive maintenance (TPM) checklist.

Types of Control and Warning Devices

Warning devices alert the operator to a problem but don't prevent the error or the defect. Control devices shut down the operation or don't allow it to proceed until it is corrected. Each category, control, and warning contain the following three methods:

Contact Device:

Contact is established between the device and the product:

- Plugs
- House and car keys
- Camcorder batteries

Fixed-value Method:

- Part must be a certain weight, or it won't work
- Lot size
- Egg carton

Motion Step Method:

- Product must pass inspection before proceeding to the next step
- Barcoders
- Garage-door sensor beam
- Motion detector lights design-out defect

The ultimate goal is to eliminate errors by designing products or processes Lean. The Lean tools and Six Sigma tools integrate well; however, Six Sigma tools are only a stepping stone to zero defects. The other secret to eliminate mistakes is to have a system that rewards surfacing the mistakes.

Design the Control Plan

We shouldn't need a control plan if our processes are capable (CPk) of making good parts all the time. However, even with Lean, control strategies are needed, as it is difficult to mistake-proof 100% of the opportunities where errors can occur even though that is the goal. The goal of the engineer is to design the product to be error-free before, during, and after assembly, beginning at the concept stage. The worst types are those defects that are unknowingly designed into the system.

Developing the control plan (see Figure 5.58) at this stage is consistent with Dr. Shingo's approach (vs. Deming) where it becomes part of the plan phase of P(control)DCA. The control plan is a spin-off of the process block diagram. At this stage, we need to ask ourselves for each process box the following:

Quality Control & Improvement Plan

Product / Process:			Approval 1 - Product / Date:								Current Expected Number of Defective Units per Day		0
Lutron Location:			Approval 2 - Process / Date:								Current RTY (Rolled Throughput Yield)		0%
Date:			Approval 3 - Quality / Date:								Future RTY (Rolled Throughput Yield)		0%

Figure 5.58   Control-plan template example. (Source: Andy McDermott & BIG Archives.)

- Who owns the process?
- What is the process capability?
- How do we make sure we are starting on a good part?
- How do we know we are not passing on a bad part?
- What are the critical inputs for the process box to obtain the Big Y (Six Sigma calls these Xs).
- Can we physically stop the process if it goes out of control?
- Do we have a review process as part of PDSA if the process goes out of control?
- Do we have visual controls in place?
- Will the process make itself immediately visible if it goes out of control?

The control plan differs from the FMEA or PFMEA. The control plan is put together after the product is launched and works to increase first time through (FTT) and rolled throughput yield (FTY) to 100%.

Mistake-Proofing Designs

Mistake-proofing should be considered throughout the design process:

- Simple inspection methods and mistake-proofing should be designed in.
- Every operation should be designed in such a way that we never pass on a bad part (i.e., built-in quality at the source or process level). The goal should be to eliminate the need for final inspection.
- Always make sure the parts can be installed only one way versus any way.

Focus on the process to get the result and do the right thing regardless of the ROI.

Zero Defects and Machining

The machine should be process capable of making zero defects, and, in the event it has a problem, should shut down and signal the shutdown with an andon light and or music or noise to make the problem immediately visible. This is one of the principles of jidoka and, in some cases, the machine can be set to text the person responsible when the machine goes down.

Implement DFMA

The motivating factors for using a DFA (design for assembly) and DFM (design for manufacturability) in the early stages of the product design are to cut the cost to produce and to reduce the complexity of assembly and fabrication. As we begin to use these methodologies, we soon realize that the product manufacturing efficiency improves dramatically. Cost and time are the common denominators, which is why most in the engineering and manufacturing community embrace design for manufacturability methods in product design.

Using DFM will guide us toward a product with fewer parts and a more efficient production line. DFM gathers all the attributes of manufacturability and quantifies them into data that can be calculated into usable metrics. We can utilize the metrics to compare different design scenarios and ensure intelligent choices and decisions will be made. The inventory turns of a company is rarely a concern of the designer during the product development, but it should be. R&D should own the product from concept to end of life. General guidelines to consider are as follows:

- Don't tie operators or customers to machines
- Semi-automate where possible
- Provide easy-to-use fixturing for operators
- Design-in mistake-proofing
- Eliminate, simplify, and combine wherever possible

We have found over and over that wherever one can video the process, we discover steps we don't find when we walk through a process with a supervisor or even the employees that do it every day. They simply forget the steps they do. When we record video, review it with the operators, and compare it to what they told us, they are surprised that they left a step out. Sometimes you will hear, "that doesn't normally happen." But our experience shows that if you capture it on video, it probably happens much more than anyone thinks or cares to believe.

Implement Total Productive Maintenance (TPM)

TPM stands for total productive maintenance and is a combination of the following:

1. *Preventative Maintenance*

    Preventive maintenance is completing routine tasks at set intervals to prolong the life of the equipment and to prevent breakdowns from happening in the future.
2. *Predictive Maintenance*

    Predictive maintenance is performing tasks based upon a historical pattern of breakdown or wear, or you can use a technology solution to predict exactly when the tire is going to go bad. Many technologies exist in the marketplace today that were not available 20 or 30 years ago. These technologies are utilized by NASA and the military. They include ultrasound and Sonics testing, infrared thermography, and vibration testing. In many cases the technology can determine if a motor bearing needs just lubrication or is going to fail in the next 30 days.

3. *Participative Management—Autonomous Maintenance*

   Participative management is employee involvement resulting in a productive maintenance program carried out by all employees. TPM is, in effect, equipment maintenance performed on a company-wide basis, and there are five goals of an effective TPM plan:

   a. Maximize equipment effectiveness (improve overall efficiency)
   b. Develop a system of productive maintenance for the life of the equipment
   c. Involve all departments planning, designing, using, or maintaining equipment in implementing TPM to include engineering and design, production, and maintenance
   d. Actively involve all employees from top management to shop-floor employees
   e. Promote TPM through motivational management (autonomous small group activities)

TPM involves everyone in the organization, from top management to the team member on the floor. With TPM, the team members share in the maintenance and upkeep of the equipment and complete day-to-day checklists (adding oil to a machine, changing over reagents), and the maintenance team ensures the complex items are completed to support operation schedules.

The analogy used is taking care of your car. You wash it, check the fluids, and put gas in it, but when there is a big problem, such as a transmission overhaul, you take it to a mechanic. As the car owner (process owner), you still own the timely completion of the maintenance or repair.

In a Lean enterprise, the team members, whether working on the shop floor or in the office, become the frontline for maintenance when reporting problems or making minor fixes to machines.

Discipline is necessary to implement and sustain a TPM program. The process owners need to ensure the equipment is maintained in their areas. Accountability and pride are required to ensure the machines are operating as planned and designed. If not, it reflects their ability to truly lead and own their area. We should clean our machines daily and check the gauges to make sure the fluid levels are proper and look for opportunities to improve the machine.

Management must remove all roadblocks to successful completion of the assigned TPM tasks by their employees. Consider painting the floors a light gray or white color to show any oil leaking from machines and then have someone not just fix the leak but root-cause the leak. Figure 5.59 shows machine-log examples to assist the TPM process. The goal is always to fix the problem so it never comes back, otherwise we can assure you it will when you least expect it.

Report of Idle Machine Time Fig. 316

Week ending ____________

Machine No.	Operating Hours	Idle Hours	Idle Time Burden Rate	Cost of Idle Time	Reason
A1	42	2	.40	.80	No job card
A2	43	1	.40	.40	" " "
A3	43	1	.40	.40	" " "
A4	41	3	40	1 20	Breakdown
A5	44	-	-		Full Capacity
B1	39	5	1 05	5 25	No job card
B2	41	3	1.05	3.15	" " "
C1	43	1	.75	.75	" " "
C2	40	4	.75	3.00	Repair
C3	42	2	.75	1.50	No job card
Total	418	22		16.45	
Cost of idle time last week				48.30	

Remarks: Planning department is to take immediate action to see that job cards are provided on time.

CCS Manual Page 234

Figure 4-14 Machine Down Time Report

Machine Problem / Opportunity Investigation

Note: Once Problem is Corrected This Sheet Should Stay With The Machine for Future References

Machine	Zone:
Supervisor	Cell No:
Date	Process
Manufacturer of Machine	
Manufacturer Contact and Phone Number	
OEE	

Follow Up Responsibilities (Most Important)	**Date**	**Responsibility**
Person Responsible to Follow Up Countermeasures:		
Person Responsible to Follow Up Countermeasures Six Months Later:		
Machine Drawing/ Description		
Part Numbers Impacted		**Program**
Symptoms Caused By: (note: become the machine)		
Countermeasures Taken	**Date**	**Responsibility**
Do We Need to Contact the Manufacturer?		
Followed Up To See If Countermeasures Corrected Root Cause		
Follow up Six Months Later	**Date**	**Responsibility**
Followed Up To See If Countermeasures Corrected Root Cause		

Figure 5.59 Machine downtime logs. (Source: *CCS Training Manual,* Charles Protzman Sr. and Homer Sarasohn, 1952, Diamond Press and BIG Archives.)

Total Productive Maintenance Goals

- Eliminate unplanned machine downtime
- Increase machine capacity
- Incur fewer defects (scrap or rework)
- Reduce overall operating costs
- Allow for minimum inventory
- Increase operator safety
- Create a better working environment
- Improve environment and sustainability
- Eliminate breakdowns
- Reduce equipment startup losses
- Faster more dependable throughput
- Improve quality

Six Big Losses In A Factory (See Figure 5.60)

The six big losses in a factory are listed below:

1. Availability.
2. Equipment failure (breakdown losses)—downtime resulting from machines breaking down.
3. Setup and adjustment (setup losses)—downtime caused by setup times.
4. Idling and minor stoppage losses that result from uneven workflow or short stoppages due to detection of defective products.
5. Operating rate—reduced speed machine is running slower than it was designed to.

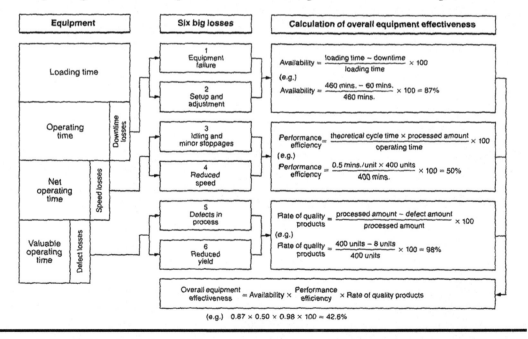

Figure 5.60 TPM—six big losses. (Source: *Introduction to TPM***, Seiichi Nakajima, 1989, 1998. Productivity Press.)**

6. Defects produced: Quality
   - Defect in process (defect losses)—waste that occurs when defective products must be thrown out or reworked.
   - Reduced yield (yield losses)—result of constant stopping and starting of equipment, including the loss from startup to stable production.

Factors Resulting in Machine Losses

Listed below are factors resulting in machine losses. The first are factors leading to machine troubles:

- Dirty machines
- Dirty oiler
- Flooded oil pan
- Oil leakage
- Empty oiler
- Overheated motor
- Uncontrolled vibration
- Scattered chips
- Difficulties in inspection
- Dirty floor
- Lack of organization

Factors Related to Operators

- Not concerned about dirty machine
- Mistakes made in operation, changeover, and maintaining
- Have no knowledge of inspection
- Incapable or unwilling to conduct easy maintenance
- Lack of knowledge of the machine itself—oiling, tool change, parts change, adjustment, etc.
- Do not ask for help even when problem exists
- Consider production more important than good machine maintenance
- Do not have control over machines

These factors, by definition, are all controllable by the process owner.

Factors Related to Mechanics and Maintenance Crews

- Replace or repair parts, but do not question why trouble occurred or root-cause the problems so they never come back.
- Do not train or work with operators on basic/easy maintenance task.
- Do not effectively communicate with operators.
- Focus efforts on major urgent troubles and forget about dealing with quality-related problems and loss of machine speed.
- Consider machine deterioration as unavoidable.
- Seek solutions in new machines or new technologies rather than in available resources. These factors and behaviors are all owned by the maintenance-process owner.

TPM Metrics Goals

Zero Breakdowns

TPM is just in time (JIT) for machines, as the machine must be ready when you need it and for however long you will need it. If not, we cannot support one-piece flow goals and meet production targets.

Part of this JIT strategy for TPM dictates the creation of a spare-parts list and on-call contact lists located at the machine, which include in-house and supplier contact information for repair and service, as well as timing (escalation protocols) based on what is happening on the machine or in the area. If one does an FMEA and a breakeven analysis, one can determine the optimum level of spare parts to carry on hand.

TPM Daily Checklist

The best way to start TPM is by creating simple checklists for just one pilot piece of equipment. Next add TPM-related metrics to the processes to ensure they are being carried out properly (see Figure 5.61). As more confidence is gained and sustained, then add the next piece of equipment. We recommend there be something the operator has to fill out, i.e., machine setting, or readout, to ensure they are actually checking. In the future, we are working on manufacturing electronic systems (i.e., internet of things—IOT 4.0), MES systems with sensors tied to motors, and air systems to automate the checking.

There must be a written process tied to ISO or QS9000 or some other formal standard documenting the process like a TPM card (see Figure 5.62). The TPM card describes how the machine is to be maintained and documents the maintenance of the machine.

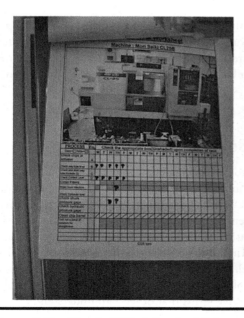

Figure 5.61   Simple TPM daily checklist example. (Source: Courtesy of Ancon Gear.)

 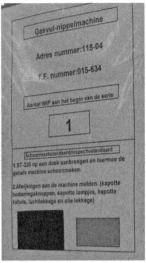 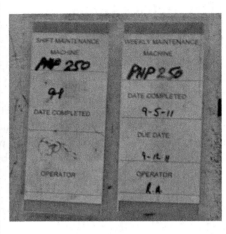

Figure 5.62 TPM cards—green is complete/red is pending. (Source: BIG Archives.)

Overall Equipment Effectiveness

The goal of overall equipment effectiveness (OEE) is to take metrics that individually might look good and review them together (see Figure 5.63). The metrics are the following:

■ Scheduled available time (any unplanned downtime or changeover time counts against this)
■ Operating rate or speed at which the machine is designed to run
■ Quality (the percentage of good parts manufactured per specification)

If one is going to utilize OEE, it is imperative that the proper data are collected and proper data collection procedures exist; otherwise the OEE analysis is based on faulty data. The machine operating rate should be based on the manufacturer's recommended speeds and feeds for the machine. It should be a cycle time–driven metric not based on some historical output or compared to a standard that hasn't been updated in years.

Rapid Kaizen Improvement—See, Solve, Tell

Rapid kaizen is a phrase we started using to help people "learn to see" simple improvements. It is an improvement that can be implemented with 30 minutes and requires no capital or purchases. We teach the team to use the PDSA process versus throwing solutions at a problem. After their observations the team or individual writes the problem statement and root cause. This allows us to teach them to "learn to solve." After the implementation of the improvement we have them report out. Here is the catch—they only get five minutes. This allows us to teach them "how to tell." This is a critical part of the learning. It allows us to coach people on how to close the communication loop and tell a simple story from the heart instead of the brain. Once they can connect with the heart, the story becomes natural and is spoken in simple terms that others can understand.

Defects	Overall Equipment Effectiveness (OEE) Calculator*		
Machine	OEE is a measure of the value added to production through equipment		
Slowed Down	Do not enter blue numbers. Blue numbers are preset formulas		
	A	Working Minutes Per Day	480	Actual time per day or per shift
Unplanned	B	Loading Time Per Day = Available Time (Min)	420	Actual time less time taken for meetings, breaks, lunch
Downtime	C	Total Output Per Day (Good and Bad Units)	15,300	Actual output per day from day by hour chart
		Types of Downtime		
	D	Setup	90	Time from last good piece to first good piece
	E	Breakdowns	60	Any time equipment is stopped due to breakdown
	F	Adjustments	15	Any time equipment is stopped due to adjustments
	G	Total Downtime Per Day	165	(D+E+F)
Time	H	Defects	153	# defects in total output per day from day by hour chart
Spent	I	Actual cycle time	0.0200	Measured at the machine via watch or videotape
Making	J	Ideal cycle time	0.0160	Cycle time the machine should be running per manufacturer's specs or speeds and feeds
Good	K	Operating Speed rate	80%	Ideal cycle time / actual cycle time (J / I))
Parts	L	Net Operating Rate	120%	[(Output per day x actual cycle time) / (loading time - downtime)] [(C x I) / (B - I)]
	M	Availability Rate	61%	[(Loading time - downtime) / loading time] [(B - G) / B)]
	N	Performance Rate	96%	Net operating rate x operating speed rate (L x K)
	O	Quality Rate	99%	[(Total output - defects) / total output] [(C - H) / C]
	P	**OEE**	**58%**	(Quality rate x performance rate x availability rate) (O x N x M)

* Based on TPM Development Program, Nakajima, Productivity Press, 1982

Figure 5.63 OEE calculator. (Source: BIG Archives.)

Key Formulas

Listed in Figure 5.64 are key formulas we have discussed in the book for your reference.

Takt Time = Available Time / Customer Demand

Available Time = Total Time less breaks, meetings etc. (weekly meetings are amortized across the days (i.e. 25 min meeting per week = 5 min per day))

Cycle Time = Total Labor Time / Number of Operators (if there is no machine bottleneck)

Cycle Time = Available Time / Factory Demand

Cycle Time = The amount of labor each operator has assuming line is balanced (if there is no machine bottleneck)

Number of Operators Required = Total Labor Time / Cycle Time (or Takt Time)

Total Labor Time = labor value added plus labor non value added time

Complete Time = labor value added plus non labor value added plus machine value added plus machine non value added

Capacity = Available Time / Complete Time

Hourly Output = 3600 sec /hour divided by the cycle time in sec

Daily Output = hourly output times available time in hours

Interruptible Work in Process (WIP) = Cycle time of the machine / cycle time or takt time of the line. If it is non interruptible then double interruptible quantity

Standard WIP = Throughput Time / Required Cycle Time

Kanban sizing = Total amount needed to cover replenishment time (includes production and delivery) plus safety stock plus yield / container size

Figure 5.64 Key formulas. (Source: BIG Archives.)

Chapter 6

BASICS Model: Check (C)

The C in our BASICS model stands for Check. The importance of "checking" is to make sure the improvements we implemented are working and sustaining (see Figure 6.1).

A System of Checks

We must build in checks to make sure the new process is meeting our expectations and to continue looking for additional improvement opportunities. We need to make sure we have active metrics in place that surface any problems within the process.

Many times, we can use similar tools to the day-by-hour chart in the office as well as the +QDIP board to monitor the process real time and implement countermeasures and root cause corrective action as necessary. It is also important to build as much of the documentation and standard work for the resulting transactional processes into ISO9000 type systems or configuration control-systems to ensure the new processes become part of the system. This way, as leadership changes, the system will not, which is part of the learning organization we are ultimately striving to create. Check includes the following:

- Do you know how to check?
- Check using the visual-management system.
- Heijunka and scheduling.
- Mixed-model production.

Do You Know How to Check?

Every company we work with has problems with inspection. When we start drilling down into why or how someone is checking, we normally find they don't know or if they do know how to check, they don't know why they are doing it that way. In many cases we are told the check is part of the quality documentation; but again, when we drill down, sometimes we find the documentation is missing or doesn't exist.

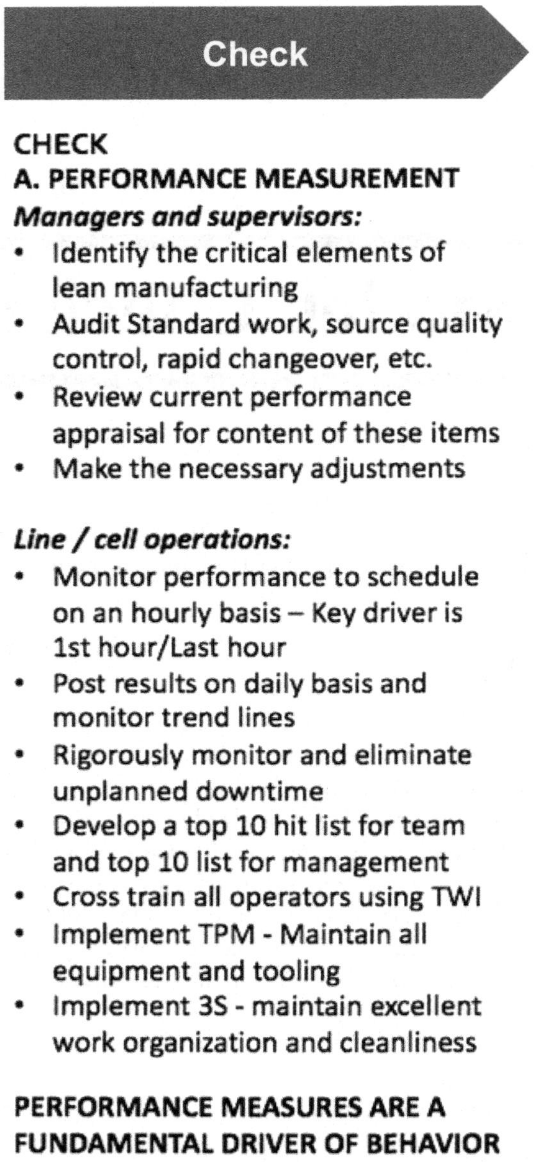

> **Check**

CHECK
A. PERFORMANCE MEASUREMENT
Managers and supervisors:
- Identify the critical elements of lean manufacturing
- Audit Standard work, source quality control, rapid changeover, etc.
- Review current performance appraisal for content of these items
- Make the necessary adjustments

Line / cell operations:
- Monitor performance to schedule on an hourly basis – Key driver is 1st hour/Last hour
- Post results on daily basis and monitor trend lines
- Rigorously monitor and eliminate unplanned downtime
- Develop a top 10 hit list for team and top 10 list for management
- Cross train all operators using TWI
- Implement TPM - Maintain all equipment and tooling
- Implement 3S - maintain excellent work organization and cleanliness

PERFORMANCE MEASURES ARE A FUNDAMENTAL DRIVER OF BEHAVIOR

Figure 6.1   The BASICS six-step model for Lean implementation—check. (Source: BIG Training Materials.)

Most of the checking is done via training by another person. In this case we find the checking is different because different people (trainers) do the check differently based on what they think is best.

So our advice is to always question what, how, and why we are checking. In the end, if we have to check, we don't trust our process and they are not capable. Checking is very expensive for companies and because humans are doing it; the checking is not reliable.

Exposing the Gaps

Finding and exposing the gap is a very important concept. If we can create a system in our companies to expose the gaps, we can surface the problems and establish targets for improvement. In a factory, we paint the floors and walls a light color. This way it makes any leaks immediately visible. In the office, we will setup visual controls and Obeya boards/rooms, which we put in place to make problems immediately visible.

Gemba Walks—Go and Watch

Gemba walks are at the heart of checking and also sustaining. The purpose of a gemba walk is to "check" in order to discover abnormalities and use these gaps for coaching, challenging, and developing your people. This is also part of developing a problem-solving culture.

Get out of your office and walk around. Conduct audits, talk to employees, and encourage suggestions, and ask employees how you can help. Create visual metric boards in each area (not in computers) and eliminate all the unnecessary reports. This not only demonstrates your desire to understand what is happening at the gemba, but also shows that you are "walking the talk" and you will gain your employees' trust and respect. Eat lunch with your employees. Encourage them to think; do not give them all the answers. Ask them what their metrics are, discuss Lean concepts with them, and most importantly, listen!

Questions You Can Ask When Doing a Gemba Walk

- What is the standard? Is there a gap?
- What are your challenges, problems, and issues?
- What have you improved today?
- Audits: Are they up to date?
- How does the material flow?
- Why is there so much WIP here?
- Please explain to me how the product flows?
- Why are you batching here?
- Please show me your standard work. (Note: You should be able to see it.)
- Where are your visual controls? (Note: If you can't see them, they are not there.)
- How many suggestions has the team implemented this month? How have they helped you personally?
- Do you have all the tools and materials you need?
- What are you learning?
- Do you like your job? Why or why not?
- What can the company do to help our team members more?
- How can I help you?

Visual Management and Checking

Visual management is a system we discussed earlier, but it is critical to checking and sustaining. In a visual management system there are devices installed to detect or prevent defects or injury from occurring. The goal of a good visual-management system is to make abnormal conditions immediately visible using the tools referenced previously; 5S, visual displays and visual controls, and taking the premise one step further by incorporating root cause, countermeasures, andon, risk mitigation, TPM, and mistake-proofing.

A good visual-management system connects all the Lean tools and allows problems no place to hide and prevents defects from occurring in the first place. The goal of the system is to prevent or mitigate the defect. Implementing a good visual-management system means one must eventually integrate the following:

■ +QDIP
■ Andon
■ TPM
■ Jidoka
■ Implement a problem-solving culture to fix gaps

MES Systems

With the advent of Industry 4.0 many companies are now implementing MES manufacturing execution (electronic) systems. These systems build in sensors to automatically check for abnormalities 100% of the time. For TPM we can even install sensors to detect problems in motors, air systems, i.e., cooling towers, etc., to let you know up to 30 days ahead of time when a bearing may need to be lubricated or replaced.

The advantages to these systems is a human no longer has to go around and "check" all the time. Checking is non–value-added. Now the machines can tell us immediately if there is a problem.

Andon

Andon is a form of signaling device (see Figure 6.2). It can be visual (see Figure 6.3) or audible in the form of an electronic counter, kanban signal (see Figures 6.4a and b), or clock, buzzer, or even music. The goal is to create a visual management, so anyone can walk around the area and know exactly what's going on and how the area is doing without asking anyone. The area should be constantly speaking to you.

Uptime or downtime clocks (see Figure 6.5) can be very helpful when working with machines to include TPM and daily production activities. The andon system and clocks can easily be tied to CNC controllers to show when the machine is working and when it is idle.

The goal of the visual-management system should be to eliminate the need for the human to check and replace it with a machine, i.e., sensor detection, and then communicate the problem to us via a signal, i.e., light, music, sound, text message, WeChat, etc. Please keep in mind, it is still checking, which means we ultimately don't trust the process.

Poka Yoke

Implementing poka yoke, i.e., mistake-proofing, eliminates the need to check, unless there is a need to check the poka-yoke device itself. This is the best path to sustaining.

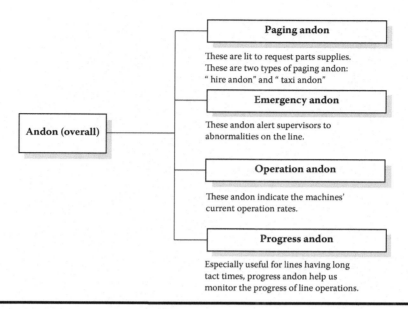

Figure 6.2   Four types of andon. (Source: The Visual Factory.)

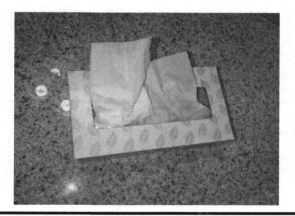

Figure 6.3   Tissue box. The darker color tissues show the end is near. (Source: BIG Archives.)

The Five Whys

Once we have the problem statement, we need to analyze the problem and identify the symptoms or point causes. One of the basic techniques leveraged when problem-solving is using the Five Whys. This widely used tool (see Figure 6.6) involves asking the question "Why?" The number five is suggested because "why" usually takes up to five times, at least, to get to the root cause of the problem. In our experience the hardest part of the Five Whys is getting people to do it properly. Many people jump to conclusions after the first one to three "whys" and don't reach the true root cause.

Figure 6.4 (a) Andon—counter. (Source: BIG Archives.) (b) Visual signal for replenishment, also visual displays in pricing and signage, etc. (Source: BIG Archives.)

Figure 6.5 Downtime clock wired into PLC. (Source: BIG Archives.)

Problem Statement: The pool is cloudy and has sediment in the bottom

1. **Why** The filter DE sediment is getting into the pool
   – Because the DE sediment is bypassing the valve
2. **Why** Why is it bypassing the valve
   – The valve is corroded
3. **Why** is the valve corroded
   – Because the water from the well is too acidic and is corroding it
4. **Why** is the water to acidic
   – Because the water is not filtered going to the pool
1. **Why** is the water not filtered going to the pool
   – Because we bypassed the filter when the pool was installed

Figure 6.6   Five Whys—real-life example. (Source: BIG Archives.)

5W2H: Another Great Tool to Get Rid of Waste

The 5 Ws are composed of asking: When? Where? What? Who? and Why? The 2 Hs are How? and How much? (See Figure 6.7).

The following questions apply:

- When is the best time to do it? Does it have to be done at a certain time?
- Where is it being done? Why is it done here?
- What is being done? Why are we doing it? Can we eliminate this work?
- Who is doing it? Would it be better to have someone else do it?
- Why is the work necessary? Clarify its purpose.
- How is it being done? Is this the best way to do it? Are there any other ways to do it?
- How much does it cost now?
- How much will it cost to improve?

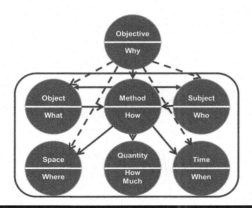

Figure 6.7   The 5 Ws and 2 Hs. (Source: Modified from *The Shingo Production Management System*, Shigeo Shingo, 1990. Productivity Press.)

Fishbone, Pareto Charts, and Lean

The fishbone tool is one of the basic TQM tools that helps identify the point causes and is somewhat of a graphical Five-Whys tool. It works by putting the problem at the head of the fishbone, then brainstorming and categorizing all the reasons for the problems (see Figure 6.8).

The first layer of problems, which are placed on the main branches of the fish, is normally only the point causes or symptoms of the problems we see. We then ask, why? For each major branch, which creates sub-branches. We continue to ask why, until we reach the bottom branch or hopefully the root cause.

This tool provides a way to see all the problems in an area at a glance. The fishbone is a great tool for collecting, categorizing, and root-causing feedback from staff.

A Pareto chart is a chart that contains a bar graph and a line graph such that the individual values are shown in descending order by bars, and the cumulative total is shown by the line. The left vertical axis is usually the frequency of occurrence and the right axis is the cumulative percentage of the total number of occurrences. The purpose of the Pareto chart is to highlight the most important factors and is used for root-cause analysis to focus on the most common sources of defects or the highest occurring type of defect. A Pareto waterfall chart is combining the Five-Why tool by creating multiple Pareto charts until the root cause is detected (see Figure 6.9).

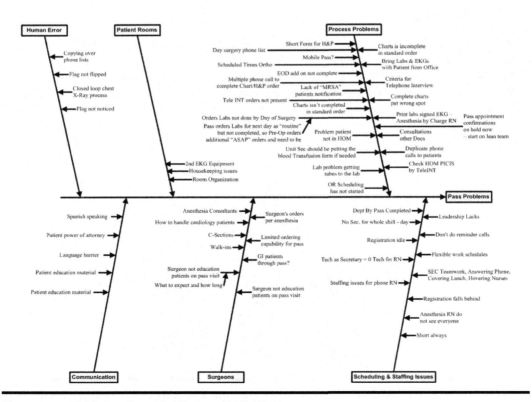

Figure 6.8 Fishbone example. (Source: BIG Files.)

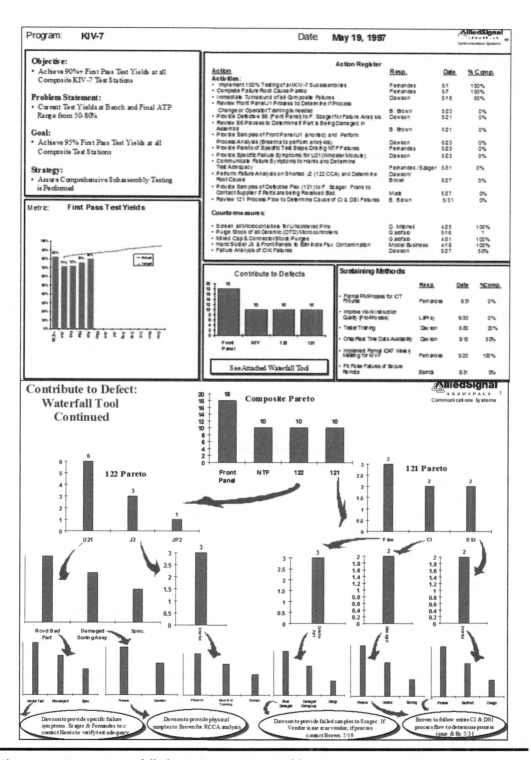

Figure 6.9   Pareto waterfall chart. (Source: BIG Archives.)

Heijunka and Scheduling

We have put heijunka and scheduling into the "check" category. We feel this is part of checking the ability of the company to level-load and where necessary handle mixed-model production. It starts with predicted capacity, as we discussed earlier in the PPCS section.

"Demonstrated Output Capacity"

We find at most companies that capacity is no longer based on any formal type of calculation but is normally based on the supervisor's experience. We developed a term for this phenomenon, which we call "demonstrated output capacity."

"Demonstrated output capacity" is when companies or departments use their actual daily or weekly demonstrated output totals as a measure of what they feel they can produce and to which they subsequently schedule.

This is opposite scientific methods like time and motion study, or published speeds and feeds, which would define exactly what should be produced. Ninety percent of companies we work with, including government and healthcare, initially have metrics based on "demonstrated output capacity."

Many companies use standard costs and earned hours to set and monitor their capacity and efficiency. The fallacy with this is the standards are seldom updated or are just plain wrong.

Scheduling Issues

Often our need to meet the end-of-the-month goals forces us to pull in shipments from weeks or sometimes months outside our current planning horizon, which creates chaos in the factory. Another issue with scheduling comes when we convert our systems over to kanban. The idea behind kanban is that the kanban signal triggers the replenishment. However, when companies insist on using material requirements planning (MRP) to trigger the orders, the kanban systems will not work properly and will not sustain.

Build to Order versus Push Production versus Pull Systems

In build-to-order systems the products are not made until an order is received. Most companies use some type of enterprise resource planning system. Within that system is a master schedule and an MRP or some type of shop-floor control system. These systems consolidate requirements, order materials, and release scheduled orders based on lead-time offsets.

Lead-time offsets are the lead times put into the system for the supplier, receipt, inspection, manufacture, etc. This creates what we call a "push"-type system. In this system, MRP (based on the planner's review and approval) is the "trigger" for the order. The work orders are released and then scheduled in the various work centers in the shop.

If the company triggers each order based on the shipment of a previous order where the shipment creates the trigger, this is considered a pull system. If the pull is from finished goods, then it is not a true "build-to-order" system, but it is still considered a "pull" system.

Takt—Flow—Pull

In Lean, there is a saying: takt ... flow ... pull, which is short for implementing a Lean system.

This means understanding the customer demand and that everything starts with the customer. Once we know the customer demand and our available time, we can calculate our takt time.

Establish flow within the factory (or service company) from raw materials to finished goods/shipping in accordance with the beat of the takt time.

Create a pull system with synchronized linkage to our customer and supply chain. As they use our parts, they let us know in real time, which then triggers an order at our workshop. The orders at the workshop then trigger orders throughout our supply chain. This system embodies JIT, jidoka, and the respect for humanity-based Lean culture (see Figure 6.10).

Production Sequencing Example

A key concept for level loading is production smoothing, which involves taking the production schedule and averaging it into daily or even hourly demand. Let's review an example: Let's say an automotive company uses a press to make parts for multiple vehicles. This concept of leveling the weeks' worth of production into smaller daily lots is called heijunka or production smoothing (see Figure 6.11) . For instance, if we have a weekly demand for part A of 1000 pieces, part B of 750 pieces, and part C of 250 pieces, we can perform a mathematical equation of dividing each part quantity by five (to obtain the daily demand). For part A, this means we need to produce a quantity of 200 pieces per day $(1000 \div 5)$; part B, 150 pieces per day $(750 \div 5)$; and part C, 50 pieces per day $(250 \div 5)$ (see Figure 6.12).

Figure 6.10 Shipping trigger board at Dana Corp connected directly to Toyota. Every time Toyota completes a car, a light turns on, on this board. Twenty-five lights signal means 25 car chassis to leave Dana. (Source: CNN News Footage Video.)

Products	Monthly Demand	Daily Demand	Takt Time
A	4,800	240 units	120"
B	2,400	120 units	240"
C	1,200	60 units	480"
D	600	30 units	960"
E	600	30 units	960"
	9,600 units	480 units	60"

Sequence Alternatives: **Segmented Batch**

Monthly 4,800 - As / 2,400 - Bs / 1,200 - Cs / 600 - Ds / 600 - Es
Daily 240 - As/ 120 - Bs / 60 - Cs / 30 - Ds / 30 - Es
Hourly 30 - As / 15 - Bs / 7.5 - Cs / 3.75 - Ds / 3.75 Es per hour

Mixed Model

Hourly 1- 2- 3- 4-5- 6-7-8- 9-10-11-12-13-14-15-16-17-18-19-20-21-22-23-24-25-26-27-28-29-30
A B A C A B A C A B A D A B A E A B A C A B A C A B A D A B
A E A B A C A B A C A B A D A B A E A B A C A B A C A B A D

Figure 6.11 Converting monthly scheduling to sequencing schedule. (Source: BIG Archives.)

	Weekly Demand	# working days per week	Daily Demand
Part A	1000	5	200
Part B	750	5	150
Part C	250	5	50

	Weekly Demand	# working days per week	Daily Demand	Time to Produce per Piece (Seconds)	Minutes Required to meet Daily Demand	FPY	Extra Parts Required	Number of Parts Needed based on FPY	New Cycle Time Minutes
Part A	1,000.0	5.0	200.0	60.0	200.0	0.99	2.0	202.0	202.0
Part B	750.0	5.0	150.0	67.0	167.5	0.90	16.8	166.8	186.2
Part C	250.0	5.0	50.0	46.0	38.3	0.98	0.8	50.8	38.9
Totals	2,000.0		400.0		405.8		19.5	419.5	427.1

Figure 6.12 Production smoothing example—calculating daily machine-time based on FPY. (Source: BIG Archives.)

When we implement heijunka for a press, line, or a plant, we must routinely review the assumptions and ensure that the actual performance meets the planned assumptions. If not, then we have the choice of either correcting the variance by problem-solving and implementing corrective actions, or as a last resort after we have exhausted our improvement opportunities, we then adjust our assumptions.

Shop-Floor Scheduling without Using the MRP System

One of the first things we do is turn off the shop-floor control sections of MRP when we implement kanbans. In Figure 6.13 one can see a simple pull system installed at final assembly. This system was designed with no kanban cards. Everything was triggered using visual controls (i.e., outlined squares on the floor, shelf gas gauges, and two-bin systems).

Once a unit goes to final assembly, it pulls from the paint kanban, the paint kanban pulls from the welding kanban, which pulls from the machine-shop kanban, which pulls from the raw-material kanban, which sends a signal back to the supplier to replenish. We also had 80% of their materials set up on VMI (vendor-managed inventory).

Establishing Flow: Order Staging Rack in Place

Once the Lean line is implemented, it is important to make sure that you are working on what is really needed. The first step is to set up a work-order scheduling rack. Some people refer to this as a heijunka rack, however, this is a misnomer; we are in effect starting to level-load the workshop. We often use a heijunka or sequencing box (see Figure 6.14) as a visual control to know when to act or how we are doing according to the plan. These boxes generally have slots that represent time. It could be hours within a day or days within a month. The box is typically stored in the shipping area where the pull is started from finished goods.

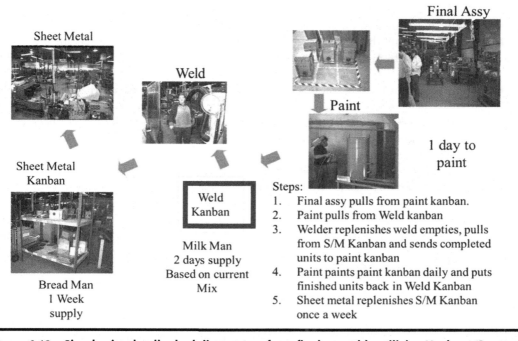

Figure 6.13   Simple visual pull scheduling system from final assembly utilizing Kanban. (Source: BIG Archives.)

Figure 6.14 Heijunka-box examples. (Source: BIG Archives.)

Scheduling Board Rules

Once the Lean line is implemented, it is important to make sure that you are working on what is needed. An initial step to setting up heijunka is starting with a visual scheduling system. The rules are:

- Planning will provide a weekly schedule to the team leaders.
- Planning will walk the floor with the team leader two times a day to review the progress of the work orders from the shipping area to final assembly, to welding, to machining, and to raw material.
- Planning will put the work orders in the visual work-order boards on the appropriate day based on the start date.
- Planning may change the work-order schedule only if the work order has not been pulled from the work-order scheduling board. Once a work order is started in the cell, it may not be stopped to start another.
- No work orders are to be put in the scheduling-board queue if they have part shortages.
- The planner and team leader are responsible to make sure that the parts are available when needed for final assembly and the staging areas with no shortages.
- Planning is responsible to create a visual queue at each machine to show what work order is in process and to determine a way to label the work in process with the appropriate work-order number.

Pitch

Pitch is the time required to supply a standard pattern of parts to a line. Pitch is calculated by multiplying the takt time (or cycle time) by the number of pieces in the pattern of parts needed for the line, which is normally a shipping box or container-size (see Figure 6.15).

Figure 6.15 Pitch marks for Boeing 737 line. (Source: Cordatus Consulting, Boeing 737 manu-facturing [video]. https://www.youtube.com/watch?v=-y0U1Qux9EA&list=PL0C5BB2A293DC D7DE.)

Capacity and Load

When determining capacity and the load on the factory, there are certain calculations we must consider. Many times, the load is based on machining hours or percent of a work center that is scheduled. Our first calculation is of excess capacity.

$$\text{Excess Capacity} = \left(\text{Capacity Load}\right)/\text{Capacity}$$

What if load exceeds capacity? If load exceeds capacity, then we must review each machine and determine if we can offload to another machine, look at speeds and feeds, look at setup times and overall equipment effectiveness.

We may have to investigate, adding a shift or working over lunches and breaks. We also some-times use a group-tech matrix to find "families" or groupings of parts, which allows us to increase capacity by reducing the number of changeovers.

Planning and Scheduling Tips

- Implement in phases.
- Consider using finished goods kanban if factory or process cannot produce make to order.
- Develop a level-loading strategy, internal and external.
- Get sales/marketing on board. They must understand the system and the need for real infor-mation (i.e., no more "padding" delivery times). Review sales strategies; does it make sense to offer a discount or price break anymore?

- Whenever you make more than you need, it prevents you from making what is really needed.
- Eliminate buffers, reduce inventory, and change MRP lead-time offsets after you have proven you can meet customer demand.
- Develop failure-modes effects analysis or risk-mitigation strategies for each process/machine.
- Keep scheduling systems as simple as possible or no one will follow them.
- Work the excess WIP off, starting closest to the customer.
- Remember, if you dry up the line, you will lose output the next cycle.

Mixed Model Production—Production Sequencing

In manufacturing, production sequencing is utilized to level out production of various or "mixed" models. This concept allows Toyota to run multiple car-types down the same line, one model after another. This can be accomplished only with flexibility built into the layout, equipment, utilities, and people.

The idea behind this concept is to schedule products evenly to avoid batches of products coming in at one time. In some areas of companies, this is easy to do, and in some areas, it may be nearly impossible to do.

This mixed-model concept could be interpreted as running multiple types of a product family at the same time. To properly sequence activities within an operation, one must understand the order of the activities and, in most cases, the information flow.

The process-flow analysis gives us this data, and then we combine it with the "amount of demand" and "type of demand" in products or services to determine the sequence. Figure 6.16 shows a sequencing worksheet.

Weekly Robot Scheduling Sheet For Product X

Model	Model Type	Available Time Hours / Min/ Sec		7.4	444	26640			Takt Time Minutes	246.7							

Model Size	RF	RG	RN	RLF	RLG	RLN	SRS	Total Weekly Demand	Total Daily Demand	Takt Time Sec	Takt Time Minutes	Takt Time Hours	Sequencing Based on TT	Pass 1	Pass 2	Total Daily	Total Weekly	Variance from Weekly	Notes
3.0	6		6	6		6	1	25	5.0	5,328	88.8	1.48	2.8	3.0	2.0	5.0	25.0	0.0	
4.0	13	1		6				20	4.0	6,660	111.0	1.85	2.2	2.0	2.0	4.0	20.0	0.0	
5.0	5		4					9	1.8	14,800	246.7	4.11	1.0	1.0	1.0	2.0	10.0	-1.0	once a week run 0 on second pass
6.0	11	1	11					23	4.6	5,791	96.5	1.61	2.6	3.0	2.0	5.0	25.0	-2.0	once a week run 1 on first pass
8.0	2	2	7					11	2.2	12,109	201.8	3.36	1.2	1.0	1.0	2.0	10.0	1.0	once a week pass 2 = 2
10.0				0				0	0	-	0.0	0.00	0.0	0.0	0.0	0.0	0.0	0.0	
12.0				0				0	0	-	0.0	0.00	0.0	0.0	0.0	0.0	0.0	0.0	
Totals								17.6	1,514	25.2		9.8	10.0	8.0	18.0	90.0	-2.0		

Sequencing for Model	3.0	4.0	5.0	6.0	8.0	9.0	10.0	Totals
First Pass	3.0	2	1	3	1			10.0
2nd Pass	2	2	1	2	1			8.0
Total Daily	5.0	4.0	2.0	5.0	2.0			18.0

Robot Machine Time	430	840	1250	1660	2070	2320	2638	
Robot Time Minutes	7.17	14.00	20.83	27.67	34.50	38.67	43.97	
Robot Time Per Size	35.8	56.0	41.7	138.3	69.0	0.0	0.0	340.8
Percent of capacity based on Avail Time								76.8%
Cell should be running (hours)								5.68
Assembly Time Sec (from time study)	2847	3244	3702	4012	4429			
Bottom head, 1st stage, 2nd stage, prep Time Minutes from System	47.5	54.1	61.7	66.9	73.8			
# people required	6.6	3.9	3.0	2.4	2.1			

Figure 6.16 Sequencing worksheet. (Source: BIG Archives.)

Mixed-Model Changeovers

We must compare the batch flows to the Lean flows. Let's assume that there are six people on the line when batching. Whenever a model changes over, the rest of the line keeps running while the first station changes over. This is the same for the second station as it changes over and so on.

Available time Hours	7.5								
	Station	Operation Description (what they do)	Model 1	Model 2	Model 3	Model 4	Model 5	Model 6	
1	Operation 1	11.0	11.0	11.0					
2	Operation 2	16.0	16.0	16.0					
3	Operation 3	40.0	40.0	40.0	54.0	42.0	54.0	42.0	
4	Operation 4	33.0	33.0	33.0	29.0	29.0	29.0	29.0	
5	Operation 5	25.0	25.0	25.0	31.0	31.0	31.0	31.0	
6	Operation 6	60.0	60.0	60.0	33.0	32.0	33.0	32.0	
7	Operation 7	50.0	50.0	50.0					
8	Operation 8	5.0	5.0	5.0	7.0	7.0	7.0	7.0	
9	Operation 9		14.0	14.0		14.0	14.0		
10	Operation 10	12.0	12.0	12.0	10.0	10.0	10.0	10.0	
11	Operation 11	19.0	19.0	29.0	9.0	9.0	9.0	9.0	
12	Operation 12	19.0	19.0	19.0	19.0	19.0	19.0	19.0	
	Total Labor Time Seconds	290.0	304.0	314.0	192.0	193.0	206.0	179.0	
	Total Labor Time Minutes	4.8	5.1	5.2	3.2	3.2	3.4	3.0	
	Units Per Hour 1 person	12.4	12.4	12.4	12.4	12.4	12.4	12.4	
	Units per Day	93.1	93.1	93.1	93.1	93.1	93.1	93.1	
	Units Per Hour 2 persons	24.8	23.7	22.9	37.5	37.3	35.0	40.2	
	Units per Day	186.2	177.6	172.0	281.3	279.8	262.1	301.7	
	Units Per Hour 3 person	37.2	35.5	34.4	56.3	56.0	52.4	60.3	
	Units per Day	279.3	266.4	258.0	421.9	419.7	393.2	452.5	
	Units Per Hour 4 person	49.7	47.4	45.9	75.0	74.6	69.9	80.4	
	Units per Day	372.4	355.3	343.9	562.5	559.6	524.3	603.4	
	Units Per Hour 5 person	62.1	59.2	57.3	93.8	93.3	87.4	100.6	
	Units per Day	465.5	444.1	429.9	703.1	699.5	655.3	754.2	

Figure 6.17 Mixed-model matrix example. (Source: BIG Archives.)

The definition of internal setup for a line like this is from the last piece completed on the last station to the first good piece of the next lot out of the last station.

When changing over a one-piece flow line, sometimes we must dry up the line each time. During the initial changeovers, no one knows what to do. The first station changes over and then the other five team members must wait for the other stations to change over. This time adds up and reduces line capacity and output.

The key here is to focus on quick changeovers for the Lean cell. The setup should be videoed and reviewed with all the operators and opportunities looked for to externalize as many tasks as possible, just like we would in a machine setup.

Mixed-Model Matrix

This figure shows what we call a mixed-model matrix. On the left side are all the different operations the product might see (see Figure 6.17). On top (x axis) is each of the model types. Then in each box is the cycle time per model per operation. When the operations are summed up for each model, it yields the TLT. This can then be divided by the number of operators to figure out the average cycle time and output per hour and per day.

Chapter 7

BASICS Model: Sustain (S)

The second S in our BASICS model stands for Sustain (see Figure 7.1). Sustaining means it is self-sustaining and improving. It means you don't have to check. It is not dependent on a person but is now part of the company's culture. It means we welcome audits and look forward to visits from any outsider that can highlight gaps and give us opportunities to improve.

Document the Business Case Study

Once we have completed the implementation we use the chrono file, which we have kept updated throughout each BASICS step, to put together the final summary and results of the project.

The Key to Sustainability—Why People Resist Change

We all resist change, it is our basic human nature. Some changes, however, are easier to accept than others. If you've ever noticed, change that agrees with our way of thinking is accepted easier, but we truly resist changes we consider as negative. If people around you don't buy into the Lean changes, and consider them as negative, what does that tell you for your chances of sustainment and long-term success?

$$\text{Back to the change equation} - C \times V \times N \times S > R_{change}$$

Think back to the change equation introduced earlier. Your organization has completed a project and is now at the sustain portion (or the S in the equation).

As we mentioned earlier, the sustainment portion is the hardest part. Undoubtedly this is not a new concept, as every book and teaching out there says the exact same thing. But why is it so hard?

Believe it or not, it references back to the same change equation we gave you earlier. If your C (compelling reason to change) wasn't truly compelling enough, then there's no way you can overcome the resistance to change. Remember, this was a multiplication equation, which means if the C becomes zero, the whole equation fails.

Sustain

SUSTAIN
A. DOCUMENT BUSINESS CASE
Compare base conditions with the projected lean condition:
• Output rates, Labor requirements (direct and indirect), Floor space, Inventory

Document cost of implementation:
• Capital, expense and training expenditures

Present findings to senior management:
• Include all stakeholders and decision makers
• Let the facts speak loudly
• Create concurrence on cost and schedule

Ongoing Daily Kaizen
• Use daily huddles to collect improvement suggestions
• Implement suggestions using PDCA
• Update Standard Work

Celebrate Success – recognize the Team
THIS REPRESENTS A SIGNIFICANT CHANGE IN HOW WE RUN THE BUSINESS

Figure 7.1 The BASICS six-step model for Lean implementation—sustain. (Source: BIG Training Materials.)

Is leadership continually using PDSA on their change equation to make sure that the organization is still on the same course of action and that the tools put in place match up with their compelling reason for change?

The other answer at the core of this sustainment issue is accountability and discipline. This starts with leadership but cannot solely rely on leadership. The system must be built upon these fundamental principles. Every operation put in place needs to ensure operators or leaders are accountable for their actions, held responsible, and given a consequence when they meet or fall short of their goals. Every action has an equal yet opposite reaction. If the workforce meets a goal, it is just as important to celebrate the success of the team or individual as it is to impose a negative consequence if we fail.

Below is a section that Fred Lee writes in *If Disney Ran Your Hospital**:

Accountabilities drive structure and structure drives culture. Because this concept is so fundamental and powerful, let me repeat that. Accountabilities drive structure and structure drives culture. Any leader who is striving to change the culture … would do well to ponder this key principle: You can't change the fruits of a tree without changing the roots. … but here is where I want to indicate how powerful Disney's simple principle of making courtesy more important than efficiency is. It strikes at a cultural root. Do you have a tree rooted in structures that support this rule, or do you have a tree rooted in structures that support primarily the fruits of unit efficiency?

But now we come to a surprising paradox: by putting courtesy and service first, our problem with phony efficiency virtually disappears. So do problems with communication and teamwork between departments. One rule, if followed by all departments, aligns the entire culture. Talk about an elegant model!

This means that we can actually get the fruits of overall corporate efficiency when we subordinate departmental efficiency for the sake of courtesy and responsiveness (the most important aspects of service). Figure 7.2 demonstrates the line of thinking behind this paradox. The ultimate shortcut to getting the best overall efficiency is to focus on service and make it more important than efficiency.

As long as department directors have to answer only for their own labor costs, cross-functional savings and teamwork are not likely to happen. And the waste will go unmeasured and unnoticed as it gets invisibly absorbed by the organization.

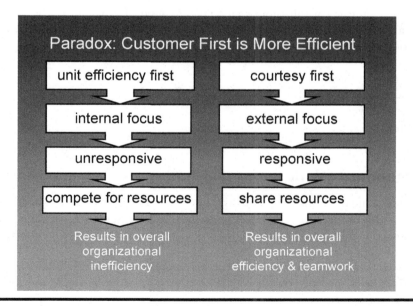

Figure 7.2 Line of thinking behind the efficiency paradox. (Source: *If Disney Ran Your Hospital: 9 1/2 Things You Would Do Differently* [Kindle Locations 765–770], Fred Lee, 2004. Second River Healthcare: Bozeman, MT. Kindle Edition, with permission.)

---

* *If Disney Ran Your Hospital: 9 1/2 Things You Would Do Differently* (Kindle Locations 765–770), Fred Lee, 2004. Second River Healthcare: Bozeman, MT. Kindle Edition. With permission.

Place service above efficiency, however, and the internal customer will speak up and document the waste caused by poor service delivery. Working together as internal service provider and customer department, these inefficiencies would be identified and addressed in a culture of teamwork and responsiveness instead of competition.

Again, this one rule can change the entire management culture more dramatically than 20 team-building retreats. What top management needs to figure out is how to foster a climate in which departments and their managers are held accountable and rewarded for service instead of being punished for it, as they would be under conventional hospital budget monitoring and accountability systems.

Sustaining Lean

The key to sustaining Lean isn't a separate step; instead, it's doing all the previous steps to the fullest. Sustainment isn't a separate concept or set of tools; instead, it is implementing the system and providing training with accountability and discipline woven throughout.

In order to sustain, one has to ensure that Lean gets built into your quality system and becomes part of the fabric of the organization. Companies must create a problem-solving culture and make sure systems are in place to problem-solve and update the standard work on an ongoing basis.

Creating the Lean Culture—The Four Things to Sustain Lean

It is interesting to note how we all know what it takes to build a Lean culture. The question is, why don't we do it? David Mann suggests in his book, *Creating a Lean Culture*,* there are four areas to focus on in order to create a Lean culture:

1. Leader standard work
2. Visual controls
3. Accountability
4. Discipline

Leader Standard Work

The concept of standard work extends to the leadership that supports the sustainment of the overall system. This means every employee, up to the CEO, has standard work as a basis for their jobs. The higher one is in the organization, the less standardized the work. David Mann describes leader standard work in detail:

"Whether you are a supervisor or CEO, you may wonder why you need leader standard work. One reason is it helps manage your day, and the other is to set an example and role model the behaviors desired from the rest of your organization."

Critical components of a Lean initiative are developing standard work for processes routinely performed, eliminating errors, providing role and task clarity, and decreasing variation within an activity, task, or process.

---

* *Creating a Lean Culture*, David Mann, 2005. Productivity Press: New York; 2013, 3rd edition, CRC Press: Boca Raton, FL.

Standard work must become part of the fabric of the workplace, which means it should be part of ISO, QS, or other standards that apply to your business. By ingraining the Lean processes in your formal policy and procedures, it will make it much more difficult to revert to the way it was before.

Once the Lean culture is in place, it is important when hiring to communicate the new Lean expectations during the initial interview. Each person must know from the very beginning they are expected to follow standard work and contribute daily improvement ideas.

Once developed and implemented, it is important to audit standard work. This ties into the CHECK part of our BASICS model (see Figure 7.3). Auditing is the job of the supervisor and leadership and produces what are called layered process audits. Once our initial Lean project is implemented, there are several sustaining tools including:

- Training within industry (TWI)
- 10-cycle analysis
- QC circles
- Point kaizen events
- Ongoing daily kaizen
- Company-chartered continuous improvement groups

The ultimate vehicle for sustaining, regardless of the approach, is capturing improvements in the standard work.

Ten-cycle analysis is the process of filming or observing a job for two to 10 cycles or more, and then obtaining the cycle times for each activity (see Figure 7.4). It is a great tool for auditing standard work or performing an operator analysis for machining or quick-cycle operations. The way the tool is designed, if one does not follow the standard work, it makes it immediately obvious. This is because it becomes difficult to fill out the 10-cycle analysis form since the operator is no longer performing the steps in the correct sequence.

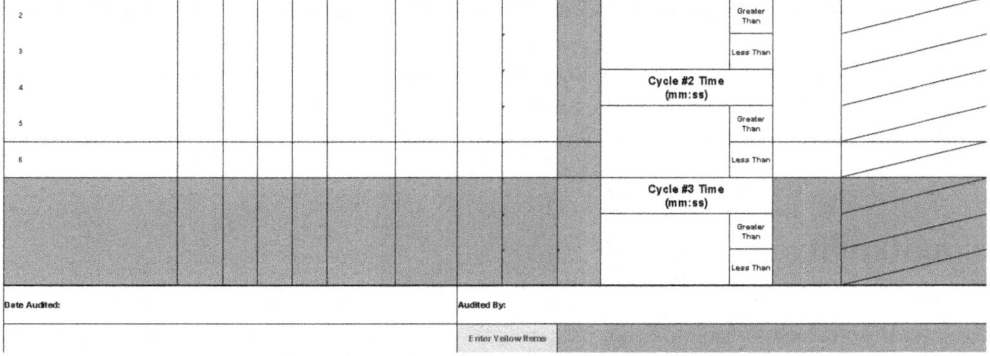

Figure 7.3 Standard work audit sheet. (Source: BIG Archives.)

NO.	Description		1	2	3	4	5 Revised flow	6	7	8	9	10	Maximum	Minimum	Average	Std. Dev.
	Total Operation Time	Cumulative	1:15:20	1:17:24	1:19:27	1:21:30	2:20:12						128	98	119.20	12.03
		Cycle Time	128	124	123	123	98									
1	Unload part	Alt. Start Time (optional)	1:13:12				2:18:34									
		Cum	1:13:28	1:15:33	1:17:35	1:19:40	2:18:45									
		Split Time	16	13	11	13	11						16	-5	12.80	2.05
2	Load part	Alt. Start Time (optional)														
		Cumulative	1:13:39	1:15:43	1:17:45	1:19:50	2:18:54									
		Split time	11	10	10	10	9						11	9	10.00	0.71
3	Cycle machine 1	Alt. Start Time (optional)														
		Cumulative	1:13:42	1:15:46	1:17:49	1:19:52	2:18:56									
		Split time	3	3	4	2	2						4	2	2.80	0.84
4	Walk to machine 2	Alt. Start Time (optional)														
		Cumulative	1:13:46	1:15:50	1:17:54	1:19:58	2:19:02									
		Split time	4	4	5	6	6						6	4	5.00	1.00
5	Load machine 2	Alt. Start Time (optional)														
		Cumulative	1:13:54	1:16:07	1:18:03	1:20:09	2:19:08									
		Split time	8	17	9	11	6						17	6	10.20	4.21
6	Cycle machine 2	Alt. Start Time (optional)														
		Cumulative	1:13:58	1:16:12	1:18:07	1:20:14	2:19:12									
		Split time	4	5	4	5	4						5	4	4.40	0.55
7	Wait	Alt. Start Time (optional)														
		Cumulative	1:14:10	1:16:24	1:18:19	1:20:26	2:19:24									
		Split time	12	12	12	12	12						12	12	12.00	0.00
8	Unload machine 2	Alt. Start Time (optional)														
		Cumulative	1:14:20	1:16:36	1:18:31	1:20:38	2:19:37									
		Split time	10	12	12	12	13						13	10	11.80	1.10
9	Walk to and place part in basket	Alt. Start Time (optional)					2:19:47									
		Cumulative	1:14:24	1:16:39	1:18:33	1:20:41	2:19:52									
		Split time	4	3	2	3	5						5	2	3.40	1.14
10	Walk back to machine 2 and remove trim excess and walk back to machine 1	Alt. Start Time (optional)					2:19:37									
		Cumulative	1:14:43	1:16:57	1:18:58	1:21:02	2:19:47									
		Split time	19	18	25	21	10						25	10	18.60	5.50
11	Oil next part	Alt. Start Time (optional)					2:19:52									
		Cumulative	1:15:06	1:17:22	1:19:25	1:21:28	2:20:10									
		Split time	23	25	27	26	18						27	18	23.80	3.56
12	Wait	Alt. Start Time (optional)														
		Cumulative	1:15:20	1:17:24	1:19:27	1:21:30	2:20:12									
		Split time	14	2	2	2	2						14	2	4.40	5.37

Figure 7.4 Ten-cycle analysis example. (Source: BIG Archives.)

Visual Controls

Visual controls, as we discussed earlier in the text, are of paramount importance to sustain Lean. Building in the ability to make the abnormal immediately obvious in all processes will highlight areas that need a quick countermeasure and then yield candidates for the PDSA cycle.

It is a given in this discussion that standard work is in place, and processes are stable and capable. The more visual the process, the easier it will be to manage and sustain the process. Visual controls should be part of our standard work.

Accountability

Accountability means you meet your commitments. We have a saying: "If you say you are going to do it, then do it; otherwise, don't say you are going to do it." It also means you will do the best job possible by the time promised. A culture of organizational accountability is critical to sustain Lean.

Once we implement Lean in an area, it should not only be sustained, but also continuously improved. There is a common phrase one often hears when discussing behaviors: "You get what you expect, you deserve what you tolerate." This saying reigns true throughout many of life's situations, including the workplace. Ultimately, as a manager or supervisor, "you get the behaviors you reward." This is part of systems thinking. These behaviors can be desired or undesired.

The goal is to convert the undesired to desired behaviors by changing the reward system. No matter what our role is in the organization, most of us want to understand what is expected and be empowered to achieve it.

To be successful, we must provide clear direction aligned with organizational priorities, and create processes to do our jobs safely and efficiently. We need to be able to obtain the right tools and supplies to do our jobs and leave our employees feeling like they accomplished something and are part of a winning team. This is impossible to achieve if processes, areas, or people are out of control and processes are not standardized. The combination of Lean and change-management tools will help make us successful.

Discipline

Discipline is welcomed in Lean thinking and can be internal or external. From an external standpoint, it is following the rules, and if not, being subjected to some type of negative reinforcement. However, internal discipline is the ability we develop in ourselves to adhere to a plan, follow the rules, get to meetings on time, adhere to standard work, follow checklists, etc.

Discipline should be viewed positively as a quality for each of us to develop. Discipline is a key ingredient in the recipe for Lean environments, as without discipline, there is chaos. We need people to have the discipline to follow standard work, put things back where they belong, get back from breaks on time, start on time, follow through on audits, conduct root-cause analysis, and create the continuous improvement environment.

Long-Term Sustainment Tools

Hoshin

Hoshin Kanri is arguably the world's foremost strategic planning system. Put in other terms, hoshin kanri is a structured planning and implementation approach to manage change in an organization to provide desired results necessary for the organization's success.

Hoshin Kanri provides an opportunity to improve performance continuously by disseminating and deploying the vision, direction, and plans of the corporate management to the top management and to all employees, so that people at all job levels can continually act on the plans and then evaluate and study the feedback results as a part of a continuous improvement process.

Hoshin Kanri is the strategic planning and execution (deployment) process designed to ensure that the vision, mission, annual objectives, goals, and resulting action items are aligned and communicated throughout the organization. It is a *systems approach* to manage change in business processes. Goals are agreed upon and implemented by everyone (consensus building) from the top management to the shop-floor (frontline) level.

In this process, the organization develops a vision statement to encourage breakthrough thinking about its future (next three to 20 years) direction. Work plans are developed based on the collectively chosen vision statement, and progress toward them is periodically monitored through performance audits. It is a system of goal definition and deployment using the plan, do, check, act (PDSA) improvement cycles that must be led by the CEO.

The senior leadership is ultimately responsible for establishing the objectives, strategies, goals, and PPMs to address the organization's issues for the coming year. The catchball process can be implemented using "issue" teams or management quality teams. These teams consist of the functional managers and senior leaders that are most involved with a particular strategic issue. Together, they formulate objectives and strategies to best address the critical business issues at hand. The organization's leadership should be convinced that successfully implementing the selected strategies will make it possible to achieve objectives and resolve issues. Listed in the following are the components of the Hoshin plan.

1. Statement of purpose
2. Determination of breakthrough objectives
3. Business fundamental objectives
4. Development of plans that adequately support the objective
5. Review of the progress of these plans
6. Changes to plans as required
7. Continuous improvement of the key business fundamentals
8. Organizational learning and alignment

Hoshin Planning Is Critical to Sustaining

Managers and employees participate in setting their annual targets and developing the strategy and detailed action plans to meet the high-level vision and goals. This provides bottom-up participation. This back and forth process is called catchball and uses something called an "X-matrix." The X-matrix visually depicts the linkages between each level in the organization and shows the person on the floor how what they are working on is directly linked to the company's vision and goals (see Figure 7.5).

Create a Sustain Plan (See Figure 7.6)

Even after we implement standard work, audits, and Hoshin planning, one of the things we are always asked by any company, or any person, is, "Yeah, we get all that ... but how do we sustain it?" Our response always revolves around the idea that there is no silver bullet. What is required is a system of accountability and discipline, driven from the top leadership. We build this accountability using a tool called a Sustain Plan, which is typically used as part of the project exit strategy but can be implemented earlier if we feel that there is a lack of leadership-driven focus.

This plan is owned by the area's manager or director and is followed up monthly or quarterly. The plan can become part of the Hoshin plan or Goal Deployment Process (GDP). The plan has the following components:

- Ongoing implementation strategy
- Deadlines
- Tools
- Training plan

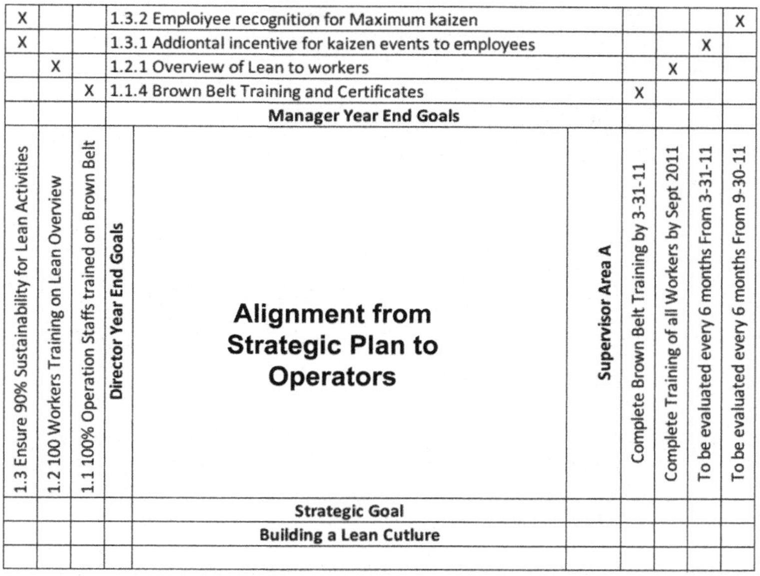

X			1.3.2 Emploiyee recognition for Maximum kaizen				X
X			1.3.1 Addiontal incentive for kaizen events to employees			X	
	X		1.2.1 Overview of Lean to workers		X		
		X	1.1.4 Brown Belt Training and Certificates		X		
			Manager Year End Goals				

Figure 7.5   Hoshin X-matrix. (Source: Pat Grounds Consulting Training Materials.)

- Communication plan
- Responsibilities
- Resources required

The plan may combine some of these elements but each element should be covered. This plan is customizable according to industry and level of success with the tools, but the concept always remains the same. This is a report card put in place by you and your company to hold yourself accountable to the system.

Leadership Coaching—See, Solve, Tell

The coach's responsibility is to coach the learner on the following:

- Learning to See
- Learning to Solve
- Learning to Tell

It can be a Lean kaizen, system implementation, or rapid improvement event. The goal of the coaching is to understand the thought process. The coach does not always give the answer; but also, does not let the learner fail.

This is the balance between system thinking, tool execution, and soft skills. The learner's mindset should not only be based on hitting the target condition; but, even more important, is to focus on how the target condition is reached.

Reaching the target condition requires going through the PDSA steps (see Figure 7.7). These small projects are repeated over and over in small PDSA cycles in order to achieve the challenge. One simple technique we use to help is called T.A.PE.—Target, Actual, Please Explain.

Actions	Due Date	Frequency	Tools	Resp.	Resources Required
Ownership and Accountability of the Sustain Plan				VP Mfg.	
Training and Implementation Plan					
Mechanics (100% time on the floor)					
Train mechanics in problem solving techniques	30-May	Monthly	TWI Training	Team Lead	Lean Practitioners
Train mechanics in their standard work process	31-May	Monthly	Standard Work	Team Lead	Lean Practitioners
Train mechanics on the metrics and visual control boards	1-Jun	Monthly	KPI Boards	Team Lead	Lean Practitioners
Create and Train in new break policy	2-Jun		P&P	Team Lead	Lean Practitioners
Team Lead (100% time on the floor)					
Train team lead on the metric boards	30-May		KPI Boards	Director Mfg.	Team Lead / LPs / ME / QE
Establish an agenda for daily team meeting start up and ending meeting	30-May			Team Lead	Team Lead / LPs Experts
Establish an agenda to communicate to second shift and determine if overlaps are required	30-May			Team Lead	Team Lead / LPs Experts
Develop checklist for pre-production startup	30-May		Walk Patterns	Team Lead	Team Lead / LPs Experts
Develop checklist for post production startup	31-May		Walk Patterns	Team Lead	Team Lead / LPs Experts
Line Manager (80% time on floor)					
Team manager needs to create a schedule / walk pattern to support team manager standard work	23-May		Standard Work Instructions	Team Manager	
Develop scheduled daily walkarounds with Team Lead, ME, QE, Materials (LPA)	23-May	Daily / Weekly		Director Mfg.	Team Lead / LPs Experts / ME / QE
MFG. Director (50% time on the floor)					
Create a schedule /walk pattern to support team manager standard work	30-May		Standard Work	Director Mfg	Team Manager / Team Lead / LPs
Train on standard work for Director and Manager	2-Jun		Standard Work	Team Director	Team manager / Team Director
MFG. Engineer (80% time on floor)					
Train in standard work for ME	30-May		Standard Work	ME Mgr.	ME / ME Manager / Team manager / Team Lead
Quality Engineer (80% time on floor)					
Train in standard work for QE	30-May		Standard Work	QE Mgr.	QE / QE Manager / Team manager / Team Lead
Materials (30% time on floor)					
Train in standard work for Materials	30-May		Standard Work	Materials Mgr.	Materials / Materials Manager / Team manager / Team Lead
HS&E (30% time on floor)					
Train in standard work for HS&E	30-May		Standard Work	HS&E Manager	HS&E Rep / HS&E Manager / Team manager / Team Lead
Planners / Production Control					
Train in standard work for Planners	30-May		Standard Work	Planner Mgr.	Planner / Planner Manager / Team manager / Team Lead
Lean Assembly and Test Person					
Identify the Lean person	22-May			Director Mfg.	Team manager / Team Lead / COE Director / BIG
Communication Plan					
Establish monthly meetings with mfg. shop floor personnel	2-Jun	Monthly	KPI Boards	Team Mgr	Team Manager / Team Lead
Establish quarterly Town Halls	2-Jun	Quarterly	KPI Boards	VP Mfg.	LPs
Establish owners for all metrics / communication boards	3-Jun		KPI Boards	VP Mfg.	LPs/ Team Lead
Lean newsletters		Weekly	KPI Boards	Lean Team	Team Manager / Team Lead
Educational and Training Plan					
Train in Training Within Industry	19-Jun	Ongoing	TWI Workbook		
Train all employees in Lean Maturity Path Assessment Tool	9-Jun		Lean Specifications		
Overarching actions required to Sustain Long Term (18 months and beyond)					
Conduct quarterly self assessment on Lean Maturity Assessment Tool	7-Jul	Quarterly	Lean Specifications	Team Lead	Team Lead
Conduct Lean Maturity Assessment with Site Leadership and compare gaps to self assessment and create actions accordingly	14-Jul	Monthly	Lean	VP Mfg.	Team Director / Team VP / Team Manager / Team Lead
Staff Satisfaction					
Survey employees formally	Aug-04	Annually	Gallop	HR.	
Skip levels monthly		Monthly		VP Mfg	
Visual controls					
Day by hour		Daily		Team Lead	
Metrics We Are Going To Track - Follow-up					
Inventory Turns					
Throughput Time					
Cycle times					
Number of People					

Figure 7.6 Sustain plan example. (Source: BIG Archives.)

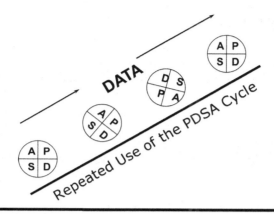

Figure 7.7 Ongoing PDSA cycles. (Source: BIG Archives.)

Using this process will help the learner articulate the gap to standard in a short concise way. This coaching process must be consistently used to help the learner gain a deeper understanding of the process and the current standard. Here are a few aspects of leadership coaching:

- Trying to understand the learners' level of knowledge.
- Going to the gemba to see what the person has learned.
- Teaching using a rapid PDSA system, i.e. countermeasures adding complexity or making the work simpler.
- How visible is the problem?
- Focusing on solving one action or obstacle at a time versus a 100-line item open-issue sheet.

Tools we can use in this process include:

- Using a block diagram to show the process steps
- Use of 10-cycle analysis
- Developing key metrics, both leading and lagging
- Understanding current condition in both KPI form as well as trying to describe in words the current condition
- Developing future state condition both in KPI and words
- Using PDSA to keep teams on pace

Keeping kaizen storyboards at the gemba will foster participation and make the work of the team visible for all to see. When developing the storyboard we always want to use pencil, and paper sticky notes to keep updates simple and real time. Use simple language like you would use when speaking to people who know nothing about the process. The storyboards should also be developed by the team, not marketing or leadership. It's not about being pretty, it's about being effective and understanding the tools.

We believe using coaching is a form of leadership development and combining it with continuous improvement helps integrate the people and the process.

Creating these habits and daily routine helps develop a culture of continuous improvement and will allow your organization to develop true Lean leaders. This mindset change is one of the keys to sustainability and long-term cultural change.

Upgrade the Organization

As we progress down the Lean maturity path, we need to focus on improving the organization. There is a tool we use mentioned in the book called *Good to Great* by Jim Collins. Once we define the new vision for the organization we need to review the organization chart and look to see if we have the right people on the bus and they are in the right seats. This is the start of succession planning. During our coaching of leaders we teach them that there is also a selfish reason to develop your people. Because if you don't develop your people, then there is no one to take your place, which means you can't move up in the organization.

We suggest reviewing the organization every six to 12 months because as the vision evolves we have to constantly ask ourselves if we have the right people in place to take us to the next level. If not, what do we need to do to develop them?

This does not mean the responsibility is totally on the company. Part of the process is training each person on the team, and that they need to be the best they can be first. This means looking for ways they can help understand where the weaknesses are in their behaviors and skill sets and look for ways they can self-improve.

The leader and the team member need to identify what they think are the gaps separately. Then the leader and team member need to meet to discuss the gaps (weaknesses) and then discuss where they have differences and agree on a development plan for the next year.

The company then needs to agree on ways to continue to develop them. Every employee should know what the plan is for them over the next one to three to five years. This assessment between the leader and employee is necessary to keep them focused and challenged to continually improve themselves. Eventually the goal is to get away from annual planning and make it a rolling 12 months.

As companies move more toward Scrum culture and teaming organizations, this assessment may become more team-based versus individual-based. Even so, the individual and the company both share in their ongoing development responsibility.

Part of the goal of ongoing leadership coaching each employee and team is to continue to help them evolve and increase their skill sets and problem-solving mindset as well as living the company's values through their behaviors.

The other change we make is to move toward value-stream or product-focused organization design and support it with a scrum-of-scrums–based culture.

Span of Control

An area where we see companies fail is in having too large a span of control for their leaders, particularly first-line leaders. We have seen direct supervisors have 30–60 people directly reporting to them for day-to-day activities. This system is unmanageable and results in lots of firefighting. Many companies have lost their shop-floor management system to implementing daily reactive solutions and chaos.

Toyota has a different system. At Toyota there are teams of six to eight people that report to a team leader. The team leader has responsibility for training, improving standard work, and responding to andons, as well as assisting the group leaders on certain tasks. They don't do disciplinary action.

The group leaders do the disciplinary piece and coach the team leaders in problem-solving. It can take 20 years or more in Japan to become a group leader. The group leader normally has five or six team leaders reporting to them. The group leader functions as a first-line supervisor over team leaders and team members. They focus on cross-training, hiring, monitoring staffing, ensuring, and appraising team-member job performance. They develop and maintain positive team-member relations, emphasizing safety, quality, efficiency, productivity, cost reduction, and morale.

To show how different this is from most companies … Do you have a team member handbook? Do you have someone focused on cross-training? Do your supervisors lead hiring decisions?

Managing by Fact

Lean is about being able to manage by fact and understanding all the data related to the as-is or current-state process and what it can deliver. The data captured in the baseline phase provides the foundation for the calculations and comparisons for the improvements as we methodically move through the phases.

In the quest of gathering accurate data, we repeatedly ask people how long it takes to complete activities within a given process. Most managers and staff provide their best estimate; however, when we video or use a stopwatch on the process, they are almost never correct. Once we walk through the tools, they are very surprised to see how far off their estimate was from the real data.

As soon as someone says, "I think" or "it was," or "it should be," we know the person is not sure and what they are stating does not meet our goal to act on fact.

We must always question the data we receive from people and computers. The data must be accurate if we are to develop measurable baseline. The baselining phase sets the stage for the Lean initiative. You can't possibly know how much you have improved if you don't know where you started.

Suggestion Systems

Suggestion boxes do not work. The best suggestions systems are where ideas are generated from the frontline staff, run by the team and team leader for discussion, and consensus is reached on how to implement it. Then the ideas are piloted, given a chance to work, and then refined and implemented. Once implemented the standard work must be updated. Truly Lean companies don't worry about ROI or even tracking the number of ideas. It just becomes part of the culture.

Do not monetarily reward team members for ideas. If you do, then people will only give you ideas if they get paid for them, will argue over what they got paid, why someone got paid more than they did, etc.

Do recognize people for giving ideas, i.e., pat on the back or public recognition etc. The culture should encourage everyone to contribute and implement ideas every day. One tenth of 1% is just fine but do it every day.

Problem-Solving Thinking

We refer to problems as "gaps." We don't focus on the good; we look for and try to surface the bad. At Toyota, they are not concerned as much with the "good," because this is expected. For us the definition of the word gap is the void between the standard, current state, and the target (future state). Thus, a discovered gap anywhere in the process becomes a starting point for continuous improvement. Toyota doesn't have the word Lean. They call it "Daily Kaizen." This is an important distinction.

Incorporate problems solving methodology into your culture—utilize small PDSA cycles over and over and over again. Work toward zero defect production and transactional processes.

How to Keep Track of Your Progress

There are many ways to keep track of your progress. One is to put together a timeline of major improvements or milestones (see Figure 7.8). You can use your value-stream maps to keep track of your progress as shown earlier in the book. The VSM will give you your overall progress with reducing process time and storage time (see Figure 7.9). You can also use a high-level assessment or health check as seen in Figure 7.10. We have also been experimenting with scrum and scrum-of-scrum techniques to accelerate implementations and keep track of overall progress.

The Authors Would Like to Leave You with this Ultimate Challenge …

We say the goal of Lean is to create a culture where 80% of your ideas come from the shop floor or office and then we implement 96% of them. This is what we call daily kaizen. Can your existing culture support this? If not, there is still work to do. Remember, having no problem is the biggest problem. No matter how much you have improved, there is still room for more.

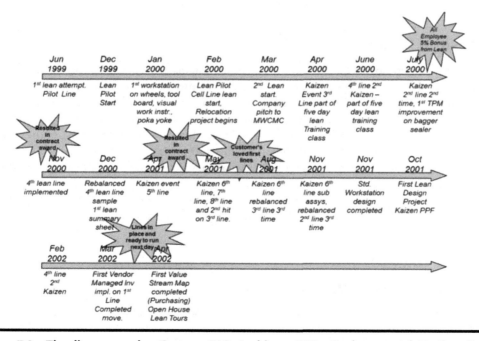

Figure 7.8 Timeline example. (Source: BIG Archives, ETG—Environmental Testing Group, Baltimore, MD. Formerly part of Bendix Communications Group.)

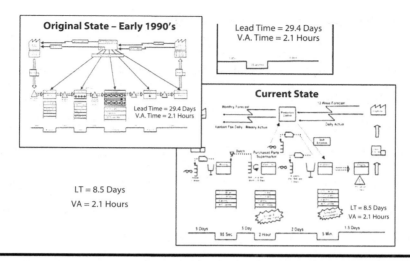

Figure 7.9 Example of tracking progress using VSM. (Source: SME Value Stream Mapping, Donnelly Mirrors Portion of the video.)

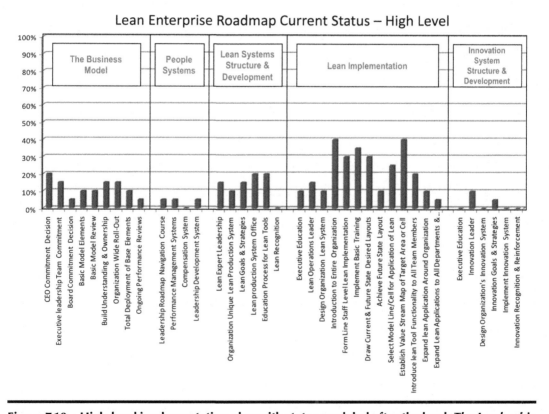

Figure 7.10 High-level implementation plan with status modeled after the book *The Leadership Roadmap*, by Dwane Baumgardner and Russ Scaffede, 2008, North River Press: Great Barrington, MA. (Source: Mike Hogan and BIG Archives.)

Dr. Shigeo Shingo used to do an exercise with his P-course classes. He would wet a towel and pass it around the class and have each person squeeze it. Toward the end each student could still squeeze out a drop of water. This was a great analogy for finding waste.

The other example we like to use is small improvements are where it's at. Every once in a while, you will get a big one, but the goal is small, incremental improvements every day. We use snow for analogy. Each snowflake may seem insignificant but eventually it turns into inches (cm) and then feet (meters) of snow. Each idea on its own may seem insignificant, but eventually we create a snow-storm.

We sincerely hope this book helps you unleash the ideas and engagement of those who do the work, while giving you a good, granular, structured approach to implementing the BASICS of ongoing Lean Improvements.

Bibliography

Akao, Yōji. *Hoshin Kanri: Policy Deployment for Successful TQM*. New York: Productivity Press, 1991.

Barnes, Ralph Mosser. *Motion and Time Study* (5th edn). New York: Wiley & Sons, 1964. Barnes, Ralph Mosser, and Marvin E. Mundel. *A Study of Simultaneous and Symmetrical Hand Motions*, University of Iowa, *Studies in Engineering, Bul. 17*, 1939.

Collins, Jim. *Good to Great* New York: Harper Business Press, 2001.

Coopers and Lybrand. Allied Signal TQ Training Course, 1994.

Dinero, Donald. *Training within Industry and Training within Industry Manual*. New York: Productivity Press, 2005

Gilbreth, Frank. Article reported in the *Journal of the American Society of Mechanical Engineering*, 1921.

Hammer, Michael. *The Agenda* (1st edn). New York: Random House, 2002.

Harris, Rick. *Making Materials Flow*. Cambridge, MA: Lean Enterprise Institute (LEI), 2006.

Hopp, Wallace, J., and Mark L. Spearman. *Factory Physics* (3rd edn). Longrove, IL: Waveland Press, 2011.

Ishiwata, Junichi. *Productivity through Process Analysis*. New York: Productivity Press, 1984.

Japanese Management Association (eds). *Kanban Just-in-Time at Toyota*. London & New York: Productivity Press, 1986.

Katzmarzyk, P. T, T. S. Church, C. L. Craig, C. Bouchard, and C. Pennington. "Sitting time and mortality from all causes, cardiovascular disease, and cancer." Biomedical Research Center, Baton Rouge, LA. http://conditioningresearch.blogspot.com/2009/04/too-much-sitting-down-is-bad-for-you.html.

Monden, Yasuhiro. *The Toyota Production System* (1st edn.) New York: Industrial Engineering and Management Press, 1983.

Ohno, Taiichi. *Toyota Production System: Beyond Large-Scale Production* New York: Productivity Press, 1978

Ohno, Taiichi. *Workplace Management*. New York: Productivity Press, 1982.

Osgood, Charles. "Don't Just Sit There—It's Dangerous." The CBS Radio Network. *The Osgood File*. June 10, 2010.

Peters, Tom. *Speed Is Life*. Co-production of Video Publishing House and KERA, 1991.

Protzman, Charles, George Mayzell, and Joyce Kerpchar. *Leveraging Lean in Healthcare* New York: CRC Press, 2011.

Protzman, Charles, Christopher Lewandowski, Fred Whiton, Joyce Kerpchar, Patrick Grounds, and Steve Sternberg. *The Lean Practitioner's Field Book*. London & New York: CRC Press, 2017.

Rath & Strong. *Time Is the Next Dimension of Quality*. American Management Association video.

Rathmore, Ranveer Singh, B.Sc (Engineering). Study of effect of angle and distance on the speed and accuracy of single hand and two hand simultaneous motions in the horizontal plane. Bihar University, India, 1959, Master's thesis.

Rother, Mike, and John Shook. *Learning To See* New York: Lean Enterprise Institute (LEI), 2003.

Rother, Mike. *Toyota Kata*. New York: McGraw-Hill, 2009.

Shingo, Shigeo, Dr. *Kaizen and the Art of Creative Thinking*. Tokyo: Hakuto-Shobo, 1959. (English translation, Enna Products Corp. and PCS Inc., 2007.)

Shingo, Shigeo, Dr. *A Revolution in Manufacturing: the SMED System*. New York: Productivity Press, 1985.

Shingo, Shigeo, Dr. *Zero Quality Control: Source Inspection and the Poka-Yoke System* New York: Productivity Press, 1986.

Shingo, Shigeo, Dr. *Non-Stock Production.* New York: Productivity Press, 1988.

Shingo, Shigeo, Dr. *A Study of the Toyota Production System from an Industrial Engineering Viewpoint.* New York: Productivity Press, 1989.

Shook, John. *Lean Lexicon.* Cambridge, MA: Lean Enterprise Institute (LEI), 2004.

Sylvester, Laurence Arthur. *The Handbook of Advanced Time-Motion Study.* New York: Mayflower Publishing Co, 1950.

Toyota Production System, Yasuhiro Monden, Productivity Press, CRC Press, 1993.

TPM Productivity. TPM Video Tapes Productivity Series.

Vinas, Tonya. Capturing the competitive advantage of employee fulfillment. *Target Magazine,* Volume 25, No. 3, 2009.

Womack, Jim, and Dan Jones. *Seeing the Whole.* Lean Enterprise Institute (LEI), 2002.

Yasuda, Yūzō. *40 Years, 20 Million Ideas* London & New York, Productivity Press, 1990.

Index

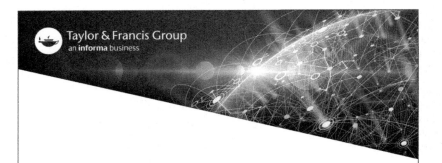

Printed in the United States
by Baker & Taylor Publisher Services